The Family Emotional System

The Family Emotional System

An Integrative Concept for Theory, Science, and Practice

Edited by
Robert J. Noone and Daniel V. Papero

LEXINGTON BOOKS
Lanham • Boulder • New York • London

Published by Lexington Books
An imprint of The Rowman & Littlefield Publishing Group, Inc.
4501 Forbes Boulevard, Suite 200, Lanham, Maryland 20706
www.rowman.com

Unit A, Whitacre Mews, 26–34 Stannary Street, London SE11 4AB

British Library Cataloguing in Publication Information Available

Library of Congress Control Number: 2015950336
ISBN: 978-0-7391-9893-3 (cloth : alk. paper)
ISBN: 978-0-7391-9895-7 (pbk. : alk. paper)
ISBN: 978-0-7391-9894-0 (electronic)

∞™ The paper used in this publication meets the minimum requirements of American National Standard for Information Sciences—Permanence of Paper for Printed Library Materials, ANSI/NISO Z39.48-1992.

Printed in the United States of America

Contents

v

List of Figures

Part I

BOWEN THEORY AND THE FAMILY EMOTIONAL SYSTEM

Chapter 1

Toward a Science of Human Behavior

Robert J. Noone and Daniel V. Papero

I believe that human behavior will one day become an accepted science that can grow and develop with all the sciences. I have presented some ideas that I hope will be helpful. When it does become a science, family concepts and relatedness to the lower forms of life will play some kind of part. Murray Bowen, 1982.

For the greater part of the twentieth century, psychoanalytic theory and its derivations formed the central paradigm in psychiatry, psychology, and the larger mental health field. By the middle of the century, however, many questioned whether this approach could move toward science. Its grounding in human subjectivity would not permit it to adequately connect with knowledge developing in the life sciences. Efforts to move toward science led to several developments in the mid-twentieth century which have continued into the present.

The introduction of psychotropic medications in the treatment of severe psychiatric disorders such as schizophrenia represents one such development. The success in decreasing some of the most disturbing symptoms and behaviors of the mentally ill and in decreasing the long-term institutionalization of many led to a rapid rise in a pharmaceutical approach to treatment. It also led to a significant shift in the central paradigm of psychiatry.

Psychiatrists and researchers came to view psychiatric disorders as brain disorders and biochemical or genetic in nature. Such problems were increasingly seen as best treated with biochemistry. The approach led many in psychiatry to see this paradigm as a hopeful move toward mainstream medicine and becoming more scientific. Its rapid growth was also to a significant degree fueled by the profitability attained by the large pharmaceutical companies which financially supported this perspective (Bentall, 2009).

While the "biological" psychiatry paradigm has come under increasing criticism, it has clearly benefited countless numbers of distressed individuals. It also led to a significant increase in brain research, so wonderfully portrayed in Eric Kandel's *In Search of Memory* (2006). The pharmaceutical innovations based on knowledge developing in the neurosciences hold promise both for more effective treatments and for their application to a wider range of disorders. As a paradigm for understanding human behavior, however, the biological paradigm in psychiatry falls short of the mark. Its narrow focus on individual psychopathology ignores a growing body of evidence linking the context of the individual to behavior expressed. And its narrow cause-and-effect perspective, derived from the breakthroughs in nineteenth- and early twentieth-century medical research, reflects a way of thinking that fails to take into consideration the emerging view of the role of systems in human behavior.

At the same time new developments were occurring in the treatment of psychiatric disorders with medications, another paradigm shift from psychoanalysis appeared. Independently, a number of investigators began to move beyond viewing emotional dysfunctions solely as individual psychopathology or as reflecting poor or inadequate parental care (i.e., the schizophrenogenic mother hypothesis) to the observation that families functioned as whole, highly integrated systems (Guerin, 1976). This paradigmatic shift led to a view that an individual's behavior was a component of a larger interdependent and interactive system. A perspective that viewed the family as a resource rather than the cause of an individual's impairment and the effort to engage the family in treatment rather than isolate individuals in psychiatric institutions (Langsley & Kaplan, 1968) also proved to be highly effective.

Most of the early family investigators focused primarily on the development of clinical interventions with families with a member experiencing psychiatric symptoms. Fueled by the excitement that the discovery of the family as a system might offer new treatment options, the field of family therapy developed rapidly over the next several decades. The new field primarily consisted of practitioners in the mental health field (psychiatrists, social workers, and psychologists) and remained primarily based in the clinical arena, largely outside of academia and research.

In the last couple of decades in the twentieth century, knowledge relevant to human behavior expanded explosively in the life sciences. Related areas of research in neuroscience, evolutionary biology, and animal behavior among others led to a wide range of discoveries in stress reactivity, attachment, emotions, social behavior, epigenetics, and the interplay of physiological regulatory systems (the central nervous, endocrine, and immune systems). Research emerging in these fields increasingly supported a bio-psycho-social paradigm (Adolphs, 2003; Carter, 2005; Fleming, 2002; McEwen, 2002; Meaney, 2010; Panksepp, 1998; Sapolsky, 2005; Suomi, 2002).

Toward the end of the twentieth century, scientists, scholars, and even some clinicians increasingly came to accept an evolutionary perspective that provided a broad conceptual framework for knowledge developing in the life sciences. Edward O. Wilson's book, *Sociobiology* (1975), generated interest among some in the social sciences that greatly expanded in the following decades. Though initially met with some resistance, Wilson's work contributed to a broader acceptance of the idea that human behavior had a basis in both biology and evolution. During this same time period, knowledge in the neurosciences grew rapidly. Technological innovations, animal studies, and the study of brain injuries shed light on the functioning and structures of the brain and its relation to behavior.

The study of the brain and its evolution generated increased interest in the remarkable expansion of the brain from that found in our nearest primate relatives to that found in Homo sapiens. The dramatic growth of the human cerebral cortex in particular occurred over a relatively short period in evolution. What kind of selective pressures could have led to this rapid development?

While previous hypotheses related to this development, such as tool use and hunting, had been discussed, a number of investigators (Allman, 1999; Byrne & Whiten, 1988; Dunbar, 2003) developed the "social brain hypothesis" that came to be the principally accepted explanation of this evolutionarily rapid development. Proponents of the hypothesis see the adaptive advantages of working in complex integrated groups, of anticipating the intentions and behaviors of others, and of regulating one's own emotional reactions in such groups, as the primary selective pressures leading to the expansion of the human brain.

The complex brains found among primates require prolonged periods of dependence and parental care. Nowhere is this more evident than with the human. And the attachments required for such prolonged relationships evolved to include larger multigenerational kin groups. In his book, *Evolving Brains* (1999), the neuroscientist John Allman wrote: "The human evolutionary success story depends on two great buffers against misfortune, large brains and extended families, with each supporting and enhancing the adaptive value of the other" (p. 203).

Given the increased interdisciplinary nature entailed in neuroscience and the recognition of the heightened social interdependence found in the human, the recent emergence of the field of social neuroscience was predictable (Cacioppo et al., 2002; 2006; Harmon-Jones & Winlielman, 2007). Yet surprisingly, the role of the family remains largely absent in the social neuroscience literature. Levels from the molecular to the social and cultural are cited, but a void exists at the level of the human family. Nevertheless a dialogue, first initiated by the family systems pioneer Murray Bowen in the mid-1970s, had begun and has continued to expand.

BOWEN'S EFFORT

Murray Bowen's original interest in a science of human behavior followed his experience as a young medical officer during WW II. He was intrigued both by the fact that psychiatric casualties outnumbered physical casualties and that knowledge about how to treat the psychiatric casualties seemed to be lacking. Following the war he entered the training program in psycho-analysis at the Menninger School of Psychiatry in Topeka, Kansas with an interest in whether he could contribute in moving psychiatry toward science.

After a number of years, his study of psychoanalysis, along with broad reading in the natural sciences, led him to conclude that psychoanalysis was not a conceptual framework that could move toward science. It was in this context that he began an original research study at the National Institute of Mental Health (NIMH) in 1954 (Bowen, 2013).

The study permitted him and his staff to observe families over the course of months and years while they lived on a research unit. The study lasted five years and consisted of 14 families with a severely psychotic adult child. Seven families lived in an inpatient unit from a range of six months to three years and seven families were studied on an outpatient basis. He began with mother/child dyads, but the initial observations led to the view that the rela-tionship involved more than just the dyad and so the fathers and some siblings became participants living on the unit.

Bowen began his research at NIMH with the assumption that the intense mutual connection between mother and child in utero and after birth was a central mammalian characteristic vital to survival. He also brought to the study the hypothesis that the intensity of this connection could impede the movement of an offspring toward autonomy. Within six months it became clear that the intensity in the mother-child relationship among the research subjects involved more than the dyad. As he wrote during the study:

> The observations described here were among those which were different from the original hypothesis, and which led to the extension of the hypothesis. The most striking was the fluid, shifting character of the mother-patient attachment. It was more than a state of two people *responding* and *reacting* to each other in a specific way but more a state of two people *living and acting and being for each other.* There was a striking lack of definiteness in the boundary of the problem as well as lack of ego boundaries in the symbiotic pairs. The relation-ship was more than two people with a problem involving chiefly each other; it appeared to be more a dependent fragment of a larger family group. There was this quality referred to as "transfer anxiety" in which the anxiety or sickness or psychosis could shift from one to the other, or to other family figures or, to a lesser degree, to staff members. The results with psychotherapy also suggested

the symbiotic pair to be a weak undifferentiated fragment of a larger group and to lack within itself the strength to differentiate into two autonomous people. (Bowen, 1978, p. 10)

This led to a shift from viewing the dyad as the unit of study to that of the family. He wrote:

Once it was possible to focus on the family as a unit, it was like shifting a microscope from the oil immersion to the low power lens, or like moving from the playing field to the top of the stadium to watch a football game. Broad patterns of form and movement that had been obscured in the close-up view became clear. The close-up view could then become more meaningful once the distant view was also possible. (Bowen, 1978, p. 50)

Bowen's observation that the family functioned as a unit led a number of investigators to begin referring to the family as a "system." For some this raised the question "What kind of system?" Several investigators attempted to use the general system theory framework which earlier had been developed by von Bertalanffy (1969). Others utilized thinking from communications theory and cybernetics to describe the interactional patterns observed in the family (Watzlawick et al., 1967). And others attempted to extend psychoanalytic theory to account for the family as a system (Ackerman, 1958). While the family could be observed to function as a system, the principal focus of these investigators remained on the development of clinical interventions. Bowen was interested in the development of more effective clinical approaches, but his primary focus was on science.

While still engaged in the NIMH study, Bowen began to consider that there might be sufficient evidence for a new theory of human behavior, one that was distinct from psychoanalytic theory and had the potential to move toward science. Once Bowen could see the interactional patterns in the families with schizophrenia, he could see the same patterns, in less exaggerated form, in other families. He later wrote: "The main part of this family systems theory evolved rather rapidly over a period of six years, between 1957 and 1963" (1978, p. 358).

In thinking about the development of a new theory, Bowen believed that it needed to be based on three principal "pillars": systems, evolution, and that part of psychoanalytic theory he believed to be factual. He incorporated "systems thinking" into the research to describe the automatic patterned behavior that could be observed to occur among the members of the family. In an effort to get beyond "cause and effect" thinking, he developed a disciplined effort by the research staff to focus on the how, what, when, and where in observations of the families and their members and to avoid speculation about their motivations. Once the family could be observed to function as a unit, interactional patterns could be seen. Change in one family member predictably led to changes in the others.

Bowen believed that the human family was a product of evolution and that if a theory were to move toward science, it would have to be based in evolution and biology. In defining what kind of system the family is, Bowen was unique among the early family researchers in the view that the human family needed to be seen as a product of evolution. In using the term similar to Darwin's use of it, he defined the family to be an "emotional system." Darwin used the term emotion to address underlying aspects of human and animal behavior which were broader than a single human culture and were evident across species. Bowen wrote:

> Man is conceived as the most complex form of life that evolved from the lower forms and is intimately connected with all living things. . . . Emotional functioning includes the automatic forces that govern protoplasmic life. It includes the force that biology defines as instinct, reproduction, the automatic activity controlled by the autonomic nervous system, subjective emotional and feeling states, and the forces that govern relationship systems. . . . The theory postulates that far more human activity is governed by man's emotional system than he has been willing to admit, and there is far more similarity than dissimilarity between the 'dance of life' in lower forms and the 'dance of life' in human forms. (1978, pp. 304–305)

The third pillar Bowen thought was important to include in a new theory of human behavior was what he believed to be factual in psychoanalytic theory. Freud was interested in science and a great observer. More than anyone else up to that time he had observed that the basis of much of human behavior operated outside of awareness. He also observed that early life experience greatly influenced adult experience and behavior.

Bowen believed that one of the principal obstacles in moving toward a science of human behavior was the degree to which feelings or subjectivity can be introduced into theory. He thought that at some time in the future it would be possible to have a total theory of the human based on the facts of human functioning, that it would be possible to distinguish between what the human is from what the human thinks the human is. Bowen considered it vital to place the human as a life form among life forms, a product of evolution.

The discovery that the family could be observed to function as a unit was a major step in moving toward a theory which had the potential to minimize subjectivity. Predictable behaviors could be observed to be repeated over and over. These observations led to the development of concepts which Bowen later developed into an integrated theory of the family. He believed that grounding the family in biology and evolution would allow it to remain open to knowledge developing in the life sciences.

A NEW THEORY

In the effort to move toward a science of human behavior, Bowen was careful to be clear in defining such terms as hypothesis, concept, and theory. He defined predictable patterns in areas of family functioning in formal concepts. It was not until the mid-1960s that he believed the interrelated concepts sufficiently constituted a coherent and integrated systems theory of the family. Bowen published the theory, consisting of six concepts (the differentiation of self-scale, triangles, nuclear family emotional process, family projection process, multigenerational transmission process, and sibling position), in 1966 (Bowen, 1978). In 1975 he added two additional concepts (emotional cutoff and societal emotional process) (Bowen, 1976; 1978).

Bowen believed it vital that theory be open to knowledge developing in the life sciences. He knew that while Freud was aware of discrepancies in his theory, many of his followers were not. Bowen thought that if the family systems theory was to avoid becoming a fixed belief system, viable contact with the sciences would be essential. Beginning in 1975, Bowen began to invite scientists from a wide range of the natural sciences to be the principal guest lecturers at the Georgetown Family Center's annual symposia. Since that time there has been an ongoing and expanding dialogue with researchers in the life sciences at symposia, conferences, and other meetings at the Georgetown Family Center and at other family centers around the country.

The integration of knowledge from evolution, neuroscience, animal studies, etc., has been a principal focus in the development of family systems theory (now known as Bowen theory). The importance of systems thinking in understanding the functioning of complex living systems has become more apparent as knowledge of systems, from the genome to ecosystems, has expanded. Conceptual frameworks that allow for the integration of knowledge are required alongside interdisciplinary efforts. As the molecular biologist James Shapiro writes: "The science of the 21st Century deals with the interactions between the multiple components of complex systems, ranging from aggregates of elementary particles to the behavior of the largest structures in the cosmos" (Shapiro, 2011, p. 145).

The concept of the emotional system, as defined in Bowen theory, represents such an integrative concept. It assumes that the human is a product of evolution and related to all of life. As a product of evolution, human behavior in all of its complexity retains the biological processes involved in the evolutionary line leading to Homo sapiens. As Michael Kerr writes:

> Defined broadly, the concept postulates the existence of a naturally occurring system in *all forms of life* that enables an organism to receive information (from within itself and from the environment), to integrate that information, and to respond on the basis of it. The emotional system includes mechanisms such as those involved in finding and obtaining food, reproducing, fleeing enemies, rearing young, and other aspects of social relationships. (Kerr & Bowen, 1988, pp. 27–28)

The concept of the family emotional system adds the instinctual "forces that govern relationship systems" as a central and interrelated element in the regulation of human behavior. It highlights the fact that human behavior, along with that of many other social species, is not only self-regulated by individuals, but co-regulated in the highly interdependent systems in which individuals are embedded.

The rapid expansion of the cerebral cortex, which occurred in the primate line leading to the human, contributes to those aspects of behavior less instinctual or automatic. It greatly enhances the human's capacity to self-regulate and develop a life course less determined by the environment or the past. At the same time, knowledge developing in the neurosciences demonstrates that our "social brains" are highly sensitive to the social environment and that we respond to social cues automatically and outside of awareness to a greater degree than had previously been known.

As remarkable as the expanding knowledge occurring in the neurosciences has been, as dramatic as the discoveries of the mind/body relationship have been, and as illuminating as an understanding of the social nature of the human brain has become, the family as context for the brain both over the course of individual development and evolution remains for the most part ignored.

The discovery by Murray Bowen and other researchers that the family operates as a unit and is involved in regulating the behavior of its members is an observable phenomenon. The sciences have greatly contributed to an understanding of the complexity of the many systems involved in the regulation of behavior. And while much of this work remains compartmentalized, the integration of knowledge of living systems at many levels has been accelerating at a rapid pace. The study of the family and the effort to integrate knowledge about the many systems involved in its functioning has been an exciting arena of investigation. And the concept of the family emotional system has provided an integrative conceptual framework in this process.

OBJECTIVES OF THE BOOK

The interdisciplinary dialogues between Bowen theory theorists, clinicians, and natural scientists have been exciting, stimulating, and productive. They have educated many on the family side of the dialogue and spurred a disciplined effort to understand and be conversant with the scientific literature emerging from many relevant disciplines. They have also contributed to clinicians becoming more interested in research and beginning pilot projects of scientifically oriented investigations with the families they interact with in their practices and more formally in small observational or descriptive studies of behavior. In turn the dialogues have provided scientists with new questions to ask of their data and even new perspectives on their own research. With this volume, the editors hope to capture some of that excitement, stimulation and motivational energy for the interested reader, whether clinician or scientist.

This volume also aims to describe and present the human family as a naturally occurring system, a product of evolution, occupying a place in the compendium of knowledge of systems alongside other emerging natural systems from single-celled organisms to broad social coalitions of animals and human societies. The human family system both embodies and expresses the response of living units to challenge and adaptation, the fundamental process of natural selection. As a natural system the family forms the immediate and most important context for individual development across the individual lifetime. In that sense the family plays a considerable role in environmental circumstances that can affect developmental processes that influence the entire organism and lead to phenotypic variation among individual family members. Specifically the family may be the most central and important environment shaping brain development across the lifetime of the individual. The notion of the family as an emotionally guided and motivated unit or system that deeply influences the behavior of each member can serve as an integrative framework within which specific factual discoveries and hypotheses from many areas of science can be brought together and understood as various manifestations of a coherent whole.

The editors hope this volume will provide the reader with some understanding of what is entailed in conceptualizing the family as an emotional system (Section I), a sense of the breadth and depth of knowledge the sciences are contributing to this effort (Section II), and examples of how this theoretical framework contributes to family research and practice (Section III). And it is hoped that some of the richness and excitement occurring in the ongoing dialogue between scientists and Bowen family systems practitioners and researchers will be captured along with the promise it holds for the study of human behavior.

In the first section an overview of the family emotional system as it has been defined in Bowen theory is presented. The theory represents, in the strict sense of the term, a paradigmatic change in how human behavior is observed and understood. The various concepts in the theory describe observable areas of family functioning, while the defining of the family as an emotional system grounds it as a natural system and a product of evolution (Papero). The family as a multigenerational phenomenon (Noone), the predictability of family functioning (Frost), and the early conceptual development of the family as an emotional system by Bowen (Butler) elaborate on the concept of the family as an emotional system.

The chapters in the second section are representative of the scientists who have participated in Bowen theory meetings and whose work has enriched a natural systems view of the family. They also illustrate some of the great strides in science in recent decades which have shed light on some of the underlying mechanisms involved in the behavior of living systems. The search for a greater understanding of the nature/nurture interplay in behavior and in individual variation has dramatically altered the view of how social interactions both regulate and are regulated by our basic biology. At present one of the more exciting areas of investigation in science is that of epigenetics. The concept of the multigenerational transmission process in Bowen theory describes a patterned and predictable family emotional process which generates wide-ranging individual variation in adaptiveness. The first two chapters in this section (Champagne & Curley; Crews & Noone) describe recent advances in the study of epigenetics and the social regulation of gene expression. This research demonstrates how the family might have such a profound effect on physiology, cognition, and behavior during the course of development and over multiple generations.

Animal research has been vital in expanding our knowledge of human behavior. With family structures similar to the human, the study of marmosets and tamarins (Snowdon) has provided knowledge about physiological mechanisms underlying the behavior of cooperative breeding and of its selective advantages. The value of animal research in understanding the emotional and evolutionary underpinnings in the development of an individual's higher cognitive processes is also highlighted (Panksepp).

The evolution of characteristics unique to the human family and some of the biological mechanisms underlying these phenomena are presented in chapter 10 (Flinn) along with some results from a 25-year study of families in a Caribbean village. The final two chapters in this section (Howard & Gordon; Gadagkar) present systems properties of insect colonies. This research provides fascinating evidence of how interactional processes regulate the structure and behavior of colonies and their members.

Section III provides examples of how viewing human behavior through the lens of Bowen theory and a family emotional systems perspective contributes to research and practice. The influence of the emotional system in regulating reproduction is described in chapter 13 (Harrison) and the contribution that knowledge of some of the biological mechanisms underlying relationships brings to clinical practice is captured in chapter 14 (Donley). Finally a study of child maltreatment in high-risk families (Skowron) demonstrates the value of incorporating biological markers, family observations, and the broad conceptual lens of Bowen theory.

REFERENCES

Ackerman, N. (1958). *The psychodynamics of family life.* New York: Basic Books.

Adolphs, R. (2003). Cognitive neuroscience of human social behavior. *Nature Reviews/Neuroscience,* 4: 165–179.

Allman, J. (1999). *Evolving brains.* New York: Scientific American Library.

Bentall, R. P. (2009). *Doctoring the mind.* New York: New York University Press.

Bertalanffy, L. V. (1969). *General system theory: Foundations, development, applications.* New York: George Braziller.

Bowen, M. (1976). Theory in the practice of psychotherapy. In P. J. Guerin, (Ed.), *Family therapy: Theory and practice.* New York: Gardner Press (pp. 42–90).

Bowen, M. (1978). *Family therapy in clinical practice.* New York: Jason Aronson.

Bowen, M. (1982). Subjectivity, Homo sapiens, and science. *Family Center Report.* Washington, D.C.: Georgetown Family Center.

Bowen, M. (2013). *The origins of family psychotherapy: The NIMH family study project.* J. Butler (Ed.). Lanham, MD: Jason Aronson.

Byrne, R. W. & Whiten, A. (Eds.). (1988). *Machiavellian intelligence.* Oxford: Clarendon Press.

Cacioppo, J. T., Visser, P. S., & Pickett, C. L. (Eds.). (2002). *Foundations in social neuroscience.* Cambridge, MA: The MIT Press.

Cacioppo, J. T. et al. (Eds.). (2006). *Social neuroscience.* Cambridge, MA: The MIT Press.

Carter, C. S. (2005). Biological perspectives on social attachment and bonding. In C. S. Carter, L. Ahner, K. E. Grossman, S. B. Hrdy, M. E. Lamb, S. W. Porges, & N. Sachser. (Eds.), *Attachment and bonding: A new synthesis.* Cambridge, MA: The MIT Press.

Dunbar, R. (2003). The social brain: Mind, language, and society in evolutionary perspective. *Annual Review of Anthropology.* 32: 163–181.

Fleming, A. (2005). Plasticity of innate behavior: Experiences throughout life affect maternal behavior and its neurobiology. In C. S. Carter, L. Ahnert, K. E. Grossman, S. B. Hrdy, M. E. Lamb, S. W. Porges, & N. Sachser. (Eds.), *Attachment and bonding: A new synthesis.* Cambridge, MA: The MIT Press.

Guerin, P. (1976). *Family therapy: Theory and practice.* New York: Gardner Press.

Harmon-Jones, E. & Winkielman, P. (Eds.). (2007). *Social neuroscience.* New York: The Guilford Press.

Kandel, E. (2006). *In search of memory.* New York: W.W. Norton & Co.

Kerr, M. & Bowen, M. (1988). *Family evaluation.* New York: W.W. Norton.

Langsley, D. G. & Kaplan, D. M. (1968). *Treatment of families in crisis.* New York: Grune and Stratton.

McEwen, B. S. (2002). *The end of stress as we know it.* Washington, D.C.: Joseph Henry Press.

Meaney, M. J. (2010). Epigenetics and the biological definition of gene x environmental interactions. *Child Development.* 81: 41–79.

Panksepp, J. (1998). *Affective neuroscience.* New York: Oxford University Press.

Sapolsky, R. M. (2005). The influence of social hierarchy on primate health. *Science.* 308: 648–652.

Shapiro, J. A. (2011). *Evolution: A view from the 21ˢᵗ century.* Upper Saddle River, N.J.: FT Press Science.

Suomi, S. J. (2002). Attachment in rhesus monkeys. In J. T. Cacioppo et al. (Eds), *Foundations in social neuroscience.* Cambridge, MA: The MIT Press. (pp. 775–795).

Watzlawick, P. et al. (1967). *Pragmatics of human communication.* New York: Norton.

Wilson, E. O. (1975). *Sociobiology: The new synthesis.* Cambridge, MA: The Belknap Press.

Chapter 2

The Family Emotional System

Daniel V. Papero

Murray Bowen's rigorous and meticulously conducted study of the human family led him to the observation that the family functioned as a whole, a unit or system. In a passage often cited by students of Bowen, he reasoned that emotion provided the energy that fueled the family system and relationship interaction reflected the expression of that emotion in family behavior.

Often active below the threshold of a person's awareness, emotion involves multiple complex interactions of physiology and psychology that deeply influence the individual's functioning (how the individual responds to the conditions he or she faces). That functioning in turn unfolds in sets of reciprocal interactions with important others, each influencing the other to form repetitive sets or patterns. These patterns can be observed and predicted in conjunction with variables in context.

Rising and falling levels of anxiety and tension in individuals and in their relationships significantly influence the particular manifestations of family emotional process displayed by a given family. Said another way, the family unit behaves much differently psychologically and behaviorally when it is calm than when it is tense and anxious. Such changes in the functioning of the family unit are predictable and signal not only the changing tension levels of the family unit but also the types of behavior and relationship processes that can be expected to emerge. Other variables in context include the particular people present, the quality of relationships among family members, the specific resources available to the family, and the presence and effectiveness of family leadership.

The flow of emotionally fueled reciprocal interactions in the human family is called family emotional process (FEP). FEP operates continuously in the family, reflecting the principle of reciprocity in action and shaping the response of individuals, particular relationships, and the network of relationships called family to the vicissitudes of life. FEP plays a particularly important role developmentally for children, as it establishes and maintains the specific relationship context of the family in which the child develops. Bowen observed that families differ in the degree to which they operate as a "oneness." That difference finds expression in the varying abilities of family members to substitute thoughtfully guided action for a more instinctive, emotionally reactive response. Some family members simply have more "differentiation of self," as Bowen (1978) called it, than others. Families with greater degrees of differentiation of self approach life challenges with a larger arsenal of response and greater flexibility of adaptation to changing conditions.

The clinical approaches developed on the basis of the Bowen theory address the family as the unit of treatment. The clinician functions as a consultant or supervisor alongside a motivated family member(s) who is working on increasing the ability to develop a thoughtful framework for guiding oneself in responding to others in the family and to life challenges that affect both oneself and the family unit. The clinician employs "systems thinking" in the efforts to assist the family, with the goal of family members themselves becoming expert system thinkers about themselves and their own family relationship system.

ASPECTS OF THE FAMILY EMOTIONAL SYSTEM

In the early 1950s (1954–1959), psychiatrist Murray Bowen led a remarkable research project at the NIMH in Bethesda, Maryland. (See chapter 5 by Butler in this volume) The initial research hypothesis proposed that certain conditions exist in the very early mother-infant relationship which impede the child's emotional maturation and set the stage for the later development of clinical schizophrenia (Bowen, 2013, p. 18).

The study initially focused on the mother-patient relationship (Bowen, 1978). However, within the first year of the study, evidence accumulated that while the mother was deeply involved in the patient's dilemma, the mother-patient relationship functioned in an interdependent manner with other relationships in the family. The father played a particularly important role. "The psychosis in the patient was now considered to be a symptom of the total family problem" (Bowen, 1978, p. 47).

EMOTIONAL ONENESS

Bowen described the relationship between mother and patient as an "emotional oneness" (Bowen, 1978, p. 72). The pair was so close that each could accurately know each other's feelings and even thoughts. Other observations made it apparent that the oneness extended beyond mother and patient to involve other family members, particularly the father. With the shift to the family as the unit of illness hypothesis, the focus of the research shifted to the "family oneness" (Bowen, 2013, p. 106).

The emotional oneness phenomenon seems to exist in all families to some degree. It occurs naturally and may serve the function of supporting connectedness among family members. For example, many parents will find themselves responding emotionally when their child expresses deep sadness. Their throats constrict and tears may come into their own eyes in response to the report of the child. Similarly one recognizes the transmission of joy, fear, and other emotions between and among family members. The difference among families appears to lie in the intensity of the emotional oneness. In less intensely connected families, individuals appreciate the situation of the other via the emotional oneness phenomenon, but are better able to distinguish between an empathic response to another and taking responsibility for another. They appear able to sustain contact with the other without needing to either intrude or withdraw from the interaction.

The family emotional oneness includes a psychological unity that Bowen, in an early effort to convey his observations to others, called the undifferentiated family ego mass (UFEM). It appears that the family reflects a common psychology involving perception, the processes of interpretation of perceptions, ways of thinking and biases that provide the infrastructure of behavior. It is as if the family presents, to one degree or another, a larger version of the folie à deux phenomenon. The members of the family appear to share a common mindset and to look at the world through the same lens. Unlike the psychotic level folie à deux, Bowen observed that this psychological oneness can be found not only in severely symptomatic families, but in all families to some degree. And some family members are more caught up in it than others. This observed variation became a part of the foundation for the development of the concept of the scale of differentiation of self, the core of the Bowen theory.

THE EMOTIONAL SYSTEM

At the core of the emotional oneness of the family, Bowen posited the idea of the *emotional system*. The term, as used in the Bowen theory, includes two domains. One is internal to the individual. It describes the automatic processes by which an organism directs its response to the challenges and opportunities it faces. This response expresses the cumulative effects of innumerable interactions: from the level of biochemistry, to the interaction of brain systems, to the interaction of interpersonal relationships that guide the processes of adaptation to challenge and change. Bowen suggests that the term emotional system can be applied to all living things, including plants. In such a broad application, the term becomes synonymous with instinct. The term refers to the force or energy that both produces and results from the interaction between discrete living entities and between a living thing and its environment.

The output of the emotional system is emotional reactiveness or reactivity. Bowen used the idea of an emotional reflex, similar to the well-known spinal reflex, in his effort to describe the process. The reflex occurs generally outside of the person's awareness automatically, that is unintentionally. Observers can note the reflex when observing relationship interactions that are moderately intense. The reacting person can become aware of the response to some degree by monitoring his or her physiological responses, shifts in feeling and mental process, and shifts in behavior. The reflex can be expressed subtly or overtly and intensely. A voice tone, a look on a face, a subtle shift in bodily position, or a range of other shifts, convey the reflex process. In intense relationships, the other persons note the reaction immediately, often again without active awareness, and respond.

The second domain to which the term emotional system applies in the Bowen theory pertains to interpersonal exchanges of emotional reactivity that occur between people in a relationship. With the reflex in one and the reactive response in the other, a relationship pattern emerges. For example, a husband may note a voice tone used by his wife and immediately become cautious and seek to withdraw from her presence. He may actively move away from her or retreat mentally, in essence disengaging from her. She, in turn, immediately notes his retreat and reacts, now agitatedly attempting to provoke a response from him. He in turn retreats further. If the cycle persists and intensifies, he may at some point launch an intense response toward her, raising his voice, driving his fist into a wall, or storming out of the room.

Bowen observed that in families four basic reactive patterns occurred—conflict, distance, an over- and under-functioning pattern, and the focus or projection of immaturity of two toward a third, usually a child. While conflict requires no further description, the other three do. Distance describes the process by which people decrease their contact with one another in response to tension in the relationship. In the over- and under-functioning pattern, one person appears to give up the effort to be responsible for oneself and allows the other to take charge of that responsibility. This pattern works well for brief periods, serving an important function for the family in allowing responsibilities to be transferred for a short time and allowing recovery from illness or response to other sorts of challenges. But when the pattern becomes chronic, the symptoms can develop in either partner.

A variant of the fourth pattern, the focus by two on a child, receives status as a concept of the Bowen theory, the family projection process, due to its role in the cross-generational transfer of differentiation of self. Tension between parents appears to decrease when both join in an anxious perception of the child as inadequate or weak. In efforts to support the child, the parental disagreements fade into a posture of joint concern and cooperation in their efforts for the child. The child in turn presents himself or herself as in need of such support. When maintained over time, the process appears to render the child vulnerable to the development of symptoms, while the parental relationship appears generally smooth and cooperative. The functional difficulties for the child shift with the degrees of anxiety in the family unit. The threesome appears to respond in predictable steps and patterns reflecting the shifting anxiety field. While the process may provide stability and a decrease of tension in the parental relationship, it appears to contribute to an increase in tension and symptoms in the child.

The family emotional system affects all family members. Family relationships cycle between too much closeness and too much distance. When overly close, family members feel another's feelings and know another's thoughts. The emotional system of the family also finds expression in physiological responses between family members. One family member may experience intense stress, and in reaction, another family member might become ill.

Functioning also reflects the effects of the family emotional system. People behave reactively, assuming roles or functioning positions in the family in response to shifting intensities of emotion. For example, one person may reactively begin to think and decide for another, who then thinks and decides less for oneself. Another person might become dramatically expressive, histrionically conveying fear and upset, and another might automatically move to smooth over the upset by appeasing the upset one and guarding against any further disturbance by restricting access to the upset person. Another family member might become the family critic, finding fault with how others are functioning, while avoiding responsibility for his or her own behavior. Family members might automatically turn to one family member, seen as the problem solver, to deal with a situation, while they themselves remain in a posture of helpless passivity.

TRIANGLES

The emotionally reactive emotional interactions involving more than two also produce patterns of interaction. Another concept of the Bowen theory, triangles, describes these predictable interactions. Bowen observed that two-person relationships become unstable when stressed (Bowen, 1978). Under tense conditions the least comfortable individual moves to involve a third person in the sequence of interactions. This move occurs predictably as the involved person approaches the third with a bid to talk about the other involved person.

With this initial movement, the tense two-person relationship expands to include three people and three possible two-person relationships. Within this context of three possible relationships, tension can shift among those relationships, with two more involved and one less involved. The involvement reduces the tension between the first two and moves it to the relationship between persons two and three. Bowen observed that the three-way configuration allowed the threesome to manage greater degrees of anxiety than the two-person configuration.

Within the three-way relationship system the pattern reflects two who are closely involved and one in a position outside the twosome. When the triangle is calm, the twosome and the outsider are relatively calm, with the position in the twosome appearing to be favored. If tension increases in the outsider, he or she will predictably act to form a twosome with one of the close insiders, leaving the other now in the outside position. Sometimes the outsider succeeds in this effort. Often, however, the outsider's move intensifies the closeness of the twosome, further extruding the outsider. When the triangle is tense, the outside position becomes the favored one, leaving the tension between the other two. Sometimes one of the twosome can gain the outside position, leaving the tension between the other two—"you two work it out and leave me out of it." But sometimes the outsider succeeds in maintaining the outside position, leaving the tension with the twosome, leading to the effort to involve yet a fourth person. The movements of people within the triangle occur continuously and predictably. With observation, a person can "see" the movements involving oneself and others and develop the ability to predict the next movements of each. That predictability provides the basis for an effort to shift functioning within the family unit.

The changing efforts of each person to seek closeness and avoid tension, underlies the shifting patterns of the triangle (Bowen, 1978). People seek closeness for comfort and the feeling benefits of the close relationships, and they use distance to withdraw from tension and the discomfort that accompanies it. The movement can occur simultaneously. One person moves away from the tense relationship toward the third seeking comfort. Sometimes it is not possible for people to move away from tension within the triangle and toward closeness. When this occurs, Bowen observed that two members of the original twosome will bring in another person, adding a fourth person to the configuration. The emotional process will then operate in this new triangle, leaving the original third person uninvolved. The original triangle is now quiet or dormant but can be reactivated at any time.

Bowen observed that the triangle characteristically has two sides or relationships that are comfortable and one that is scratchy or conflictive. He gives as an example the phenomenon of sibling rivalry. The mother generally has a positive relationship to each child, but the relationship between the siblings has a negative feeling tone. Another example might involve a woman who has a positive relationship with her husband and her mother, but the relationship between son-in-law and mother-in-law reflects the negative tone.

Within the family, through repetition over long periods of time, the triangle can assume a general configuration to which the family returns repeatedly. A frequently seen example involves mother, father and child, with mother and child in the favored twosome and father in the outside position. The closeness-distance movements will occur within it, but when the dust settles, mother and child remain in the close position with father on the outside. Another example invokes a parent and two siblings. The close twosome may come to involve the parent and one of the children with the other child in the outside position. Bowen uses the term *fixed* to refer to this recurrent configuration in the triangle. One can find other examples of this process in the family.

Bowen noted that the primary function of the triangling process appears to lie in shifting anxiety and tension across three relationships, allowing the configuration to manage and tolerate greater degrees of tension and anxiety than the single two-person relationship can. Consequently, each person in the triangle can maintain a relatively stable degree of functioning so long as the capacity of the triangle to manage and distribute tension is not exceeded. At the point when the quantity of anxiety and tension exceeds a given triangle's capacity, additional people are brought in, using the process described above and creating a series of interconnected or interlocking triangles.

THE INTELLECTUAL SYSTEM

Alongside the emotional system, Bowen hypothesized that the human has an intellectual system that operates in conjunction with the emotional system to facilitate response to the world. The two systems function alongside one another, each influencing the other. Bowen proposed that the feeling system, through which one gains subjective awareness of deeper emotions, links the two. He explained what he meant by the term *intellectual system* in the following manner:

> The *intellectual system* is a function of the cerebral cortex which appeared last in man's evolutionary development, and is the main difference between man and the lower forms of life. The cerebral cortex involves the ability to think,

reason, and reflect, and enables man to govern his life, in certain areas, according to logic, intellect, and reason. (Bowen, 1978, p. 356)

While one might easily conclude that Bowen's term *intellectual system* might be synonymous with the more current term *cognitive system*, Bowen had something else in mind. While the intellectual system clearly must be a product of cognition, the term reflects the acquired ability of the person to access and utilize cognitive processes freely (i.e., in different contexts and under different emotional conditions) to address life problems and adaptive challenges. If the cognitive system could be thought of as a set of tools, then the intellectual system could be considered the developed skills in using the toolset.

THE SCALE OF DIFFERENTIATION OF SELF

The interplay between the emotional and intellectual systems forms a part of the concept of the scale of differentiation of self. From an evolutionary perspective, the older and more fundamental emotional system influences virtually any aspect of life, often operating outside of awareness. The evolutionarily younger cognitive and intellectual systems usually function in a cooperative or coordinated manner with the emotional system. The intensity of emotional system activity can override the intellectual system, however, rendering it ineffective in guiding behavior. Under conditions of emotional system override, emotional reactivity captures the cognitive system and cancels out the ability of the intellectual system to influence behavior, more specifically to regulate the expression of emotional reactivity.

According to the concept of the scale of differentiation, individuals differ in their ability to access and utilize the intellectual system to regulate the emotional system. People lower on the scale have little ability or practice in the use of the intellectual system. They confuse feeling with fact, subjective perspective with more objective reality. Small quantities or degrees of stress and anxiety quickly incapacitate the intellectual system, resulting in behavior that is automatic, reactive and poorly regulated with thought and a consideration of consequences.

The concept of the scale of differentiation of self captures this range of variation among individuals in a family in terms of the ability to step outside of the automatic reactivity and respond on the basis of thinking and knowledge. A more differentiated person can access and utilize the intellectual system to achieve greater objectivity and thoughtfulness than less well differentiated family members. The somewhat more differentiated person, the theory implies, has more response flexibility available than the less well differentiated person. The theory also hypothesizes that although family members do not vary greatly from one another, the degree of variation finds expression in how individuals process and respond to challenges in the relationship system and in their adjusting to the larger environmental context.

Bowen's observations led him to propose that better differentiated individuals in a family display greater inner-direction, principle-based, and goal-directed behavior than their less differentiated relatives. They are more secure in their beliefs and principles, but not fixed in their thinking. They are able to hear and evaluate the opinions and perceptions of others and discard old beliefs in favor of new ones. Better differentiated people appear to navigate through the family relationship system with greater freedom from constraining emotional reactivity. They can maintain and reflect their beliefs in behavior while remaining in contact with important others. Their lives appear to be more orderly than those of less well differentiated people, and they can be productive while alone or in the context of relationships.

THE FAMILY RELATIONSHIP SYSTEM

Bowen came to refer to the family unit or organism as the family system or family relationship system (Bowen, 1978). The terms attempt to capture the fluid, shifting nature of relationships in the family. "The family is a system in that a change in one part of the system is followed by compensatory change in the other parts of the system" (Bowen, 1978, pp. 154–55). As such, the family responds to the larger systems of which it is a part (society, ecology, evolution, and so forth) and also to the subsystems that comprise it, down to the most complex levels of the physiological functioning of individuals. From this perspective, symptoms of any sort (emotional, social, or physical) in an individual, or in a component relationship within the family system, become evidence of family disturbance. Bowen went on to describe the family system as a combination of emotional and relationship systems (Bowen, 1978). Emotion provides the energy or force that underlies and motivates the behavior of any individual, and relationships define the arena in which such motivational forces find expression.

ANXIETY AND STRESS

The family unit reflects rising and falling degrees of anxiety and stress. Anxiety expresses the activation of the fear system, and stress reflects the mobilization of the organism's resources to meet the challenge. Bowen defined anxiety as the response of the individual to real or imagined threat. Anxiety increases in individuals and spreads from one to another rapidly. As it rises and spreads, behavior (defined broadly to include mental process and physiology as well as behavioral action) shifts in well-known, predictable ways. People become more sensitive to the world around them and focus more intently on the perceived threat. The intense focus on threat in effect regulates the information that flows into the central nervous system. Broad awareness becomes limited and only information directly relevant to the perceived threat reaches processing areas of the brain. This process leads to a confirmation bias. The individual perceives and interprets the situation in a way that confirms and continues the emotional response. Behavior becomes much more automatic and instinctive as people attack, defend, and freeze in place. Patterns of mentation change, as apprehension, worry, and fear come to dominate the active mind. With increasing anxiety, people shift into cause-and-effect thinking, losing a broad perspective. People blame others for their own difficulties, and the process of blame and counter-blame becomes the content of relationship interaction.

Anxiety also spreads from one to another within the relationship network. As it spreads, reciprocal interactions produce patterns with observable shifts in individual behavior. One person may begin to present self as incapable of coping with the shifting anxiety, developing a deep helpless posture and possibly presenting a symptom (physical, emotional or even social). Reciprocally another may attempt to function for the one acting helpless, and others may come in to support or distance from the perceived symptom and tense interaction. The symptom in one person or in a relationship expresses the disturbance in the family unit or system.

In presentations of his observations and theory, Bowen introduced the idea of *anxiety binding*. Anxiety binding emerges from the phenomenon of anxiety transfer among members of the family system. Bowen observed that anxiety appears to pass or transfer from one to another rapidly within the relationship system. It appeared to come to rest disproportionately in one person or perhaps in one relationship that then expressed the anxiety in anxious behavior. As the anxiety came to rest in this localized fashion, it appeared as if a quantity of anxiety had been bound or absorbed by a small part of the larger system. The anxiety had been "bound" and contained. The remaining system members appeared freer from the effects of the anxiety in the system and were able to pursue their activities with less anxious constraint than those who appeared to absorb the anxiety.

The idea of anxiety binding reflects the notion that a quantifiable amount of anxiety exists within the system. That amount becomes unevenly distributed across members of the system, with some receiving/accepting significantly more than others. Those who receive more display the markers and effects of anxiety in their behavior, and those who receive less are freer to pursue their lives.

The interpersonal patterns rooted in emotional reactiveness occur reciprocally. Each person plays a part in initiating and continuing the pattern. Each reacts and responds to the other emotionally, and the pattern in established family relationships repeats frequently, responding to context and tension levels within the relationship system. The relationship interaction can be described as a chain reaction, with each response predictably leading into the next.

Within the context of the family the shaping power of such predictable and repetitive relationship patterns is enormous. The quotidian nature of the patterns establishes frequent opportunities for reinforcement of a pattern, with each repetition increasing the likelihood that the pattern will repeat in the next engagement between the involved people. The process can involve more than two people, with each person reacting reciprocally to another and to the interactions between others.

FAMILY EMOTIONAL PROCESS

Bowen used the term *emotional process* in the family or *family emotional process* to refer generally to the dynamically shifting transfers of emotion, particularly anxiety, among the members of the family and the reciprocally linked movements toward and away from one another that form the patterns and triangles described above. The natural series of changes and responses of family emotional process include phenomena at all levels of the individual (e.g., biochemical, cellular, the interaction of physiological systems, mentational, etc.) as well as the more directly observable movements and patterns of the family relationships.

The behaviors reflect the activation of emotional programs within and between persons expressed in relationship interaction. The emotional response and reactivity programs have been shaped by the reciprocal process of relationship interactions across developmental time and modified to some degree by life experience, interaction by interaction. The interactions and behaviors emerge in the relationship context of the present. The relationship patterns tend to repeat and reinforce the response patterns developed over years of development and life experience. They are not caused by any given past event, including trauma, but past events help shape the nature of the present expression.

While all family members experience and participate in FEP, some appear to be less intensely connected than others and are able to think with less emotional reactivity than others. Individuals with this capability appear better able to use their thinking capacities to direct their behavior than their relatives, who react automatically with little ability to use their thinking capacities to assess and evaluate situations, determine beliefs about the nature of the world, or to apply that assessment to regulate themselves in the FEP. Bowen captured this differing ability to use the thinking capacities in the central concept of *differentiation of self*.

Bowen proposed that such variation among siblings in a family reflects an unintended process that he called the family projection process (see above). Some children are more intensely attached to their parents than are their siblings. These children, as the hypothesis goes, receive more anxious parental attention than their siblings. The parents' either jointly or singly focus attention on the perceived inadequacy of the child, who reciprocally responds in behaviors that confirm the perceptions. The more the parent focuses on a particular aspect of the child, the more the child develops symptoms that reflect the parental preoccupation. In addition to decreasing parental tension, the focus on one child appears to leave siblings freer to develop greater autonomy from the parents and to pursue a more independent life course than that of their focused upon brother or sister.

FAMILY PSYCHOTHERAPY

The discovery of the family emotional oneness and the family emotional system opened the path to the development of family psychotherapy. The family became the patient rather than any one family member. The effort focuses on the functioning of people rather than their feelings. In observing the mix of maturity and immaturity in individuals, Bowen characterized the effort as one of placing the mature side of the person in charge of the immature or infantile side and allowing the mature side to guide the person through the web of family relationships (Butler, 2013).

The mature side of the person contrasted decidedly with the immature side that Bowen characterized as "...synonymous with infantile strivings for dependent security." The mature side included general motivational components that reflected an innate or instinctive desire to be responsible for oneself in life, to become a competent adult, able to think for oneself, act for oneself, and manage oneself with others in the family without forcing one's own need on the other or irresponsibly responding to the infantile presentation of the other.

The NIMH study revealed the importance of the family leadership structure. Bowen observed that effective family treatment began when a leader emerged from the family oneness. That leader possessed the courage to think for him self or herself and act on the basis of that thinking within the family system. Neither angry nor dogmatic, the emerging leader focused on changing him self or herself in the relationship system. He or she could respect the strengths of other family members, but could also recognize irresponsible opinions and not be influenced by them. Bowen described the leader as invested in the family as much as in him or herself. In the 1958 annual report on the project to the NIMH, Bowen described the leadership process in the following way:

> In each family there is an active one who gets things done. In the therapy, the active one works at the problem and the others play a defensive game. Then the other becomes active. The lead keeps shifting from one to another until, as we would postulate it in mature parents, they can shift the lead easily as the situation demands. (Bowen, 1958; 2013)

The clinician served as a consultant, supervisor, or coach of the family's effort to move from a position of anxious helplessness to active processes of problem-solving and adaptation to life challenge. Rather than analyzing the individual in the therapeutic hour, as had been the case in psychoanalytic treatment, the clinician worked with the family to assist their analyzing their own relationship processes *in situ* rather than the process between clinician and individual. The family made the effort to shift functioning outside of the therapeutic hour with one family member at a time, beginning an effort to shift his or her thinking about the problems and the family process, and managing oneself differently in the relationship system. In a sense, each person has the capacity to become the family leader, and that role can shift among family members as each begins an effort to change self in the family relationship system.

During the course of family psychotherapy, family members engaged in a process of differentiation of self. The process involved two basic efforts. Emotional differentiation involved the ability of people to separate their feeling states from one another, so that each could feel his or her own feelings and not incorporate the feelings of the other. This also involved the ability to be responsible for one's own feelings and actions and to allow the other to be responsible for self in a similar fashion. The second, basic self, Bowen described as the establishment of identity. In the process, the family member began the effort to think about situations for him or herself, to be him or herself freely and without guilt. The family member could then act on the basis of his or her convictions inside of self in the family. After initial resistance, the family would respond positively to such efforts.

The role of consultant or coach required that the clinician avoid intense attachments with any family member. He or she worked to remain aware of one's own emotional responsiveness to the family and regulate that tendency with conscious control. Bowen came to describe the mindset of the clinician as involving the effort to be emotionally objective and emotionally neutral.

From a position of emotional objectivity and neutrality the clinician could offer observations to the family about the emotional process among them.

The efforts of the clinician assisted the family members to identify or define the problem in the family (not in the individual patient) and then to remain alongside as the family took responsibility for resolving the dilemma. The task for the clinician, Bowen wrote, was to be helpful without becoming responsible for solving the problem. Family psychotherapy aimed to address the functional helplessness displayed by the family and their attempt to place responsibility for solving the problem outside themselves. When one member can shift his or her part of the family problem and sustain that change, the entire family system can change as well. That is the magic of family psychotherapy.

CONCLUSION

The concept of the family emotional system describes the context of reactive interaction, from the level of molecular interaction to that of interpersonal interaction. It proposes that each sort of interaction influences all others to some degree. From that perspective, consequently, one can propose that the nature of interpersonal interaction can influence the interplay of various systems within the individual and influence the development and course of illness and behavioral disturbance. Reciprocally those illnesses and behavioral disturbances influence the nature of interpersonal interaction. This broad conceptual framework, a natural system framework of the human, permits the incorporation of findings from many areas of biological science and may allow the development of an integrated scientific theory of the human, one that links the biochemistry of cellular interaction to the behavioral reciprocity of relationship interaction.

REFERENCES

Bowen, M. (1978). *Family therapy in clinical practice.* New York: Jason Aronson.
Bowen, M. (2013). *The origins of family psychotherapy: The NIMH family study project.* J. Butler (Ed.). Lanham, MD: Jason Aronson.

Chapter 3

Multigenerational Family Emotional Process as a Source of Individual Differences in Adaptiveness

Robert J. Noone

The human enterprise of science has had a remarkable impact on knowledge of the natural world and how it is currently understood. Observations of the natural world, conceptualizations of how observations might or might not fit with views of the time, and returning to further observations to confirm, refine, or discard earlier observations, have engaged human minds over the millennia. Though the human mind may be intrinsically subjective, curiosity about the natural world has allowed the human to climb beyond subjectivity in certain areas and to grasp a more factual view.

Given the limitations of the subjective mind, it is not surprising that the veil of subjectivity has been most difficult to lift the closer the effort comes to viewing human behavior. Discoveries of planetary movements and the place of our own planet in the solar system were highly disturbing to a view of the human's central place in the cosmos. Darwin's discovery that not only had life, including human life, evolved, but that it was not intelligently guided, contributed to the erosion of a subjective view of ourselves and the world in which we live.

No longer viewed as separate and above life, we can now grasp our exquisite interdependence with all of life, both in the present and over its long history. Mendel's discovery and the later discovery of DNA shed light on how characteristics can be transmitted from one generation to the next. Knowledge of how variations in these characteristics arise and are transmitted has allowed us to further understand the astounding variety found among life on earth and even within our own species. Discoveries in the emerging field of epigenetics (see chapters 6 and 7 in this volume) are dramatically altering an understanding of the interplay between genes and the environment and the influence of previous generations on the present.

Our subjectivity is evident in the difficulty we have in truly grasping the degree to which our individual selves are interdependently embedded in the present and with the past. Far from being the autonomous, free-willed individuals our subjective experience can lead us to believe we are, the facts of life indicate our lives and our behavior are shaped by countless interacting elements. Our lives are rooted not only in our evolutionary past, but in the lives and experiences of the individuals and families from which we descend. Astronomer Carl Sagan and writer Ann Druyan nicely capture some of the difficulty in observing this process in writing:

> A vast chain of beings, human and nonhuman, connects each of us with our earliest predecessors. Only the most recent links are illuminated by the feeble searchlight of living memory. All the others are plunged into varying degrees of darkness, more impenetrable the farther from us they are in time. . . . For most of us, the searchlight progresses forward as the generations do, and as the new ones are born, information about the old ones is lost. We are cut off from our past, separated from our origins, not through some amnesia or lobotomy, but because of the brevity of our lives and the immense, unfathomed vistas of time that separate us from our coming to be. (Sagan & Druyan, 1992, p. 5)

One of the hypotheses derived from the five-year NIMH study of the family by Murray Bowen was that family interactions and emotional process in the family unit, which govern varying degrees of maturity attained by children, also shape variation in the range of maturity levels attained in the next generation. With further study and the development of the concept of differentiation of self, this observation was refined into the formal concept of the multigenerational transmission process. The concept posits that the level of maturity or differentiation of self an individual attains occurs not only over the course of development, but is also a product of the preceding generations. It was based on observations and the gathering of factual multigenerational data of families. In the decades since the original presentation of the concept, the study of multigenerational families has continued and knowledge from the sciences has both lent support and contributed to the development of this rich concept.

Bowen's theory of the family emotional system and the concept of the multigenerational transmission process represented another shift away from the subjective view of self and one's conscious experience as central to behavior. Individuals can be seen to represent not only four and a half billion years of genetic transmission and natural selection, but as occupying a functional position in a multigenerational family process. His observation was that this multigenerational process entailed more than genes:

> My concept, multigenerational transmission process, defines a very broad pattern in which certain children emerge with lower levels of differentiation than the parents, and others emerge with higher levels of differentiation, while most

continue at about the same level as the parents. . ... From a strict definition of genetics, this process follows a genetic-like pattern but it has nothing to do with genes as they are currently defined. (Bowen, 1978, pp. 410–411)

FAMILY, PARENTAL CARE, AND THE BRAIN

The complete dependency of an infant on caretakers at birth, preceded by a prolonged gestational period and followed by future years of extended parental involvement over the course of development, are vital elements in the extraordinary growth and development of both the brain and the individual. The family and the development of the brain have been inextricably woven together over the course of primate and human evolution and are central to the capacity of individuals to successfully navigate through the social complexity of human life.

The remarkably rapid evolution of the human brain, doubling in size in the last half million years, occurred in the context of an evolving family environment (Flinn, Quinlan, Coe, & Ward, 2007). Together, large extended families and large brains have been central to the successful adaptation to the wide range of environments the human species has adapted to (Allman, 1999). Large brains are nutritionally expensive and require prolonged periods of caretaking over the lengthy course of maturation. The mother-infant relationship itself depended on others to provide significant levels of alloparental care (Hrdy, 2005). Clans or extended kin networks were the principal social environment during development, influencing both caretaking and the developing brain. It has been suggested that the rapid expansion of the neocortex during evolution was itself selected due to the selective advantage it provided in adapting to the social complexity involved in and between large clans (Dunbar, 2002).

The reciprocal interdependence between mother and child is evident when the placenta attaches to the uterine wall and mother's blood supply to obtain nutrients and oxygen. While the developing embryo is completely dependent on its mother-host, it also triggers physiological processes which regulate the mother's immune, endocrine, and other responses. The reciprocal influencing during the prenatal period extends beyond the mother-embryo dyad to include the social environment as mother's experience has been found to have an effect on her passenger. During the course of the pregnancy, for example, mother's own physiological reactivity to stress can influence the developing neuroendocrine stress response system of the embryo, an influence which can extend into its adult life (Champagne & Meaney, 2006).

Remarkably, among primates that engage in biparental care, the developing embryo has been found to regulate not only some of the mother's hormonal and behavioral functioning, but the father's as well (see Snowdon in this volume). In a study of tamarins and marmosets, primates in which the fathers are active in the parental care of their offspring, fetal adrenal glands have been found to secrete a hormone halfway through the pregnancy which results in mother secreting the same hormone into her urine. This then activates the hormonal system in expectant fathers, preparing them for infant care (Ziegler et al., 2004).

A new phase of interdependence begins as mother and infant physically separate at birth as a host of interactive processes, from the genetic to the psychological, continue to reciprocally influence the pair. As neuroscientist Stephen Porges, in describing what he calls the "symbiotic regulation" between caregiver and infant, writes:

> The caregiver becomes part of a complex feedback system supporting the biological and behavioral needs of the infant. Within this model of symbiotic regulation, the caregiver is not solely giving to the infant. The behaviors of the infant also trigger specific physiological processes (e.g., neural and endocrine feedback circuits) that help establish strong bonds, provide emotional comfort for the caretaker, stimulate neural pathways, and support the health of the caregiver. (Porges, 2011, p. 281)

During the maturational process a child moves toward greater autonomy, but the independence is relative. The degree of mother-child involvement is governed not only mother's experience and her current relationship environment, but from her own experience of being parented (Champagne, 2008; Fleming, 2005). Each generation then is influenced by the previous generation and will have some effect on the succeeding generation. And as will be mentioned later in this chapter and other chapters in this volume (Champagne; Crews & Noone), this influence occurs not only at the psychological level but at multiple physiological levels as well.

Maturation entails interactive processes, from the genetic to the societal. Indeed the genome is now regarded as entailing a good deal more plasticity than previously believed. Knowledge developing in epigenetics is leading to a view in which development is seen as an ongoing and mutually influential interactive process between the genome and the environment (Meaney, 2010). Separation in the mother-child relationship during the maturational process, then, is seen as occurring at multiple levels and in the context of the larger family.

In adapting to one another family members are subject to constraints in their functioning. They also engage in constraining the functioning of others as well as their own functioning as they adapt. Over the course of development, this process results in variation among the children in their maturation. Each child can be seen as born into an emotional amalgam which influences the level of maturity attained and the degree to which a child moves from "other-regulation" to "self-regulation." Given the length and degree of emotional dependence, the family is seen as the primary context shaping both the developing brain and the individual.

If the Bowen theory of the family is accurate, the family/brain co-evolution led to a nonrandom transmission process, beyond that of genomic transmission, in generating basic differences among individuals. The study of the family by Bowen led to the observation that family interactions and attachments over the course of development and over multiple generations differentially shape the basic adaptiveness of individuals.

INITIAL FAMILY RESEARCH OBSERVATIONS

Bowen began his NIMH study with the objective of gathering data on mother-daughter dyads and their impact on the development of the child (Bowen, 2013). Originally, a basic premise in the study was that while the mother-child symbiosis was a basic mammalian characteristic vital to the growth and survival of offspring, it could also be observed to constrain the maturation of some children. The initial hypothesis of the study was that schizophrenia was a result of an intense mother-child symbiosis in which the sustained emotional dependence of the mother on a child for her own well-being, and the reciprocal dependence of the child on the mother, resulted in a failure of the child to attain the maturity necessary for autonomy to occur.

As Bowen wrote in 1957, "It (the original hypothesis) considered that the mother physically gives up her child in the birth process but that she is unable to psychologically give up the child. . . . According to the thinking, the process is initiated by the emotional immaturity of the mother who uses the child for her own emotional needs" (Bowen, 1978, p. 4).

The mother-child dyad hypothesis was later modified when the relationship was seen to be a fragment of the larger family. The inclusion of fathers and siblings living on the research ward led to the observation that the family functioned as a unit and to a further modification of the hypothesis. The intense emotional involvement and reciprocal regulation of behavior observed in the mother/child relationship was then observed to exist in varying degrees among all of the members of the family unit. As Bowen later described it:

> As the research was supplemented by clinical work with outpatient families, new and unanticipated discoveries could be made. The mother-patient relationship was more intense than hypothesized and it was not a circumscribed entity confined to the mother-and-patient relationship. Instead it was a fragment of a larger family emotional system in which fathers were as intimately involved

as the mothers, which was fluid and shifting, and which could extend itself to involve the entire central family unit, and even nonrelatives. (Bowen, 1978, pp. 104–105)

When Bowen expanded his observational lens to include the fathers, he observed how differently the interactions, what he later came to call the parental triangle, were in relation to each sibling. In describing the research families he wrote:

> There is an intense interdependence between father, mother, and patient which we have called the "interdependent triad." It is usual for normal siblings to become rather involved in the family problem, but not so deeply that they cannot separate themselves from the triad, leaving the father, mother, and patient interlocked in the family oneness. (Bowen, 1978, p. 77)

The "stuck togetherness" observed in the families varied among its members. The siblings of the schizophrenic were seen as less involved in the central triangle and as having attained a level of maturity similar to that of the parents. It became clear that the child with whom the parents were most emotionally involved had been most constrained in the development of emotional autonomy. The mothers were seen as primarily involved, while the fathers were more distant.

In his study of families with a member with schizophrenia, his observations led Bowen to question whether such a significant impairment could occur in the course of just one generation. He could see that the parents functioned at a better level than their adult child with schizophrenia, but only to a degree. He also observed the remarkable interdependence existing in the parent-child triangle. He described it as a "three-legged stool" with a level of emotional dependence overshadowing the autonomy among the members of the threesome. The other siblings in the family were found to have attained more emotional autonomy than their sibling with schizophrenia.

The study of less impaired families led Bowen to observe that such interdependence existed in all families, but in varying degrees. Bowen stated that originally the idea that schizophrenia represented a multigenerational process was suggested by Lewis Hill (1955). Between 1959 and 1962 a detailed multigenerational study of several families with sufficient historical data was undertaken including one with detailed information going back over 300 years. During this period Bowen also began a multigenerational study of his own family stating "I decided that my own family would provide as much detail as any and would be more accessible" (Bowen, 1978, p. xv).

The study of families with schizophrenia, of families functioning at a higher level, and of the multigenerational histories of a small number of families, resulted in the observation that each generation appeared to generate individual differences in the degree to which children move toward maturity or emotional autonomy. The refinement of the concepts of differentiation of self, the nuclear family emotional process, and the family projection process shed light on how this variation occurred and the myriad ways in which it is manifested.

AN INTERRELATED CONCEPT

By the end of the NIMH study, Bowen believed there was sufficient knowledge for the development of a new theory. During the next five years (1960–1965) the six interlocking concepts of the theory were developed and in 1966 the unified theory of the family was first published (Bowen, 1966). The multigenerational transmission process was one of those concepts. At that point the "postulations for this concept were derived from historical material covering three to four generations on approximately 100 families, and ten or more generations on eight families." (Bowen, 1966, p. 169).

The concept of the multigenerational emotional process necessarily entails seeing it in the context of the other interlocking concepts in the total theory. The observation of this process required the observation of the nuclear family emotional patterns and variation in the process of differentiation of self among siblings. It also required the observation that individuals mate with others at similar levels of differentiation. In each generation, then, a baseline is formed from which children remain at levels similar to the parents or vary to some degree.

The principal nuclear family patterns consist of the four adaptive mechanisms the family utilizes to manage the emotional intensity or fusion. One of the mechanisms, the family projection process, describes the automatic manner in which one child is more involved in the intensity of the nuclear family. The family projection process describes the functioning of the parental triangle in which one child disproportionately becomes the focus of parental anxiety. Parental over-involvement with a child can be expressed with anxious concern or negative reactivity. The emotional involvement results in a constraint in development of a child's self. The child absorbs more of the parental immaturity and anxiety, and emerges with a lower level of differentiation of self than that of the parents. This process was most easily observed in the families with schizophrenia in which emotional intensity was most exaggerated, but found to be present in varying degrees in all families.

In an early paper, Bowen (1978) described this process as it was observed in the research families:

According to our present thinking, the child becomes the "important other" to the mother. Through the child, the mother is able to attain a more stable emotional equilibrium than had otherwise been possible for her. The "tiny helplessness" of the infant permits her to function securely in the overadequate position. The emotional stabilization of the mother then enables the father to have a less anxious relationship with the mother. (p. 63)

He goes on to describe the reciprocal nature of the process:

I believe the child is automatically protecting his own interests by doing the things that will insure a less anxious and more predictable mother. However, once the child enters into this "being (helpless) for the mother" and the mother enters into the opposite "being (strong) for the child," they are both in a functional bind of "being for each other." When the child's self is devoted to "being for the mother," he loses the capacity of "being for himself." (p. 63)

The child most involved has a stabilizing effect on the family. Neither parent wants this to happen. It is automatic and occurs outside the awareness of those involved. The other siblings are then a bit freer to 'be for self' and have a greater capacity to devote energy toward moving forward in their own lives. The child who remains most outside of the family emotional intensity may emerge from the family with a level of differentiation of self that is slightly higher than that of the parents, while the others will likely have levels similar to the parents.

From this perspective, the level of maturity parents arrive at over the course of their development, determines the degree of maturation, with some variation, their own children will attain. When followed over a number of generations, families can be seen to generate descendants with a range of maturity or basic adaptiveness. Each nuclear family, then, represents a source point for branches which lead to further branches of families manifesting higher levels of functioning, lower levels, and those which remain about the same. If the concept of the multigenerational emotional process is accurate, it accounts for the wide range of human functioning from the most resilient of individuals and families to those who are least adaptive.

The observation that siblings vary in the level of maturation attained by young adulthood, along with the observation of a broader range of families varying in their level of functioning, led Bowen to move away from the diagnostic frame of reference found in psychiatry. From a systems perspective, individuals could be seen to vary in the developmental process, but only in degree. The shift from categorical thinking to simply observing individual variation along a continuum represented a major shift in thinking about behavior and illness in psychiatry.

Bowen developed a conceptual continuum (scale of differentiation of self) along which individuals could be placed according to their basic level of adaptiveness in life. In searching for a characteristic in which individuals vary and which relates to basic differences in adaptiveness, Bowen observed that people varied in the degree to which they could distinguish between their thinking and their feelings. He posited that individuals vary in the degree to which their "intellectual system" could be involved in regulating self and behavior. In describing the scale he writes:

> It defines all people, from the lowest to the highest possible level of human func-
> tioning, according to a single common denominator. This has to do with the way
> the human handles the intermix between emotional and intellectual functioning.
> At the highest level are those with most "differentiation" between emotional and
> intellectual functioning. (Bowen, 1978, p. 424)

At lower levels of the scale individuals are principally governed by the relationship environment. Their sensitivity to the reactions and expectations of others leaves them in the position of heightened responsiveness and what social neuroscientist John Cacioppo (2008) refers to as "other-regulation". Their "thinking systems", or higher cortical processes, appear to be largely determined by the more automatic emotional responsiveness to the environment. When the relationship system is relatively calm, they can function less reactively. But the "ups and downs" in their functioning depend on the environment.

At the other end of the continuum of adaptiveness, the behavior of individuals is less other-regulated. While still responsive to the relationship environment, individuals have a greater capacity to withstand pressures from the group. In more stressful situations they are able to respond less automatically. They have more ability to access their "thinking system" to assess the reality of the situation and to distinguish, for example, whether a "felt" threat has a basis in reality. They have more flexibility in whether they choose to go with the group or not, to go with their feelings or not.

Bowen based this continuum on two principal observations. One is that individuals appear to vary in the degree to which they emotionally separate over the course of development in their families. And related to this separation, Bowen observed that individuals varied in the degree to which they could utilize their intellectual system in directing their life course. On reaching young adulthood an individual's level of differentiation of self remains quite stable throughout life and largely influences one's capacity to respond effectively to life's myriad challenges. Other factors, of course are at play, but this characteristic is seen as central.

The stability of an individual's differentiation of self is at the heart of the predictability of the multigenerational family emotional process. The relationship processes observable in the family emotional system predictably

generate variation in the maturational process of children. This variation will
then be manifested in the functioning of the families created in the next generation. From generation to generation a stable, nonrandom process can be
seen to unfold, shaping the behavior of its interacting members. This process
can be observed when a family and its descendants can be followed over
several generations. In many families it can be evident in as little as three to
four generations.

The concept of the multigenerational family emotional process also has
important clinical implications (Bowen, 1978; Kerr & Bowen, 1988). Once
individuals begin to have more knowledge about the functioning of at least
several of their families from preceding generations, their view of their own
behavior and that of their immediate family members begins to change.
Obtaining knowledge of the family requires that an individual engage members of the extended family to not only obtain facts, but to learn of the variety
of views members have of family events and other members, past and present. A view of the broader context of their lives leads to less blaming of others
and to an increased awareness not only of the influence of others on self, but
greater curiosity of one's influence on others. Knowledge and observations
of the multigenerational emotional process leads to a less subjective view of
self and others and, paradoxically, more flexibility in how one can respond to
others. Often many of the emotional biases one has arrived at over the course
of development in one's family become more apparent. When one develops
such knowledge they generally become a different person, one who becomes
more of a resource to the family and a bit more "grown-up" in their everyday
life.

RECENT FINDINGS IN NEUROSCIENCE

In the decades since Bowen made these behavioral observations of families,
knowledge developing in the neurosciences and other disciplines has contributed to an increased understanding of the influence of parental care on
brain development and on the role of higher cortical processes in regulating
the emotional system (Meaney, 2010; Roth & Sweatt, 2011). Several chapters in Section II of this volume describe some of the remarkable research
shedding light on the influence of parental care on neuroendocrine systems
of offspring which are basic to adaptiveness. It is now evident that systems
involved in parental care, stress reactivity, immune responsiveness etc., are
significantly shaped by parental care and that this influence can be transmitted
over generations.

Neural systems contributing to the functioning of what Bowen described as
the "intellectual system" are involved in the regulation of the more automatic

emotional processes involved in human behavior. In describing the emergence of "consciousness" in evolution, neuroscientist Antonio Damasio (2010) writes:

> Prior to the appearance of self and standard consciousness, organisms had been perfecting a machine of life regulation, on whose shoulders consciousness came to be built. . ... The difference between life regulation before consciousness and after consciousness simply has to do with automation versus deliberation. Before consciousness, life regulation was entirely automated; after consciousness begins, life regulation retains its automation but gradually comes under the influence of self-oriented deliberations. (p. 176)

The concept of the emotional system in Bowen theory refers to this "automation" in life. It is a premise in the theory that more of human behavior is governed by this automation than man is generally willing to admit. The evolution of higher cortical systems has allowed the human to be less determined by the past and the present environment, but only to a degree. As neuroscientist Jaak Panksepp (1998) writes:

> Although higher forms of human consciousness (namely, awareness of events and our role in them) surely emerge from the cortex and higher reaches of the limbic system, they are not independent of the lower reaches of the brain, which generate our basic emotions, feelings, and other instinctual tendencies. (p. 300)

Bowen theory posits that individuals vary in the degree to which the "basic emotions, feelings, and instinctual tendencies" determine their behavior and basic adaptiveness over their life course. The theory further posits that this variation is principally a result of maturational processes shaped by the family emotional system over the course of development and over multiple generations. Although as Michael Meaney (2010) suggests "certain genomic variants exist which (may) alter neuronal function of the child, affecting the response to environmental conditions" (p. 52), the family can still be seen as central in how such polymorphisms might be expressed. When viewed through the lens of the family emotional unit, the behavior and biology of individuals can be seen as fitting into a dynamic whole, each influencing and being influenced by the others.

The shift from a view of the individual to the symbiotic regulation between mother and child to the larger family unit requires a shift to a systems perspective. The concept of the multigenerational emotional process is far from being established as a fact. But the development of knowledge in the sciences appears to be moving in the direction of establishing the mechanisms through which the family relationship system can be seen as a self-regulating system influencing and being influenced by the functioning of its members.

The concept of differentiation of self entails genetic, epigenetic, physiological, psychological, and relationship variables which interact both over the course of development and over multiple generations. A multigenerational view of development provides a broader framework for the study of human behavior and allows for the inclusion of considerably more variables in understanding individual differences in adaptiveness.

REFERENCES

Allman, J. (1999). *Evolving brains.* New York: Scientific American Library.

Bowen, M. (2013). *The origins of family psychotherapy: The NIMH family study project.* J. Butler (Ed.). New York: Jason Aronson.

Bowen, M. (1978). *Family therapy in clinical practice.*, New York: Jason Aronson.

Bowen, M. (1966). The use of family theory in clinical practice. *Comprehensive Psychiatry,* 7: 345–374.

Cacioppo, J. T. & Patrick, W. (2008). *Loneliness: Human nature and the need for social connection.* New York: W.W. Norton & Company.

Champagne, F. (2008). Epigenetic mechanisms and the transgenerational effects of maternal care. *Frontiers in Neuroendocrinology,* 29, 386–397.

Champagne, F., & Meaney, M. J. (2006). Stress during gestation alters postpartum maternal care and the development of the offspring in a rodent model. *Biological Psychiatry,* 59: 1227–1235.

Damasio, A. (2010). *Self comes to mind: Constructing the conscious brain.* New York: Pantheon Books.

Dunbar, R. I. M. (2002). The social brain hypothesis. In J. T. Cacioppo et al. (Eds.) *Foundations in social neuroscience* (pp. 69–87). Cambridge, MA: The MIT Press.

Fleming, A. S. (2005). Plasticity of innate behavior: Experiences throughout life affect maternal behavior and its neurobiology. In C. S. Carter, L. Ahnert, K. E. Grossman, S. B. Hrdy, M. E. Lamb, S. W. Porges, & N. Sachser. (Eds.), *Attachment and bonding: A new synthesis* (pp. 137–168). Cambridge, MA: The MIT Press.

Flinn, M. V., Quinlan, R. J., Coe, K., & Ward, C. V. (2007). Evolution of the human family: Cooperative males, long social childhoods, smart mothers, and extended kin networks. In C. A. Salmon and T. K. Shackelford, (Eds.), *Family relationships: An evolutionary perspective* (pp. 16–38). New York: Oxford University Press.

Hrdy, S. B. (2005). Evolutionary context of human development. In C. S. Carter, L. Ahnert, K. E. Grossman, S. B. Hrdy, M. E. Lamb, S. W. Porges, and N. Sachser, (Eds.) *Attachment and bonding: A new synthesis* (pp. 9–32). Cambridge, MA: The MIT Press.

Hill, L. B. (1955). *Psychotherapeutic intervention in schizophrenia.* Chicago: University of Chicago Press.

Mayr, E. (1991). *One long argument.* Cambridge, MA: Harvard University Press.

Meaney, M. J. (2010). Epigenetics and the biological definition of gene x environment interactions. *Child Development,* 81, 41–79.

Panksepp, J. (1998). *Affective neuroscience: The foundations of human and animal emotions.* NewYork: Oxford University Press.

Porges, S. W. (2011). *The polyvagal theory.* New York: W.W. Norton & Company.

Roth, T. L., & Sweatt, J. D. 2011. Epigenetic mechanisms and environmental shaping of the brain during sensitive periods of development. *Journal of Child Psychology and Psychiatry, 52,* 398–408.

Sagan, C., & Druyan, A. (1992). *Shadows of forgotten ancestors.* New York: Random House.

Ziegler, T. E., Washabaugh, K. F. & Snowdon, C. T. (2004). Responsiveness of expectant male cotton-top tamarins, *Saguinus oedipus,* to mate's pregnancy. *Hormones and Behavior, 45,* 84–92.

Chapter 4

The Predictability of the Family Emotional System

Randall T. Frost

The ability to predict natural phenomena is a hallmark of science. The development of children undergoes a predictable process from the time of conception to the time children leave home and begin to function on their own. As children grow physically, however, they vary in the degree to which they separate from an emotionally dependent relationship with their parents. Margaret Mahler (1975) observed that in the very first year of life the infant and mother gradually move from a normal state of what Mahler called "symbiosis"—in which mother and child are highly sensitized to each other—to what she called "differentiation," as the child and mother gradually move away from the original "oneness." The growing away from parents Mahler studied in the first several years of life is a process that continues throughout childhood and adolescence. When all goes well, the infant gradually becomes a unique person with his or her own thoughts, feelings, perceptions and memories. Children and parents, however, vary in the degree to which the emotional attachment between child and family gradually resolves as the child grows up physically. According to Bowen theory, the intensity of the unresolved emotional attachment between adult children and their original families predicts vulnerability to dysfunction for each person and the nuclear family they establish (Bowen, 1978). This chapter will explore some of the ways Bowen theory can be used to predict family functioning and to guide family psychotherapy.

Bowen studied the most intense possible clinical examples of attachment he could find between schizophrenic patients and their mothers in landmark research at the NIMH from 1954–59. He did this on the grounds that it would be "easier to first observe the characteristics of the symbiotic relationship in the most exaggerated possible form. . . . (And) that this degree of symbiosis would imply a maximum degree of personality impairment"

(Bowen, 1978, p. 4). His original hypothesis held that "the basic character problem on which clinical schizophrenia is later superimposed is an
unresolved symbiotic attachment to the mother. . . . Symbiosis was seen
as a developmental arrest (of what) was at one time a normal state in the
mother-child relationship" (Bowen, 1978, p. 4). Bowen brought mothers
and young adult daughters diagnosed with schizophrenia to live on the
research ward of the hospital for the first year of the project. In such a live-
in arrangement, researchers had an unparalleled opportunity to observe
patterns of family functioning that reflected the unresolved emotional
attachment between mother and child. One recurring observation in this
setting was the transfer of anxiety from mother to patient. Bowen described
the pattern as follows:

> When the mother became anxious her thinking would focus on the sickness in
> the patient. The timing of this seemed more related to the mother's own func-
> tioning rather than to the reality of the patient's functioning. Mother's verbal-
> izations would include repeated emphasis on the patient's sickness. Very soon
> the mother's anxiety would be less and the patient's psychotic symptoms would
> be increased. This mechanism was so common that any increase in mother's
> anxiety would alert the staff for an increase in the patient's psychosis (Bowen,
> 1978, p. 6).

Such repeated observations led to the awareness of a pattern of transferring
anxiety between mothers and daughters in which both played *active* roles
(Bowen, 1978, p. 7).

Even more surprising was the observation that the intensity of the symbiosis was not confined to the mother-child relationship but that the anxiety
could shift to other family members, or even temporarily envelop members
of the staff. Repeated observations of the intensity of the symbiotic attachment shifting to involve other members of the family led to an extension of
the original hypothesis. By the end of the first year the extended hypothesis
regarded schizophrenic symptoms to be part of an "active dynamic process
that involves the entire family" (Bowen, 1978, p. 7), not just the mother and
patient. Accordingly, fathers and siblings began to live on the research ward
as well. New observations lent further support to the extended hypothesis of
the family as an emotional unit. Researchers began to observe how intense
unresolved emotional attachments could govern behavior in the entire family
unit.

These observations are illustrative of Bowen's methodology. The theory
grew out of direct observations of how family members actually function in
relation to one another. Bowen constructed the theory based on what he called
"*facts of functioning* in human relationship systems. . .*what* happened, and
on *how* and *when* and *where* it happened, insofar as observations are based

on *fact*. It carefully avoids man's automatic preoccupation with *why* it happened" (Bowen, 1978, p. 416). When the clinical evidence did not support the thesis that the problem was confined to the mother-patient relationship, the hypothesis was extended.

The hypothesis also predicted the changes that would occur with the psychotherapy. "When research observations were not consistent with the hypothesis, the hypothesis was modified to fit the new facts, the psychotherapy was modified to fit the hypothesis, and new predictions were made about the results of the psychotherapy" (Bowen, 1978, p. 470). When the hypothesis shifted to the family as the unit of illness, the therapy was directed to the family unit and individual psychotherapy for the mother and daughter was discontinued.

UNRESOLVED EMOTIONAL ATTACHMENT
AND DIFFERENTIATION OF SELF

Considerable therapeutic effort went into "helping the individual define his own 'self' and to differentiate self from others" (Bowen, 1978, p. 12). Bowen noted that some individuals in the research families did go through a process of "differentiation of self" from other family members. An important part of the process was "emotional differentiation" when family members began to disentangle their feelings from one another. As one mother said, she "was putting an invisible wall between herself and her daughter so I can feel what I feel and she can feel what she feels; I can have my life and she can have hers" (Bowen, 1978, p. 86).

Another part of differentiation was establishing one's own identity in the family. One father said, "If we spent less time on working on our son and more time trying to find out what we believe and stand for, it would be easier for him to find himself" (Bowen, 1978, p. 86). Moreover, when one member of the family began to define themselves more clearly, it was followed by immediate complementing changes in other family members. Bowen described one family in which the father "slowly changed from a passive compliant fellow to a man of more strength and conviction" (Bowen, 1978, p. 28). When he began to assert his different point of view in spite of his wife's intense opposition:

> Within a few days, (his wife) became tremulous, tearful, and overtly anxious. She was fearful and felt helpless. The father maintained his position in spite of her anxiety, and within two weeks she had changed to a calm, objective, firm motherly person. She said, "If he can keep on being a man then I can be a woman." The emotional divorce (between the parents) was resolved and the

father and mother were as devoted to each other as a teenage couple in love for the first time. They were so much invested in each other that neither was overinvested in the patient. Both were then able, for the first time, to be more objective toward patient. At this point the schizophrenic daughter began some significant changes toward more adequate functioning. The new functioning level lasted a month and then the family suddenly reverted to the old way of functioning; but thereafter, it was easier for the father to pull up to more adequate functioning and less threatening for the mother to give up the over adequate position. (Bowen, 1978, pp. 28–29)

Bowen elaborated on the concept of differentiation of self over time by defining various parts that make up the concept. He defined solid self as the part of self that is made up of "clearly defined beliefs, opinions, convictions and life principles on which one will take action even in situations of high anxiety and duress" (Bowen, 1978, p. 365). Pseudo self, on the other hand, is made up of beliefs and principles acquired from others and it is negotiable in relationship to others to enhance ones image or oppose the other (Bowen, 1978, pp. 200–201). The husband described above had been pretending to agree with his wife when he actually did not. He was operating out of pseudo self. When he slowly began to become a man of greater "strength and conviction" and began to assert his different point of view in spite of his wife's intense opposition, he was slowly moving toward increasing his solid self. However, the fact that he faltered after a month indicated that he had not yet arrived at a durable increase in solid self. Predictably, when one family member has thought through his or her beliefs and principles sufficiently that they do not modify their principles, but act consistently with their beliefs even under duress, the level of emotional arousal in the family unit will subside after the family vigorously tests the resolve of the differentiating one (Bowen, 1978, p. 176).

Bowen eventually defined the core of his theory as "the degree to which people are able to distinguish between the feeling process and the intellectual process" (Bowen, 1978, p. 355). People with better levels of differentiation are better able to distinguish between the more subjective feeling process and the more objective thinking process. He added, "Those with the most ability to distinguish between feeling and thinking, or who have the most differentiation of self, have the most flexibility and adaptability in coping with life stresses, and the most freedom from problems of all kinds" (Bowen, 1978, pp. 355–356).

Bowen also defined differentiation as "the degree to which one self fuses or merges into another self in a close relationship" (Bowen, 1978, p. 200). Emotional fusion is the opposite of differentiation. The attachment between people can be so intense that the fusion represents a state of two people "living and acting and being for each other" (Bowen, 1978, p. 10). One mother in the NIMH study recalled an incident when:

> The daughter, then a child, had injured her head. Instantly her own head started to hurt in the exact spot where the daughter's head was injured. . . . The daughter confirmed this fusion of feelings. She had never been able to know how she herself felt. She had depended on the mother to tell her how she felt. When she occasionally had some feeling different from what the mother said she discounted it and felt the way her mother said she felt. (Bowen, 1978, p. 41)

The early observations about the transfer of anxiety in families and the importance of differentiation for better functioning by families were later found to hold for families with less severe problems than schizophrenia and even in families without diagnosable symptoms. The crucial differences had to do with the intensity of the emotional attachment between family members, the amount of anxiety the family had to manage and the fixedness of the family patterns of relating to one another. Eventually the variables of degree of anxiety and the degree of differentiation of self became the two main variables in Bowen's theory of family emotional functioning (Bowen, 1978, p. 361). An accurate assessment of these two main variables helps to predict a family's ability to adapt to stress.

UNRESOLVED EMOTIONAL ATTACHMENT AND TRIANGLES

Triangles, another key concept of the theory, also grew out of the early research. In the first year of the NIMH study, Bowen described a common pattern that recurred between mothers and their schizophrenic daughters. He described it as a closeness-distance cycle. The mothers and daughters would "get over-close, fight, separate, come back together again and repeat the cycles over and over" (Bowen, 1978, p. 5). Bowen noted:

> During a very intense period the family could go through as many as two complete cycles in one day. The time for the average cycle varied between several days and several months. In the closeness phases the mother and patient seemed interested only in each other, and their relationships to outside figures were calm. As the closeness increased, the anxiety would increase to intense incorporation anxiety. Then they would fight and separate until separation anxiety set up a reunion and a new cycle. In the distance phase, each was hostile to the other and each attempted to duplicate the symbiotic relationship with outside figures. These outside relationships are difficult, demanding and anxious for the outside figures. (Bowen, 1978, pp. 5–6)

The pattern of mother and daughter exhibiting an "intense cohesiveness" during the closeness phase and an "equally intense disruptiveness" during the distance phases, followed by the effort to form outside relationships of equal intensity with other family members and/or staff, characterize the basic pattern of a triangle. When anxiety is low, two people can have a calm relationship with each other and a third person is in the outside position of the triangle. Under conditions of low anxiety, the outside person can actually be the most uncomfortable person in the triangle. When anxiety increases in the intense twosome, one or the other or both try to pull in a third to side with them and form a new intense togetherness. Under moderate tension the more uncomfortable position is in the intense togetherness and the more comfortable position is the outside position. A person in the outside position under these conditions often tries to take the posture "You two fight and leave me out of it." At high levels of anxiety, the tension cannot be contained in a three-person system and spills over to involve multiple interlocking triangles. It is interesting to note in the NIMH study, that when a staff member would become involved in a triangle with a family member, turmoil could spread to the entire staff through a chain of inter-staff relationships. The family would then become freer of anxiety (Bowen, 1978, p. 9).

Triangles interlock with the two main variables of the theory, level of anxiety and level of differentiation. Triangles function differently depending on the level of anxiety in the system and the level of differentiation (Bowen, 1978, p. 307). The variation in functioning of triangles is highly predictable under careful observation of the system. One pattern of a triangle can be fixed and predictable until anxiety increases at which time the triangle goes into another fixed pattern of functioning. A husband, for example, can be on the outside of an intense relationship between his wife and a child until the anxiety reaches a certain level in the mother-child relationship at which point the mother can involve the father with the child and move to a more comfortable outside position while the emotional intensity plays out between father and child. If the intensity gets too great between father and child, the mother criticizes the father at which point the conflict shifts to the relationship between husband and wife and the child is in the outside position. When the conflict between husband and wife subsides and anxiety decreases in the triangle, the pattern returns to the over-close togetherness between mother and child with father once again in the outside position of the triangle. Such moves in an intense triangle are automatic and without intellectual awareness (Bowen, 1978, p. 307). The pattern can be so predictable, it repeats over and over as anxiety builds or decreases. But to make predictions about each move in the triangle requires the ability to observe the pattern. The predictability is present, but careful observation is necessary to see the pattern.

The level of differentiation in a family also influences the functioning of triangles. A higher level of differentiation predictably results in more flexible, less automatic functioning of triangles in a family (Bowen, 1978, p. 307). This can best be seen by the effort to increase level of differentiation in a family. To change an engrained pattern of functioning in key triangles in a family requires that the person working on differentiation see the automatic pattern of which he or she is a part. Next, the person has to accurately observe his or her part in the pattern. Then the person has to develop the ability to control his or her own emotional response which interrupts the automatic chain reaction of events. If the father in the previous example can see the repetitious operation of the triangle and convey to his wife that she and the child will have to work out the problem between them, he is beginning to modify his part in the pattern. Also predictable is the responses of his wife who will challenge his interruption of the pattern with some version of (1) you are wrong, (2) change back, and (3) if you don't, these are the consequences (Bowen, 1978, p. 216). The ability not to react to the heightened pressure and revert to the usual automatic response requires the slow process of increasing intellectual control over one's part in the automatic emotional processes of the triangle (Bowen, 1978, p. 307). Better ability to observe more objectively helps to decrease the intensity of the emotion for the husband. When the emotion begins to subside, it is easier to get beyond blaming his wife, child, or himself for the problem. Lowering emotion, in turn, improves the ability to observe more objectively. As the husband achieves more emotional neutrality about the problem between his wife and child, he can relate actively to both, without taking sides with either. When the husband can do this, his wife and child will predictably go on to resolve the problem between them, once each recognizes he will not take sides in spite of pressure from each to do so (Bowen, 1978, p. 307). Any failure to achieve the predicted result is considered an error in emotional control rather than an error in the predictability of the system (Bowen, 1978, p. 234). In this example, the fixed pattern of the triangle will change if there is the ability to observe the pattern accurately, see one's part in perpetuating the pattern, become able to control one's automatic emotional response and override the urge to react emotionally to the predictable "change back or else" response of the system. Also important is keeping the process confined to the three-person system. If important others get triangled into the process and do take sides, it can undermine the effort. For the change to become permanent requires an increase in solid self, a thought through belief that the modification of self in the triangle is a responsible act that is not negotiable in the system. The predictability of triangles enables the ability to predict the outcome of an effort to change the pattern if, and only if, the requisite conditions to increase the level of differentiation in the family unit are met.

ANXIETY BINDING MECHANISMS IN THE NUCLEAR FAMILY

The interaction of the main variables of anxiety and level of differentiation within the triangles of a nuclear family help determine how the nuclear family adapts to stress. The early research at NIMH and subsequent observations led to the identification of mechanisms families use to adapt to the intensity of emotional attachments as they play out in the nuclear family. Bowen described a major dilemma for spouses with poor levels of differentiation after they marry. "Both have intense longings for closeness but when they are close, their individual 'selfs' fuse together in an emotional oneness with a 'common self'. This results in loss of individual identity, turmoil and conflict" (Bowen, 1978, p. 93).

The challenge of being an individual in an intense togetherness generates its own anxiety. One mechanism for trying to adapt to the dilemma is that couples "retreat to sufficient aloofness and distance from each other for each to maintain as much identity and autonomy as possible. This emotional distance. . .helps prevent the loss of identity that comes with closeness" (Bowen, 1978, p. 93). Emotional distance is one of the mechanisms that couples use to adapt to the anxiety created by the intense need for the other and the way it can conflict with the equally intense need to be an individual in one's own right (Bowen, 1978, p. 377).

Another mechanism couples use to deal with their "dependent attachment" to one another is marital conflict. "In marriages in which both work actively to maintain identity, neither will give in to the other and there is constant marital conflict" (Bowen, 1978, p. 93). If the conflict is contained in the marriage, children can be relatively unaffected so long as the child does not become involved in the problems the parents are having with each other (Bowen, 1978, p. 378).

A third mechanism comes into play when couples avoid conflict by one "giving in" to the other. When this happened Bowen observed:

> An exchange in which the dominant one "gains strength" at the expense of the other who "loses strength." The one who gives in often spontaneously describes a "loss of identity," "confusion," and "inability to know who I am and what I stand for" while the other functioned with greater confidence and effectiveness. The process in which the dominant one becomes stronger at the expense of the weaker one can continue until the weaker one becomes incapacitated with a physical illness, with an emotional illness, or with impaired social and personal functioning such as drinking, irresponsibility and work inefficiency. (Bowen, 1978, p. 93)

The mechanism of going along with one's spouse on matters of importance—even when one disagrees—avoids conflict but can result in the adaptive spouse becoming more vulnerable to developing symptoms.

The final mechanism used by families to manage the anxiety created by emotional fusion is what Bowen called the family projection process. This is a process by which parents reduce their own anxiety and insecurity by focusing on a perceived defect in one or more of their children. The mechanism enables the mother to be less anxious by focusing on the child and the father to be less anxious by having a less anxious wife. Bowen noted that the process

> Begins with an overanxious mother devoted to being the best possible mother and having the most wonderful child. The child becomes anxious in response to the mother's anxiety. Instead of controlling her own anxiety, she anxiously tries to relieve the child's anxiety by more anxious mothering which makes the child more anxious which further drives her anxious mothering etc. (Bowen, 1978, p. 434)

The intensity of the family projection process varies but it is a "process through which most parents permanently impair one or more of their children to some degree" (Bowen, 1978, p. 434).

The use of these mechanisms to adapt to the anxiety created by the lack of differentiation parents bring to the marriage can shift over time. When one mechanism absorbs more of the chronic anxiety generated by emotional fusion, there is less anxiety that has to be absorbed in the other mechanisms (Bowen, 1978, p. 377). If the basic lack of differentiation doesn't change, but the use of one mechanism diminishes, it is predictable that the anxiety will get redistributed to one or more of the other mechanisms (Bowen, 1978, p. 377). In the NIMH study when the schizophrenic adult child began to pull up to more independent functioning, it was not unusual for the mother to become more anxious and even develop physical or emotional symptoms (Bowen, 1978, p. 42). When a husband who had consistently deferred to his wife began to define his differences with her, the formerly calm marital relationship became intensely conflictual and the husband often developed a physical illness of some sort (Bowen, 1978, p. 40). Lack of differentiation is evident in the use of each of the four mechanisms but there is a fixed amount of immaturity in the unit that gets absorbed in one or more of the four mechanisms.

BASIC AND FUNCTIONAL LEVELS OF DIFFERENTIATION

Another component of the concept of differentiation is the difference between functional and basic level of differentiation. Basic level of differentiation is estimated by taking an average of a person's functioning over long periods of time under relatively calm and more stressful conditions (Bowen, 1978, p. 371). A person's functional level of differentiation can range above and below his or her basic level of differentiation depending on the level of

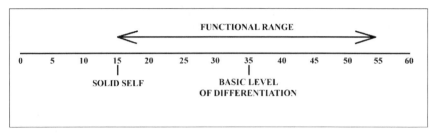

Figure 4.1   Scale of Differentiation

anxiety he or she is experiencing. Solid self refers to the part of basic level of differentiation that doesn't change. People usually have a little more solid self in some areas of functioning than others. People who make decisions easily at work according to reasonably well-defined principles may be bogged down at home if principles are less well defined and the emotional intensity is greater. The most challenging arena to define a more solid self typically is in our own families. Solid self serves as a fire wall that can halt an anxiety driven regression in functioning in the family as well as in other emotional systems.

Figure 4.1 shows a basic level of differentiation at 35 on the scale of differentiation, a functional range from 15–55 depending on the level of anxiety, and a solid self of 15. The author has located solid self at the bottom of the functional range to indicate that this is the point when nonnegotiable principles inform action that can halt a functional slide. The specific values given to basic level of differentiation, functional range, and solid self are intended to illustrate the relationship of these variables to one another, and not to imply we have as yet a way to assign fixed values to these aspects of differentiation. Nonetheless, Bowen theory holds that estimates of basic level of differentiation, functional range of differentiation, and solid self, as well as level of anxiety and the degree of flexibility of key triangles can be used to predict the ability of a family to adapt to stressors as well as a family's response to the therapy effort (Bowen, 1978).

UNRESOLVED EMOTIONAL ATTACHMENT AND EMOTIONAL CUT OFF

Another concept in Bowen theory found to have considerable predictive value is what he called the degree of emotional cut off between adult children and members of their original family, especially their parents. Emotional cut off refers to the way in which people distance from their family of origin to manage the anxiety created by the amount of unresolved emotional attachment the person has with his or her original family. Bowen noted the degree of our unresolved emotional attachment to family of origin is equivalent to our degree of un-differentiation (Bowen, 1978, p. 534). Cut off is reflected in the amount of personal contact adults maintain with their original family, how far away from each other they live, how openly family members communicate about significant developments in each other's lives, and the degree to which each is able to speak about self to the other who can reciprocate. Just increasing the amount of contact with the family of origin can reduce the amount of anxiety that has to be handled in the nuclear family. Bowen reported that among the NIMH research families, "marriage tensions would be reduced when one went to his or her parents for a visit" (Bowen, 1978, p. 54).

This early observation became amplified when Bowen began to teach psychiatric residents about working on differentiation with their families of origin based on a breakthrough he had achieved in his own family. The first year he began to do such teaching, he was surprised that the group of residents began doing better clinical work as family therapists than any previous residents. When he inquired further, "it became clear that it was precisely those residents who had done best in the effort with their parental families who were also doing best in their clinical work" (Bowen, 1978, p. 531). Moreover, none of the residents mentioned emotional problems in his or her own nuclear families. "In retrospect", he wrote, "this was also unusual since it was common for residents to seek consultation about their own emotional problems" (Bowen, 1978, p. 532). A year after he began the process, he began to ask questions about the residents' spouses and children. Bowen wrote:

> They reported the usual range of problems in their marriages and with their children, but to my amazement, they had made as much progress in dealing with the problems as similar residents whom I had been seeing in once-a-week formal family therapy with their spouses. They had automatically been using things they had learned from their parental families in the relationship with their spouses and their children. This surprise development was a turning point in my professional life. (Bowen, 1978, p. 532)

Subsequent years of close observation and "clinical experiments" supported the validity of the initial observations. He concluded that the experience since 1969 has closely paralleled the initial observations in the period from 1967–1969 (Bowen, 1978, pp. 533–34). When people can begin to bridge the emotional cut off with their family of origin and to work toward defining a more separate self in the original family, the intensity of emotional problems in the nuclear family predictably decreases.

Two families can have the same degree of unresolved emotional attachment but maintain different amounts of contact with the original family.

Bowen wrote, "One family remains in contact with the parental family and remains relatively free of symptoms for life, and the level of differentiation does not change much in the next generation. The other family cuts off with the past, develops symptoms and dysfunction, and a lower level of differentiation in the succeeding generation" (Bowen, 1978, p. 383). A husband whose own mother had been hospitalized for depression during his growing up years began to treat his fiancée as if she were likely to become symptomatic like his mother. When he began to work on engaging his mother in a more mature manner, he also changed his attitude toward his fiancée. Families that maintain viable emotional contact with their families of origin handle some of the anxiety generated by the unresolved emotional attachment to the original family in the ongoing interaction with those family members. This can result in placing members of the person's nuclear family in the outside functioning position of triangles with the original family. When a husband's mother and her second husband become critical of how their daughter-in- law was parenting their grandchild, the husband addressed the matter with his mother. This increased the tension between the husband and his mother and step-father, but it relieved the anxious focus on his wife. The wife moved to the more comfortable outside position in the triangle with the anxiety more appropriately playing out between mother and son. Indeed, in the author's experience, most conflicts with in-laws reflect the lack of differentiation between the biological parents and their adult children. The more lack of differentiation and the anxiety it generates plays out between the adult child and their family of origin, the less the amount of anxiety that has to be handled in the nuclear family. The more adults cut off from their family of origin, the more anxiety there is that has to be bound in the four mechanisms of the nuclear family. When a person can go beyond maintaining contact with families of origin and use the contact to work on defining more of a self with the original family, the nuclear family benefits. Bowen theory holds that reducing emotional cut off with the original family and using the increased contact to work on improving level of differentiation predictably decreases the amount of anxiety generated by fusion in the nuclear family and improves a nuclear families' ability to adapt to stress (Bowen, 1978, pp. 434, 545).

CLINICAL RESEARCH

The very predictability of the family emotional system allows for the ability to conduct clinical research in a more scientific way. Bowen theory enables clinicians to formulate a series of conditional predictions for each research family based on an accurate assessment of the intensity of the unresolved attachment to the original family, the patterns of functioning within the nuclear and extended family, and the ability of the therapist to carry out a course of therapy consistent with theory. The predictability of the family emotional system makes possible a series of "if. . .then" predictions. For example, if anxiety comes down in a family, then the emotional stuck togetherness in the nuclear family will relax a bit and symptoms will begin to attenuate. If people are successful in modifying the degree of emotional cut off with their family of origin, then anxiety will come down in the nuclear family which in turn will also attenuate the severity of symptoms in the nuclear family, unless the family experiences additional stressors that heighten acute anxiety in the system. If a person is able to modify his or her part in a key fixed triangle in specifiable ways, then the emotional system becomes more flexible, less stuck together and the family is better able to adapt to stress. If people over time are able to differentiate more of a self in their family of origin and resolve some of the unresolved emotional attachment to the original family, then the underlying adaptiveness to stress in the nuclear family will improve. However anxiety will increase and symptoms may get worse during initial efforts to function as more of a separate self with the original family. Predictions for outcome in therapy also have to be conditioned on the functioning of the therapist. The therapist must be able to remain emotionally neutral with a family, convey systems thinking in a way it can be heard by the family, and define and de-triangle self as needed with the family. The motivation of at least one member of a family to work on self is another variable that needs to be taken into account in predicting the outcome of a course of therapy with a clinical family. The predictability of emotional systems in Bowen theory allows for making nuanced predictions of outcome that can be tested by the actual outcome of therapy over time.

To assess clinical outcomes requires the ability of a clinician to define markers of change. How are we to know when a family is making headway in modifying the intensity of emotional attachments? One marker is how people think about self in relation to other members of the family. When one member of a family feels and thinks they are responsible for fixing the problems of another, they blur the boundary between self and the other. When family members anxiously focus on what is right or wrong about the other, they tighten the emotional attachment. Over positive or over negative focus on the other is a sign that the intensity of the attachment is not changing. Predictably such focus on the other heightens anxiety in the family and fuels the development of symptoms. On the other hand, when an anxious focus on others shifts to trying to understand and modify the part self plays in family problems, people can start a process that potentially can lead to one person separating more of a self from others, while still maintaining emotional contact with them. When at least one family member can begin to take more responsibility for self and less over responsibility for others, family members can begin to grow up. A sign that the intensity of an emotional attachment is beginning to resolve is when people are able to contain their anxiety without transferring it to others. When families gradually increase emotional separation and decrease the amount of anxiety they transfer to one another, symptoms predictably improve. The ability to focus responsibly on managing self and not trying to manage the other is one important marker of change in a family. Tracking such markers of change enable a better ability to predict change in family functioning and evaluate its solidity. The predictability of the family emotional system permits the process of family therapy to proceed with more sureness. When clinicians can consistently demonstrate the efficacy of theory in clinical research, Bowen theory will take another important step toward science.

PREDICTABILITY IN SCIENCE AND IN BOWEN THEORY

Scientists define predictability differently. Some scientists, for example, define the relationship between genotype and phenotype by statistical probabilities. Within the biological sciences, however, according to Michael Meaney, "the mere statistical relation between a genomic variation and a phenotypic outcome would not be considered as sufficient basis for the establishment of a functional link between the gene (or its product) and the relevant variation in phenotype" (Meaney, 2010, p. 4).

In contrast, Meany describes findings that variation in licking and grooming by rat mothers of their offspring during the first week of life influences the hypothalamic-pituitary-adrenal (HPA) responses to stress in adulthood. Offspring of mothers who "naturally exhibit increased levels of pup licking and grooming show more modest behavioral and endocrine responses to stress compared to animals reared by low licking and grooming mothers. Specifically, the offspring of high-LG mothers show reduced fearfulness and more modest HPA responses to stress" (Meaney, 2010, p. 21). Meaney describes in detail how variations in mother-pup licking and grooming in the rat "alter the extra-and intracellular environments of neurons in selected brain regions. Such alterations directly modify the epigenetic marks on regions of the DNA that regulate the transcription of glucocorticoid receptors, which in turn regulate the HPA response to stress" (Meaney, 2010, p. 26). Meaney also documents the operation of "multiple cofactors each of which can alter glucocorticoid receptor function" (Meaney, 2010, p. 11). The ability to track such biological pathways constitutes the basis for making predictions in biology according to Meaney.

Predictability at the level of the family as described by Bowen theory is closer to the understanding of predictability in the biological sciences. Multiple variables govern the development of intense attachments and the degree to which the attachment resolves by the time a young person leaves home. One variable is the degree to which a person's own parents and grandparents resolved the emotional attachment to their parents. Another variable is the amount of anxiety in the emotional field of the family at the time of conception, pregnancy, birth, and the first few years of life. Another variable is how the person's family handles anxiety, both the anxiety that is created by acute stressors and the chronic anxiety generated by parents' own unresolved attachment to their original families. When acute and chronic anxiety is absorbed more in conflict and distance between the parents or dysfunction in a spouse, it means there is less anxiety focused on the children. When more of the parental immaturity is focused on children, those children are less able to separate a self from their parents as they grow older; they retain a greater degree of unresolved emotional attachment to their parents. The mechanisms of marital conflict and distance, the emotional process contributing to dysfunction in a spouse, and the family projection process can each be observed and documented, much like the operation of biological mechanisms. So can the degree of emotional cut off with family of origin. Bowen summarized this set of observations by writing, "All things being equal, the life course of people is determined by the amount of unresolved attachment, the amount of anxiety that comes from it and the way the parents deal with this anxiety" (Bowen, 1978, p. 537).

Oddly enough, variation in the intensity of unresolved emotional attachment in human families may represent the functional equivalent of variation in maternal licking and grooming behavior in rats. Such different behavior in the two species each strongly influence stress reactivity in offspring. Bowen described the way in which the adolescent period for children who become psychotic is particularly stressful:

Adolescence activates intense anxiety in the symbiotic relationship. Before adolescence, the mother had remained calm as long as the child was infantile. He had handled his wishes to grow up with fantasies of future greatness. The growth period causes anxiety in the child and anxiety in the mother, until the symbiotic relationship itself becomes a serious threat. When the child is more grown up, the mother infantilizes. When he is more childish, she demands he grow up. After years of functioning as a helpless child, he has little "self" of his own and he is poorly equipped to do anything without the mother. . . . The child in this dilemma has to deal first with the mother's effort to hold him back and then with his own urge to return to her, before he can get to the problems of the normal adolescent. Once free of the mother, he faces outside relationships without a self of his own. Of this dilemma a male patient said, "It takes a lot of doing to hold your mother's hand and play baseball at the same time." (Bowen, 1978, p. 65)

Similar patterns were observed in families with less intense emotional attachments to their children, who in turn developed less severe problems. For humans, the inability to assume increasing responsibility for self as one is growing up generates its own anxiety. The chronic anxiety that results impairs functioning when one tries to function more independently as an adolescent and eventually as an adult.

The predictability of the family emotional system allows for two-way traffic between Bowen theory and the life sciences. Facts discovered about human physiological functioning can help to refine and further extend Bowen theory. The concepts of Bowen theory, in turn, can help to explain anomalies of research primarily focused on the individual. Much of the very valuable research on the stress response, for example, centers on the physiology of the individual. Bowen theory, with its focus on the family as an emotional unit, describes how the unit functions to determine which member or members of the family end up carrying more of the physiological response to stressors. From a family systems perspective, the intensity and duration of the stress response for each individual is heavily influenced by how family members interact within the triangles of the unit. The cascade of responses that occur physiologically in the stress response for an individual cannot be separated from how emotional process is playing out in the family.

The developing field of epigenetics studies the way in which specific environmental conditions can affect the expression of genes. Variation in the intensity of the family projection process stands out as a possible variable influencing the expression of genes in children that is relatively independent of variables like socioeconomic status. The family projection process operates in every family to a greater or lesser degree regardless of income and social status. Children who have been part of an intense family projection process, and emerge with a more intense level of unresolved emotional attachment to the original family, are far more vulnerable to poorer health and educational outcomes than their siblings. The day may come when well-trained family systems therapists collaborate with researchers in the natural sciences to build family variables into longitudinal research and experimental protocols.

The development of science relies on predictability in nature. The family emotional system offers a rich opportunity to exploit the predictability of emotional process in the family to move closer to a science of human behavior.

REFERENCES

Bowen, M. (1978). *Family therapy in clinical practice*. New York: Jason Aronson.

Mahler, M. E., Pine, F., & Bergman, A. (1975). *The psychological birth of the human infant*. New York: Basic Books.

Meaney, M. J. (2010). Epigenetics and the biological definition of gene x environment interactions. *Child Development*, 81: 41–79. doi:10.1111/j.1467-8624.2009.01381.x

Chapter 5

The Family as an Emotional Unit Concept

Origins and Early History

John F. Butler

This chapter reviews the seminal concept of the family as an emotional unit, discovered and developed during the NIMH Family Study Project by Murray Bowen, M.D. The chapter is based on several papers in the Bowen Archives, now housed in the History of Medicine Division of the National Library of Medicine in Bethesda, Maryland. However, the Archives are a recent source of information about the Family Study Project. Bowen's classic text *Family Therapy in Clinical Practice* has several early chapters with details about the project. In addition, there are two recently published papers about this effort (Butler, 2011, 2013), and some of the original papers about the Family Study Project with commentaries have also been recently published (Bowen, 2013). The concept of the family as an emotional unit is the chief finding of the Family Study Project and remains an enduring contribution for family systems theory and practice.

Bowen's interest in families and family theory did not begin with the Family Study Project. His thinking actually started during his tenure at the Menninger Foundation from 1946 to 1954, where he was first in training and later functioned as a staff psychiatrist. At Menninger's he began to formulate a new science of human behavior based on cross-disciplinary reading and extensive clinical experience with schizophrenic patients and their families. His interest in how psychological symbiosis operates in dyads began with his thinking and clinical experiences at the Menninger Foundation.

Bowen's Family Study Project was conducted at the NIMH campus in Bethesda, Maryland from 1954 to 1958. There were two parts of this innovative research effort: (a) the first year and (b) the last three years. The project began with a focus on the process of psychological symbiosis in mother-child dyads. Toward that end, mother-daughter pairs were hospitalized in a special ward designed to accommodate families. The dyads were admitted based on two primary criteria: (a) the intensity of psychological symbiosis and (b) a child diagnosed with schizophrenia. The initial goal was to observe these dyads with little staff interference and provide mothers and daughters with the standard treatment at that time, individual psychoanalytic psychotherapy.

However, based on systematic observation, the research protocol was revised. With the experiences during the first year, two important discoveries were made. First, the level of emotional intensity of the families and staff over-involvement with them was much unanticipated. Second, it became clear that the mother-daughter dyads were simply a piece of a larger emotional system that included fathers and other siblings. Thus, the family as an emotional system concept was born. Consequently, during the last three years of the project entire families were hospitalized and a method of working with families later called *family psychotherapy* was developed and refined. With the development of a central new theory and its emphasis on the family as an emotional unit, a new methodology became necessary, since no model existed for working with the family.

The remainder of this chapter will review steps in the development of Bowen's thinking in more detail, describe in greater detail the methods and findings of the Family Study Project, and review several of the obstacles to applying the concept of the family as an emotional unit.

THE MENNINGER YEARS

Bowen reviews this important time at Menninger's from 1946 to 1954 in his article entitled "Odyssey," his contribution to the book *Family Evaluation* written with his student, Michael E. Kerr, M.D. The book is unusual in that Bowen and Kerr wrote independently of one another rather than as joint authors of a single piece. About this period, he commented:

> The Menninger Foundation merely stimulated a lifelong interest. The attitude of the Menninger leaders played a vital role. They were more interested in helping young people develop their own capacities than in communicating a fixed body of knowledge. The early motivation toward theory and science might not have occurred in another setting. (Kerr & Bowen, 1988, p. 349)

Bowen thought about whether Freudian psychiatry could be a science like the other accepted sciences: "My theory at the Menninger Foundation was designed to help Freudian theory move toward the status of an accepted science" (Kerr & Bowen, 1988, p. 351). Bowen (1988) lauded Freud's "ability to remain relatively outside the emotional process" with patients (p. 353). It was this position that Bowen would later call emotional nonparticipation, and he would find this effective when working with families.

Bowen determined "the scientific facts of evolution have been chosen to replace many of the ideas in Freudian theory" (Kerr & Bowen, 1988, p. 360). He concluded:

> I fashioned a natural systems theory, designed to fit precisely with the principles of evolution and the human as an evolutionary being. There was a dramatic increase in my effectiveness as a psychiatrist and therapist. In retrospect, it was the broad view of the human and the emotional neutrality that made it possible. (Kerr & Bowen, 1988, p. 360)

Bowen searched for a setting where he could put some of his ideas into operation. The NIMH in Bethesda, Maryland became the site for his research.

THE NIMH FAMILY STUDY PROJECT

Overview

Bowen was the principal investigator for the Family Study Project from 1954 to 1959. The project initially consisted of hospitalizing mothers and their daughters who were diagnosed as schizophrenic. Standard psychoanalytically oriented individual treatment was offered to both mother and daughters. As mentioned above, during the second phase of the project focus of the research changed significantly. Entire families consisting of parents, a symptomatic child, and a non-symptomatic sibling were admitted. The limitations of space on the ward determined the size of families selected. The average length of stay was about one year (Bowen, 2013). Throughout the project the researchers made meticulous daily observations and documentations of the interactions of the dyads and their relationship with the staff. We are fortunate that a great deal of documentation exists about this innovative research effort.

In 2002 Dr. Bowen's family donated his papers to the History of Medicine Division of the National Library of Medicine located on the campus of the NIMH. The Bowen Archive collection includes his unpublished and some published papers, clinical case summaries, other documents, and an extensive video collection. Anyone who has the privilege of examining the collection cannot help but be captivated by their content.

Catherine Rakow, MSW, of the Western Pennsylvania Family Center, continues to devote countless hours in organizing and cataloging the collection. She is the original Bowen Archivist. The collection contains, among many other things, important annual summaries completed during each year of the project.

My work in the archives focused on those documents relating to the origin and development of family psychotherapy and the concept of the family as

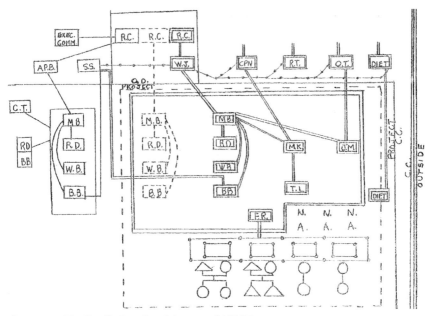

Figure 5.1   The Family Emotional System of NIMH

an emotional unit rather than a study of the individual family charts. One of my favorite documents from the Bowen Archives is a diagram of the family emotional system of NIMH (see Figure 5.1). There were several dozen copies of this diagram in a folder with other archive folders.

Since the chapter concerns the family as an emotional system, it is appropriate that this figure highlights the NIMH Project as a complex, interactive emotional system. As the reader can see, a dotted line surrounds the Family Study Project and displays the initials of the primary staff along with their connection to their own administrative emotional systems. Notable on the figure are the initials of the principal investigators: Murray Bowen (MB), Robert Dysinger (RB), Warren Bodey (WB), and Betty Basamania (BB).

Of significant interest, on the lower right, are the diagrams of the four rooms for the families on the project. Beneath each room, from left to right, family diagrams for each of the families have been added: parents with two daughters, parents with two sons, and two single parents with their daughters. The diagrams of these families are early versions of what is now known as family diagrams. The symbols for males are not the squares as they are depicted today but triangles. At some point early in the project, a change in male figures was made from triangles to squares, which is how they are depicted today. Research projects like this do not exist in isolation; they consist of many interacting emotional systems and this diagram graphically displays these complex relationships

The formulation of the concept of the family as an emotional unit, the main finding of the Family Study Project, led logically into the development of family psychotherapy, a method of working with the family units. Realizing the importance of the family as an emotional unit, the treatment efforts were directed to the family units and individual psychoanalytic psychotherapy was discontinued for all participants. One can only imagine the significant adjustments the professional staff had to make because their job descriptions changed so drastically. No longer were they in the familiar role of individual therapy; they were suddenly going down the unknown road of family psychotherapy. The staff had to learn by trial and error how best to work with family units. This was a significant challenge for everyone and involved, among other things, learning to manage their over-involvement with individual family members. Bowen (2013) commented that the staff who did the best with the families where the ones who had the good control over their countertransference reactions.

The next section will provide additional details about the first year and the last three years of the Family Study Project.

The First Year (1954)

Information about the first year of the project is taken from the first annual summary written in 1954 (Bowen, 2013). This short summary mentions the critical issue of the difficulty the staff had in managing the emotional intensities of the project families. The reader should recall that during that first year there were only three mother-daughter dyads. Managing the problems of staff reactivity and emotional over-involvement directly threatened the existence of the project. It was not an insignificant issue.

The other important finding during the first year was the recognition of the importance of other family members to the mother-daughter dyads. It became clear that the emotionality was not confined just to the dyad. A larger emotional system existed.

The Final Three Years (1955–58)

The last three years of the Family Study Project witnessed a change in the overall direction of the research effort. During this phase the investigators begin the clinical application of the concept of the family as an emotional unit and the first treatment of the family. If the theory conceptualized the family as an emotional unit, then the treatment must be directed to the family unit rather than one individual in the family who may be symptomatic. This is a dramatically different approach than the typical inpatient program on psychiatric units at that time, where the focus was on helping family members better manage one of their own having emotional problems.

With no clinical model to follow and with trial and error, Bowen and his colleagues made a significant shift from abandoning their role as individual therapists to working with the families. Daily family councils, as they were first known, were held on the unit for all the families and staff. No problem was off-limits; every issue was brought to the group. Over time it was found that the daily group meetings solved two recurring problems.

In early 1956 seminal paper Bowen saw the group meeting as serving both operational and therapeutic functions (Bowen 2013). First, the family groups fulfilled operational functions by effectively managing daily family problems. With the family groups, staff over-identifications or over-involvements could be easily identified. Second, the family groups were therapeutic endeavors. The goal was to contain the emotionality within the family units rather than the therapeutic relationship, and the daily groups accomplished that. Family psychotherapy was found to be an effective method of clinically working with families. In addition, it was the event that drew the most attention from numerous visitors to the project (Bowen, 2013).

CHALLENGES IN THE APPLICATION OF
THE FAMILY AS A UNIT CONCEPT

A basic challenge for clinicians accepting the concept is that it is not the prevailing mode of clinical practice today. The individual model remains the predominant orientation for today's clinical practice, followed by eclecticism. One has to look no further than the DSM-V to see this; the focus is on the individual. Early on in my private practice after leaving the Air Force, my partner, a child and adolescent psychiatrist, called my work with families a "foreign approach," and to some extent he is correct. From the vantage point of the individual model it is a foreign perspective.

In an editorial for the journal *Family Systems*, the journal of the Bowen Center for the Study of the Family, Kerr (2012) draws important distinctions between the individual or multicausal model and a systems theory perspective. For example, an adult male patient is referred both for medication and individual psychotherapy for his depression. In this case, the assumption is that his clinical presentation stems from multiple independent causes. A family systems model, on the other hand, assumes that there are many factors contributing to clinical problems, but none directly cause the problem. In addition, a systems approach supposes that if the present relationship functioning improves, clinical problems resolve. In Bowen theory, "a current disturbance in a system's balance is required to trigger and sustain symptoms" (Kerr, 2012, p. 4). The present family relationships, not the past, contribute to symptom development (Kerr, 2012).

It is an ongoing challenge for clinicians operating from a Bowen systems theory perspective to do their best to represent a family systems perspective. This is especially challenging in view of the current emphasis on medication. For example, medicating one person may make it more difficult to entertain the idea that the identified patient's problems are related to events within the family emotional unit.

Bowen wrote in several papers in his book, Family therapy in clinical practice (1978) and in the archives papers (Bowen, 2013) about obstacles or levels of awareness for clinicians embracing the concept of the family as an emotional unit. It is a difficulty for parents to *hear* that their child's symptoms may be related to problems within their family. Some parents cannot hear this. The concept must be presented in a non-pejorative way. The *hearing* represents certain thinking about the origin and nature of clinical problems. How we think about clinical problems reflects a person's underlying theoretical orientation.

Intellectual Awareness

The first challenge for clinicians to master is achieving an intellectual awareness of the concept of the family as an emotional illness. An intellectual understanding of the concept is relatively straightforward. Many students in undergraduate and graduate courses on the family or family therapy have come to understand this concept makes sense on an intellectual level.

Clinical Awareness

A more formidable challenge is to apply the concept on a clinical level. Most people can achieve an intellectual understanding of the concept but stumble in applying the concept clinically. The clinician may be eclectic and utilize family therapy as a technique with families and individual therapy with individuals. Highlighting the difficulties involved in an eclectic approach, a clergy member of the Bowen network remarked that it is difficult for a person to be a rabbi on Saturday and a priest on Sunday! Applying the concept of the family as an emotional unit means seeing this concept regardless of who is in the consulting is a definite challenge. tx fidelty ?

Emotional Awareness

The last hurdle to embracing family systems theory is having an emotional awareness of the concept. An emotional awareness first depends upon the clinician mastering the previous two challenges. How can the concept be internalized? How does a therapist shift from an individual orientation to a systems theory perspective? A clinician can utilize the standard mental health language and also operate strictly from a family systems theory perspective.

Bowen provided a suggestion how to successfully make a shift from seeing the individual to seeing the family unit using emotional detachment. He meant that the clinician must relate to the family unit and not be over-involved with any one individual in order to assist with emotional awareness of the family as an emotional unit. It is useful to think of walking upstairs one step only at a time but never skipping any step!

IMPLICATIONS FOR CLINICAL PRACTICE

Theory as a Critical Component of Practice

Bowen's Family Study Project highlights the importance of theory. Based on observation, the theory about psychological symbiosis in mother-daughter dyads was extended to family units when it became apparent that these dyads were a segment of a large system involving significant others. The concept of the family as an emotional unit was born during the first year of Bowen's NIMH project. Throughout all phases, theory guided the project. The theory was not an abstraction but meant to adapt to clinical situations. It was family systems theory that was seen as more significant than clinical techniques-theory always guides practice.

A Guide for Individual & Family Assessment

The concept provides a guide for clinical assessment. It orients assessment towards the multigenerational family, preferably across three generations. Although important, individual assessment is seen as incomplete because the family context for a person is often omitted. The family diagram is a graphic method to display functioning and emotional processes in families. The family diagram continues as a staple of family therapy and related disciplines today.

Placing the Therapeutic Relationship in a Broader Perspective

This view is clearly seen when working with a family. The therapist must establish and maintain *viable emotional contact* with all family members (Bowen, 1978). She or he cannot become over-involved or have alternating over-involvements with any one person. The focus must be on the family unit. Based on his experiences in the Family Study, Bowen felt that viewing the family as an emotional unit by definition places the therapeutic relationship in a broader perspective when compared to the traditional patient-therapist relationship (see Bowen, 1978, p. 346).

Re-defining the Nature and Function of Therapeutic Involvement

In all psychotherapy there is always therapist-patient involvement—the question is what is the nature of the involvement? Two factors were primarily responsible for Bowen and his colleagues departing from the traditional therapeutic relationship based on psychoanalytic theory and practice. First, there were the ongoing challenges experienced by the staff when working to manage the emotionality in the project families. As Bowen colorfully remarked, "the symbiosis tended to get stuck to the ward staff" (Bowen, 2013, p. 49). He was referring to the ongoing emotional intensities of the families and the staff-family challenges in managing these. This emotionality presented significant challenges. Bowen commented that the staff who could best manage themselves with this had the best control over their counter-transferences (Bowen, 2013).

Second, based on detailed observations it became apparent that the mother-daughter emotional difficulties were merely a small part of a larger emotional system involving people close to the mothers and daughters. Thus, the orientation changed to the family emotional units from only the mother-daughter dyads. Now that the focus was on the family unit, the treatment must be on that unit. But, there was no literature or training on working with families. Family psychotherapy was developed as one method to work clinically with families. This change altered the therapeutic role and function. This undertaking was itself monumental for that period of time and within an institution like the NIMH with its orientation to the individual.

A new type of therapeutic involvement called for relating to all family members and avoiding over-involvement with any one person. It also required placing intense emotionality into the family units rather than into the therapeutic relationship. Clinicians underestimate the extent of emotionality in clinical work and overestimate their ability to successfully manage these processes. There were two other functions that became critical. These were finding and nurturing family leaders and avoiding psychologically replacing parents.

Finding and Nurturing Family Leaders

With the degree of therapeutic involvement changing and with clinicians working to avoid replacing parents, then who should take the place of the therapist? The answer was the family headed by a family leader.

In my years of asking families to identify the family leader, I have never encountered a family that did not know who that person was. The family leader is most often the person who makes the initial mental health appointment. Bowen (2013, p. 118) made the family leader responsible for follow-up appointments and for the end-of-session summary. It was most often the case that the family leader was the first person that began working to improve their own differentiation of self (Bowen, 2013). Even if the family leader came by him or herself, the focus remained on the family unit or the leader's part in the overall family difficulties. The subject of family leadership is an area seldom mentioned in the area of clinical practice. From the Family Study Project onward, nurturing family leaders remains an important activity.

Minimizing Psychologically Replacing Parents

In a seminal paper, Bowen noted that in traditional psychoanalytic psychotherapy, "it might be said that it is a goal that the therapist replace the parent in psychological importance and that a major therapeutic principle is the analysis of this relationship" (Bowen, 2013, p. 46). Bowen realized the challenges involved in this endeavor, and through experience decided not to follow this path. He commented:

> One point would be that the therapist might develop techniques in which he did not lend himself to the patient's bid that he do a certain amount of "replacing of the parent." Experience would indicate that the patients do in fact need such a figure. If this be so, who should this figure be? (Bowen, 2013, p. 47)

Based on the experiences of the project, especially during the first year, a decision was made that the therapists try to avoid the role of psychologically replacing parents. Bowen felt that "it took great skill and training" to manage the emotionality with the families and that most staff were not trained to handle this level of intensity (Bowen, 2013, p. 46). The goal was to have the family unit absorb the emotionality rather than the therapeutic relationship.

SUMMARY

Bowen's eight interlocking theoretical concepts are often thought of as just that—purely theoretical. But often overlooked is that the theory is grounded on extensive observational research conducted during the Family Study Project. His research is an early example of single case experiments with families. One purpose of bringing to light Bowen's unpublished papers is to detail these efforts (Bowen, 2013).

Discovering and refining the family as an emotional unit concept was the chief finding of the Family Study Project. Intertwined with this concept was family psychotherapy, perhaps the first effort to work clinically with families in a much different way than traditional practice.

However, the concept is not universally accepted; the dominant mode of thinking and practicing remains the individual model. As Kerr (2013) concluded, this method is a multicausal model that assumes independence of causes for clinical presentations, often necessitating different treatments for different problems. The systems theory view is that if relationship functioning improves, symptoms will decrease.

The concept of family psychotherapy departs from traditional practice in many important ways. For the Bowen therapists, theory is a necessary and sufficient reason for clinical practice (Kerr, 2012). Clear guidance is also provided for assessment and the degree of involvement in the therapeutic relationship.

REFERENCES

Bowen, M. (1978). *Family therapy in clinical practice.* Lanham, MD: Jason Aronson.
Bowen, M. (2013). *The origins of family psychotherapy: The NIMH family study project.* J. Butler (Ed.). Lanham, MD: Jason Aronson.
Butler, J. (2011). The NIMH family study project & the origin of family psychotherapy. *Family Systems,* 8, 2, 135–143.
Butler, J. (2013). Family psychotherapy: The first evolutionary stage during the NIMH family study project. *Family Systems,* 10, 1, 29–42.
Kerr, M. E. & Bowen, M. (1988). *Family evaluation.* New York: Norton Press.
Kerr, M. E. (2012). From the editor. *Family Systems,* 9, 1, 3–7.

Part II

SCIENTIFIC CONTRIBUTIONS TO AN EMOTIONAL SYSTEMS PERSPECTIVE

Chapter 6

Epigenetic Effects of Parental Care within and across Generations

Frances A. Champagne and James P. Curley

Parents can have an enduring impact on the development of their offspring. Converging evidence from animal and human studies suggest that variation in or disruption to the quality of parent-offspring interactions can lead to divergent trajectories in brain development and behavior. These developmental effects may have far-reaching consequences that extend across generations. Though there are likely multiple pathways that contribute to these effects, epigenetic mechanisms have been proposed as a critical biological link between the experience of parenting and these within and across generation consequences. Here we will consider the emerging evidence supporting this epigenetic hypothesis and the complex routes through which multigenerational effects are achieved.

In mammals, the early life environment typically consists of dynamic interactions between parents and offspring that promote growth, survival, and behavioral development. Within-species variation in parental care is typical across a broad range of species creating a unique early life environment for developing offspring. This variation is a reflection of a variety of environmental signals, such as resource availability, social support, and stress. Thus environmentally induced changes in parent-offspring interactions allow for the quality of the environment to influence the process of development and this "responsivity" to environmental cues may serve as a mechanism to promote adaptation and evolutionary fitness. A critical question is regarding the nature of the biological pathways through which this "responsivity" is achieved. There is increasing appreciation of the role of gene regulatory mechanisms in generating plasticity in response to the environment, and these mechanisms may be engaged by the experience of variation in parent-offspring interactions. These epigenetic mechanisms consist of factors that can increase or decrease gene activity (i.e., expression) without changes to the underlying

DNA sequence. Though our understanding of these mechanisms continues to evolve, it is clear that these pathways may confer both plasticity (i.e., change in response to environmental experiences) and stability (i.e., that maintenance of these environmentally induced changes across the lifespan). Moreover, due to the stability and potential heritability of epigenetic variation, these mechanisms may play a role in the multigenerational consequences of parenting that have been observed across species.

In this chapter we will explore evidence from animal and human studies of an impact of parental care on epigenetic pathways. We will also describe the potential role that these pathways may play in the transmission of parental care effects across generations. Finally, we will describe the interplay between maternal, paternal, and offspring characteristics that are an important consideration in epigenetic studies.

DEVELOPMENT IN THE CONTEXT OF VARIATION IN PARENTING .

Though parenting can involve characteristic patterns of behavior that reflect the changing needs of offspring, there is tremendous variation in parental behavior. In humans, this variation reflects the socioeconomic demands of parents and broader ecological factors that influence the physical and psychological stress of parents. For example, parental sensitivity to infant cues may be reduced in parents that experience high environmental stress/demands (Crittenden & Bonvillian, 1984) and this reduced sensitivity may impact developmental trajectories in offspring, leading to increased negative affect, aggression, and fear responses (Hane & Fox, 2006; Hane et al., 2010). These long-term outcomes of parenting are further demonstrated in studies of childhood neglect and abuse. Cognition, social behavior, and psychiatric health are impacted by these adverse early life experiences (Trickett & McBride-Chang, 1995). Moreover, our increasing ability to study the human brain has permitted appreciation of the profound neurobiological impact of parenting. Perceived low levels of maternal care predict heightened dopaminergic response to stress in the ventral striatum (Pruessner et al., 2004) and elevated maternal and paternal overprotection predicts reduced gray matter volume in the prefrontal cortex (Narita et al., 2010). Childhood neglect, in the form of institutional rearing, and abuse are associated with heightened amygdala reactivity to threat cues (Tottenham et al., 2011; McCrory et al., 2013). A common theme of these neurodevelopmental studies is the impact of disruption to the parent-child relationship on the response to stress, and it is clear that these experiences have a lasting impact on hypothalamic-pituitary-adrenal (HPA) function, rendering individuals more vulnerable to stressors (De Bellis, 2005).

Though studies in humans provide a compelling case for the enduring impact of parents on offspring, experimental models in animals are needed to determine the causal links between childhood experience and neurobiological outcomes. In primates, increased socioeconomic stress, in the form of variable foraging demands, can reduce maternal sensitivity and lead to reduced brain volume of the corpus callosum and hippocampus (Coplan et al., 2006; Jackowski et al., 2011). Similar to humans, there is an interaction between genetic risk and environmental risk in studies of variable foraging in non-human primates, leading to increased corticotropin-releasing factor (CRF) levels—a marker of increased HPA reactivity (Coplan et al., 2011). Similar gene-environment interactions are observed among nonhuman primates that have experienced maternal deprivation through nursery rearing (Kinnally et al., 2010). In macaques that have been deprived of maternal contact through peer-rearing, there are alterations in the volume and serotonin receptor density of several brain regions which may contribute to the increased anxiety observed as a function of this early life stress (Spinelli et al., 2010). Abusive caregiving, particularly involving high levels of maternal rejection, also impacts the serotonergic system and interacts with risk alleles within this system to predict stress reactivity of offspring (Maestripieri et al., 2006).

Experimental studies of parent-offspring interactions in rodents have contributed significantly to our understanding of the molecular, cellular, and neurobiological pathways that contribute to the long-term outcomes observed in humans and nonhuman primates. Low levels of maternal care, particularly licking/grooming (LG) of pups, can lead to increased stress responsivity in offspring, and this effect is attributed to reduced glucocorticoid receptor (GR) levels in the hippocampus (Meaney, 2001). Cross-fostering studies suggest that reduced levels of LG, rather than genetic or prenatal factors, contribute to these developmental outcomes (Francis et al., 1999). Maternal separation, involving prolonged daily absences of the mother, is associated with heighted stress responsivity (Andersen et al., 1999). Elevated hypothalamic CRF and vasopressin (AVP) as well as reduced hippocampal GR induced by these disruptions contributes to this elevated HPA response (Lehmann et al., 1999; Murgatroyd et al., 2009). Postpartum female rodents can be induced to reduce their nurturing behavior and increase abusive mother-infant interactions through removal of bedding material from the home-cage, and this manipulation increases stress responsivity and reduces neurotrophin levels in the prefrontal cortex (Rice et al., 2008; Roth et al., 2009). Conversely, nurturing mother-infant interactions can be induced through brief maternal separations or through use of a communal rearing paradigm in which multiple females care for litters of biological and nonbiological offspring in a communal nest (Liu et al., 1997; Curley et al., 2009). These rearing experiences lead to reduced stress responsivity, increased neurotrophin levels within the hippocampus, and increased oxytocin receptor levels in offspring (Curley et al., 2009; Branchi et al., 2011). Overall, these studies illustrate the plasticity of the developing brain in response to the quality of parent-offspring interactions.

SHAPING THE EPIGENETIC LANDSCAPE OF OFFSPRING

During development, the brain is changing rapidly and cascades of changes that occur within the brain are dependent on the ability to dynamically alter gene expression. Though the DNA sequence encodes for the mRNAs and proteins needed for the developmental process, the timing of increases and decreases in these DNA products is of critical importance for normal development. The "turning on" or "turning off" of gene activity is accomplished through a complex process of gene regulation. Epigenetic mechanisms are central to this process and involve molecular modifications either directly to the DNA or to proteins/molecules which interact with the DNA (i.e., DNA methylation, post-translational histone modifications, and non-coding RNAs). DNA methylation is a molecular change to cytosine nucleotides within the DNA sequence. The addition of methyl groups to cytosines is generally associated with reduced gene silencing (Razin, 1998). DNA methylation patterns within cells are copied following cell division and this process is essential to cellular differentiation, whereby cells with the same DNA can generate multiple different tissue types (i.e., neurons, muscle, liver cells) (Taylor & Jones, 1985). Histones form a protein core around which DNA is wrapped and these proteins can be altered through the addition or removal of multiple chemical groups. Acetylation, methylation, and phosphorylation of histone proteins can alter the accessibility of DNA through histone-DNA interactions. Both the location and type of histone modification will uniquely predict the impact of gene activity, creating a complex "histone code" (Jenuwein & Allis, 2001). Finally, small RNA molecules that do not encode for a protein have been determined to be key players in gene regulation. These microRNAs have the capacity to alter many target genes and thus can have a widespread epigenetic impact (Sato et al., 2011).

Though our understanding of epigenetic mechanisms and their function continues to evolve, there has been increasing appreciation of the role of these mechanisms in generating environmentally induced changes in the developing brain. In rodents, the experience of low levels of LG is associated with increased DNA methylation and decreased histone acetylation (an epigenetic mark that increases gene expression) in several target genes within the hippocampus, including the gene encoding GR (*Nr3c1*) (Weaver et al., 2004). However, it is important to note that low versus high levels of LG are associated with changes in the expression of hundreds of genes within the hippocampus (Weaver et al., 2006), and genome-wide profiling of epigenetic variation within the hippocampus of these offspring reveals broad increases and decreases in DNA methylation and histone acetylation (McGowan et al., 2011). High levels of maternal LG induced through communal rearing can also induce epigenetic variation within the hippocampus. Increased histone acetylation is observed in the brain-derived neurotrophic factor gene (*Bdnf*) which may alter the plasticity of this brain region and account for rearing environment effects on cognition and anxiety-like behavior (Branchi et al., 2011).

Rodent models of neglect and abuse have also been revealing regarding the role of epigenetic mechanisms in generating the long-term consequences of early life adversity. Within the hippocampus, maternal separation decreases DNA methylation of *Crf* (Wang et al., 2014), increases DNA methylation of *Nr3c1* (Kundakovic et al., 2013), and leads to age-dependent effects on the methylation of histones associated with the *Bdnf* gene (Suri et al., 2013). Within the hypothalamus, early life maternal separation is associated with decreased DNA methylation of the *Avp* gene that leads to increased *Avp* expression and heightened neuroendocrine response to stressors (Murgatroyd et al., 2009). In rats, abusive caregiving is associated with increased DNA methylation of the *Bdnf* gene in the prefrontal cortex of offspring (Roth et al., 2009). This epigenetic disruption is also present in the hippocampus and amygdala, with effects varying dependent on the sex and age of offspring (Roth et al., 2014).

Since the discovery of hippocampal epigenetic changes induced by maternal care in rats, there has been increasing exploration of the translational relevance of these findings. In postmortem hippocampal brain tissue, epigenetic analyses have revealed increased DNA methylation of the *Nr3c1* gene associated with a history of childhood abuse (McGowan et al., 2009). Similar to the case of epigenetic variation induced by LG in rats, childhood abuse in humans is associated with genome-wide increases and decrease in DNA methylation within the hippocampus (Labonte et al., 2012). However, reliance on postmortem brain tissue for the study of epigenetics in humans limits the application of this approach and so there has been increasing focus on epigenetic variation present in peripheral tissues (i.e., blood or saliva). In nonhuman primates, it has been established that maternal deprivation can have genome-wide epigenetic consequences in both the brain and the blood (Provencal et al., 2012), suggesting the utility of blood as an epigenetic biomarker of early life adversity. Similar to what has been demonstrated within the hippocampus, increased DNA methylation of the *Nr3c1* gene has been observed in blood samples of individuals that have experienced childhood abuse or maltreatment (Tyrka et al., 2012; Perroud et al., 2014). Genome-wide

DNA hypermethylation is observed in blood samples of orphanage-reared compared to family-reared children (Naumova et al., 2012) and both hyper- and hypo-DNA methylation has been observed in genome-wide analyses of blood samples of individuals with a history of childhood abuse (Suderman et al., 2014). Thus, across species, the quality of the parent-child relationship can have a lasting epigenetic impact.

Though epigenetic variation provides critical information regarding the functional activity of the genome, it is important to consider the interplay between genetic and epigenetic variation when predicting sensitivity to adversity and long-term neurodevelopmental outcomes. In humans and nonhuman primates, genetic variation in the gene encoding the serotonin transporter (*SLC6A4*) interacting with environmental adversity (i.e., maternal deprivation, childhood maltreatment) has been found to predict heightened stress reactivity and psychiatric risk in adulthood (Caspi et al., 2003; Suomi, 2006). In macaques, this interaction has been found to be associated with DNA methylation, such that individuals with the risk genotype and maternal deprivation have elevated *SLC6A4* DNA methylation (Kinnally et al., 2010). In humans, genetic variation in the *FKBP5* gene, which encodes for a protein that impacts GR function, has been found to predict psychiatric outcomes (Binder et al., 2008). Among individuals that experience childhood abuse, presence of the risk genotype is associated with DNA hypomethylation of *FKBP5* with consequences for stress reactivity (Klengel et al., 2013). Thus, combining genetic studies with epigenetic analyses may serve as a promising research avenue for expanding our understanding of vulnerability to child-hood adversity.

TRANSMITTING TRAITS ACROSS GENERATIONS: BEYOND THE INHERITANCE OF DNA

Though the concept of inheritance has become synonymous with the trans-mission of DNA, it is becoming increasingly clear that there are multiple biological routes through which the transmission of traits can occur. Epigen-etic mechanisms are emerging as an important player in this expanded notion of inheritance and may provide a pathway through which environmentally induced changes are transmitted to subsequent generations of offspring. In the case of parental care, it is evident that both offspring and grand offspring can be altered in their developmental trajectories. In many cases, these mul-tigenerational effects can be attributed to the transmission of variation in parental care across generations. In humans, variation in parental care (Miller et al., 1997) and abusive caregiving (Egeland & Susman-Stillman, 1996) dis-play multigenerational continuity. Similarly, in nonhuman primates, abusive caregiving is transmitted across generation and cross-fostering studies suggest that it is the experience of adverse parent-infant interactions that mediate this transmission (Maestripieri, 2005). Due to this environmentally induced transmission of parental care, the broad neurodevelopmental consequences of parenting are likewise transmitted.

Epigenetic mechanisms play a critical role in the behavioral transmission of maternal care across generations. In rats, the experience of low levels of LG during postnatal development leads to epigenetic silencing of hypothalamic estrogen receptors in female offspring. Increased DNA methylation and repressive histone modifications of *Esr1*, the gene encoding estrogen receptor alpha, emerge during the postnatal period in offspring that experience low compared to high levels of maternal LG (Pena et al., 2013). As a consequence of these epigenetic changes, adult female offspring that experienced low levels of maternal care are less sensitive to hormonal priming of maternal care and display low levels of LG toward their own offspring (Champagne et al., 2001). This transmission of LG behavior can persist across multiple generations. Similarly, in rats, abusive caregiving experienced by female offspring leads to increased abusive mother-infant interactions by these females and this transmission is associated with the increased *Bdnf* DNA methylation in the frontal cortex (Roth et al., 2009). The stability of epigenetic changes within the brain allow for these developmental effects to alter maternal/reproductive behavior in adulthood and shape the development of the next generation.

In addition to these maternal routes of epigenetic transmission, there is increasing evidence for the transgenerational impact of fathers on offspring development, likely mediated through epigenetic inheritance *via* the germline. Studies in laboratory rodents, in species where fathers do not contribute to the direct care of offspring, suggest that the experience of fathers prior to mating can impact offspring, grand offspring, and perhaps even subsequent generations. Male exposure to toxins, stress, and nutritional manipulations have revealed these transgenerational effects (Curley et al., 2011) and disruption in mother-offspring interactions may likewise trigger this unconventional route of inheritance. In mice, males exposed to maternal separation during postnatal development have epigenetic alterations within their sperm in adulthood, including increased DNA methylation in the *Mecp2* gene (which encodes a protein that binds to methylated DNA) and decreased methylation of the *Crf* receptor gene (Franklin et al., 2010), as well as increased expression of several microRNAs (Gapp et al., 2014). This epigenetic variation is also observed in the brain of offspring of these males and may account for the behavioral characteristics of descendants of maternally separated males. Though it is unclear how this epigenetic variation is maintained during the early stages of reproduction, this route of transmission may serve as a key pathway for males to influence the development of their offspring.

DYNAMIC INTERACTIONS BETWEEN
MOTHERS, FATHERS, AND OFFSPRING

Though maternal and paternal influences on offspring development are often considered separately, it is important to consider the interplay between both parents and offspring when examining epigenetic and neurobiological outcomes. In biparental species, there is evidence that fathers can facilitate increased mother-infant interactions (Libhaber & Eilam, 2002) and that mothers can likewise stimulate males to engage in paternal care (Liu et al., 2013). In the case of species that do not engage in paternal care, the paternal influences on offspring development that have been observed may also involve paternal-maternal interplay. In behavioral ecology, it has been established that male mates can shift the maternal investment of females, leading to either increased or decreased maternal care (Burley, 1988; Gowaty et al., 2007). Male mice that are exposed to communal rearing and who also experience complex social environments in later life have been found to have reduced anxiety-like behavior. Females that mate with these males engage in higher levels of maternal LG and nursing toward offspring, even though males are absent during these mother-infant interactions (Mashoodh et al., 2012). The potential role of mothers in the transmission of paternal effects is further supported by studies using artificial reproductive technology. Males that experience chronic stress have been found to sire offspring that exhibit increased anxiety-like and depressive-like behaviors. However, if the sperm of stressed males is used to generate these offspring with *in vitro* fertilization, the behavioral phenotypes in offspring are not completely transmitted (Dietz et al., 2011). This finding suggests that though there may be some epigenetic marks inherited *via* the germline, there may also be maternal *in utero* or post-natal influences that account for paternal influences. Studies of this interplay suggest that the transgenerational effects of maternal separation in males can, in some cases, be accounted for by variation in maternal behavior (Schmauss et al., 2014).

Though the interplay between mothers and fathers is clearly an important factor to consider in offspring development, the active role of offspring in their own development is also critical. Increasing use of *in vitro* fertilization, egg donation, and surrogacy has allowed for the study of the unique contributions of mothers and offspring in neurodevelopment and behavior. These studies illustrate the role of offspring genotype in evoking differences in postnatal maternal care (Harold et al., 2013). Offspring are not passive recipients of parental care and rodent studies suggest that sensory and behavioral cues from offspring are important triggers of the onset of maternal behavior (Stern, 1997). Even during the prenatal period, offspring are soliciting resources from the mother through hormonally induced shifts in endocrine regulation that can increase respiration, food intake, and glucose availability. Interestingly, the placenta, which serves as an interface between the mother and fetus, is dependent on dynamic epigenetic changes for normal functioning and is influenced by fathers (Fowden et al., 2011). Paternally expressed genes (i.e., genes that are only expressed from the father's copy) are highly expressed in the placenta and also have the capacity to alter postnatal maternal behavior (Isles & Holland, 2005). Thus, the interplay between mothers and fathers can even be observed at a molecular level of analysis.

CONCLUDING REMARKS

Advances in our understanding of gene regulation may have far-reaching consequences for the study of parenting and its influences as well as the transmission of traits across generations. The field of epigenetics continues to expand and evolve but will certainly reveal new insights into the molecular basis of parental effects on offspring. However, these elegant molecular studies must also be coupled with an appreciation of the complex bi-directional interactions that occur within the family between mothers, fathers, and offspring. Though animal studies will continue to be invaluable to furthering our understanding of the causal pathways linking parental care to developmental trajectories, advances in the use of epigenetic biomarkers and brain imaging in humans will be essential to establishing the translational relevance of the groundbreaking work being done in the basic sciences.

REFERENCES

Andersen, S. L., Lyss, P. J., Dumont, N. L., & Teicher, M. H. (1999). Enduring neurochemical effects of early maternal separation on limbic structures. *Annals of New York Academy of Sciences,* 877:756–759.

Binder, E. B., Bradley, R. G., Liu, W., Epstein, M. P., Deveau, T. C., Mercer, K. B., Tang, Y., Gillespie, C. F., Heim, C. M., Nemeroff, C. B., Schwartz, A. C., Cubells, J. F., & Ressler, K. J. (2008). Association of FKBP5 polymorphisms and childhood abuse with risk of posttraumatic stress disorder symptoms in adults. *JAMA,* 299:1291–1305.

Branchi, I., Karpova, N. N., D'Andrea, I., Castren, E., & Alleva, E. (2011). Epigenetic modifications induced by early enrichment are associated with changes in timing of induction of BDNF expression. *Neuroscience Letters,* 495:168–172.

Burley, N. (1988). The differential-allocation hypothesis-An experimental test. *American Naturalist,* 132:611–628.

Caspi, A., Sugden, K., Moffitt, T. E., Taylor, A., Craig, I. W., Harrington, H., McClay, J., Mill, J., Martin, J., Braithwaite, A., & Poulton, R. (2003). Influence of life stress on depression: Moderation by a polymorphism in the 5-HTT gene. *Science,* 301:386–389.

Champagne, F., Diorio, J., Sharma, S., & Meaney, M. J. (2001). Naturally occurring variations in maternal behavior in the rat are associated with differences in estrogen-inducible central oxytocin receptors. *Proceedings of National Academy of Science,* U S A 98:12736–12741.

Coplan, J. D., Smith, E. L., Altemus, M., Mathew, S. J., Perera, T., Kral, J. G., Gorman, J. M., Owens, M. J., Nemeroff, C. B., & Rosenblum, L. A. (2006). Maternal-infant response to variable foraging demand in nonhuman primates: Effects of timing of stressor on cerebrospinal fluid corticotropin-releasing factor and circulating glucocorticoid concentrations. *Annals of New York Academy of Sciences,* 1071:525–533.

Coplan, J. D., Abdallah, C. G., Kaufman, J., Gelernter, J., Smith, E. L., Perera, T. D., Dwork, A. J., Kaffman, A., Gorman, J. M., Rosenblum, L. A., Owens, M. J., & Nemeroff, C. B. (2011). Early-life stress, corticotropin-releasing factor, and serotonin transporter gene: A pilot study. *Psychoneuroendocrinology,* 36:289–293.

Curley, J. P., Mashoodh, R., & Champagne, F. A. (2011). Epigenetics and the origins of paternal effects. *Hormones and Behavior,* 59:306–314.

Curley, J. P., Davidson, S., Bateson, P., & Champagne, F. A. (2009). Social enrichment during postnatal development induces transgenerational effects on emotional and reproductive behavior in mice. *Frontiers in Behavioral Neuroscience,* 3:25.

De Bellis, M. D. (2005). The psychobiology of neglect. *Child Maltreatment,* 10:150–172.

Dietz, D. M., Laplant, Q., Watts, E. L., Hodes, G. E., Russo, S. J., Feng, J., Oosting, R. S., Vialou, V., & Nestler, E. J. (2011). Paternal transmission of stress-induced pathologies. *Biological Psychiatry,* 70:408–414.

Egeland, B., & Susman-Stillman, A. (1996). Dissociation as a mediator of child abuse across generations. *Child Abuse and Neglect,* 20:1123–1132.

Fowden, A. L., Coan, P. M., Angiolini, E., Burton, G. J., & Constancia, M. (2011). Imprinted genes and the epigenetic regulation of placental phenotype. *Progress in Biophysical Molecular Biology,* 106:281–288.

Francis, D., Diorio, J., Liu, D., & Meaney, M. J. (1999). Nongenomic transmission across generations of maternal behavior and stress responses in the rat. *Science,* 286:1155–1158.

Franklin, T. B., Russig, H., Weiss, I. C., Graff, J., Linder, N., Michalon, A., Vizi, S., & Mansuy, I. M. (2010). Epigenetic transmission of the impact of early stress across generations. *Biological Psychiatry,* 68:408–415.

Gapp, K., Jawaid, A., Sarkies, P., Bohacek, J., Pelczar, P., Prados, J., Farinelli, L., Miska, E., & Mansuy, I. M. (2014). Implication of sperm RNAs in transgenerational inheritance of the effects of early trauma in mice. *Nature Neuroscience,* 17:667–669.

Gowaty, P. A., Anderson, W. W., Bluhm, C. K., Drickamer, L. C., Kim, Y. K., & Moore, A. J. (2007). The hypothesis of reproductive compensation and its assumptions about mate preferences and offspring viability. *Proceedings of National Academy of Science,* U S A 104:15023–15027.

Hane, A. A., & Fox, N. A. (2006). Ordinary variations in maternal caregiving influence human infants' stress reactivity. *Psychological Science,* 17:550–556.

Hane, A. A., Henderson, H. A., Reeb-Sutherland, B. C., & Fox, N. A. (2010). Ordinary variations in human maternal caregiving in infancy and biobehavioral development in early childhood: A follow-up study. *Developmental Psychobiology,* 52:558–567.

Harold, G. T., Leve, L. D., Barrett, D., Elam, K., Neiderhiser, J. M., Natsuaki, M. N., Shaw, D. S., Reiss, D., & Thapar, A. (2013). Biological and rearing mother influences on child ADHD symptoms: Revisiting the developmental interface between nature and nurture. *Journal in Child Psychol Psychiatry,* 54:1038–1046.

Isles, A. R., & Holland, A. J. (2005). Imprinted genes and mother-offspring interactions. *Early Human Development,* 81:73–77.

Jackowski, A., Perera, T. D., Abdallah, C. G., Garrido, G., Tang, C. Y., Martinez, J., Mathew, S. J., Gorman, J. M., Rosenblum, L. A., Smith, E. L., Dwork, A. J., Shungu, D. C., Kaffman, A., Gelernter, J., Coplan, J. D., & Kaufman, J. (2011). Early-life stress, corpus callosum development, hippocampal volumetrics, and anxious behavior in male nonhuman primates. *Psychiatry Research,* 192:37–44.

Jenuwein, T., & Allis, C. D. (2001). Translating the histone code. *Science,* 293:1074–1080.

Kinnally, E. L., Capitanio, J. P., Leibel, R., Deng, L., LeDuc, C., Haghighi, F., & Mann, J. J. (2010). Epigenetic regulation of serotonin transporter expression and behavior in infant rhesus macaques. *Genes, Brain and Behavior,* 9:575–582.

Klengel, T., Mehta, D., Anacker, C., Rex-Haffner, M., Pruessner, J. C., Pariante, C. M., Pace, T. W., Mercer, K. B., Mayberg, H. S., Bradley, B., Nemeroff, C. B., Holsboer, F., Heim, C. M., Ressler, K. J., Rein, T., & Binder, E. B. (2013). Allele-specific FKBP5 DNA demethylation mediates gene-childhood trauma interactions. *Nature Neuroscience,* 16:33–41.

Kundakovic, M., Lim, S., Gudsnuk, K., & Champagne, F. A. (2013). Sex-specific and strain-dependent effects of early life adversity on behavioral and epigenetic outcomes. *Frontiers in Psychiatry,* 4:78.

Labonte, B., Suderman, M., Maussion, G., Navaro, L., Yerko, V., Mahar, I., Bureau, A., Mechawar, N., Szyf, M., Meaney, M. J., & Turecki, G. (2012). Genome-wide epigenetic regulation by early-life trauma. *Archives in General Psychiatry,* 69:722–731.

Lehmann, J., Pryce, C. R., Bettschen, D., & Feldon, J. (1999). The maternal separation paradigm and adult emotionality and cognition in male and female Wistar rats. *Pharmacology Biochemistry and Behavior,* 64:705–715.

Libhaber, N., & Eilam, D. (2002). Social vole parents force their mates to baby-sit. *Developmental Psychobiology,* 41:236–240.

Liu, D., Diorio, J., Tannenbaum, B., Caldji, C., Francis, D., Freedman, A., Sharma, S., Pearson, D., Plotsky, P. M., & Meaney, M. J. (1997). Maternal care, hippocampal glucocorticoid receptors, and hypothalamic-pituitary-adrenal responses to stress. *Science,* 277:1659–1662.

Liu, H. X. et al. (2013). Displays of paternal mouse pup retrieval following communicative interaction with maternal mates. *Nature Communications,* 4:1346.

Maestripieri, D. (2005). Early experience affects the intergenerational transmission of infant abuse in rhesus monkeys. *Proceedings of National Academy of Science,* U S A 102:9726–9729.

Maestripieri, D., Higley, J. D., Lindell, S. G., Newman, T. K., McCormack, K. M., & Sanchez, M. M. (2006). Early maternal rejection affects the development of monoaminergic systems and adult abusive parenting in rhesus macaques (Macaca mulatta). *Behavioral Neuroscience,* 120:1017–1024.

Mashoodh, R., Franks, B., Curley, J. P., & Champagne, F. A. (2012). Paternal social enrichment effects on maternal behavior and offspring growth. *Proceedings of Nationall Academy of Science,* U S A 109 Suppl 2:17232–17238.

McCrory, E. J., De Brito, S.A., Kelly, P. A., Bird, G., Sebastian, C. L., Mechelli, A., Samuel, S., & Viding, E. (2013). Amygdala activation in maltreated children during pre-attentive emotional processing. *British Journal of Psychiatry,* 202:269–276.

McGowan, P. O., Suderman, M., Sasaki, A, Huang, T. C., Hallett, M, Meaney. M. J., & Szyf, M. (2011). Broad epigenetic signature of maternal care in the brain of adult rats. *PLoS One,* 6:e14739.

McGowan, P. O., Sasaki, A., D'Alessio, A. C., Dymov, S., Labonte, B., Szyf, M., Turecki, G., & Meaney, M. J. (2009). Epigenetic regulation of the glucocorticoid receptor in human brain associates with childhood abuse. *Nature Neuroscience,* 12:342–348.

Meaney, M. J. (2001). Maternal care, gene expression, and the transmission of individual differences in stress reactivity across generations. *Annual Review of Neuroscience,* 24:1161–1192.

Miller, L., Kramer, R., Warner, V., Wickramaratne, P., & Weissman, M. (1997). Intergenerational transmission of parental bonding among women. *Journal American Academy of Child and Adolescent Psychiatry,* 36:1134–1139.

Murgatroyd, C., Patchev, A.V., Wu, Y., Micale, V., Bockmuhl, Y., Fischer, D., Holsboer, F., Wotjak, C. T., Almeida, O. F., & Spengler, D. (2009). Dynamic DNA methylation programs persistent adverse effects of early-life stress. *Nature Neuroscience,* 12:1559–1566.

Narita, K., Takei, Y., Suda, M., Aoyama, Y., Uehara, T., Kosaka, H., Amanuma, M., Fukuda, M., & Mikuni, M. (2010). Relationship of parental bonding styles with gray matter volume of dorsolateral prefrontal cortex in young adults. *Progress in Neuro-psychopharmacology & Biological Psychiatry,* 34: 624–631.

Naumova, O. Y., Lee, M., Koposov, R., Szyf, M., Dozier, M., & Grigorenko, E. L. (2012). Differential patterns of whole-genome DNA methylation in institutionalized children and children raised by their biological parents. *Development & Psychopathology,* 24:143–155.

Pena, C. J., Neugut, Y. D., & Champagne, F. A. (2013). Developmental timing of the effects of maternal care on gene expression and epigenetic regulation of hormone receptor levels in female rats. *Endocrinology,* 154:4340–4351.

Perroud, N., Dayer, A., Piguet, C., Nallet, A., Favre, S., Malafosse, A., & Aubry, J. M. (2014). Childhood maltreatment and methylation of the glucocorticoid receptor gene NR3C1 in bipolar disorder. *British Journal of Psychiatry,* 204:30–35.

Provencal, N., Suderman, M., Guillemin, C., Massart, R., Ruggiero, A., Wang, D., Bennett, A.J., Pierre, P. J., Friedman, D. P., Cote, S. M., Hallett, M.,

Tremblay, R. E., Suomi, S. J., & Szyf, M. (2012). The signature of maternal rearing in the methylome in rhesus macaque prefrontal cortex and T cells. *Journal of Neuroscience*, 32:15626–15642.

Pruessner, J. C., Champagne, F., Meaney, M. J., & Dagher, A. (2004). Dopamine release in response to a psychological stress in humans and its relationship to early life maternal care: A positron emission tomography study using [11C]raclopride. *Journal of Neuroscience*, 24:2825–2831.

Razin, A. (1998). CpG methylation, chromatin structure and gene silencing-a three-way connection. *The Embo Journal*, 17:4905–4908.

Rice, C. J., Sandman, C. A., Lenjavi, M. R., & Baram, T. Z. (2008). A novel mouse model for acute and long-lasting consequences of early life stress. *Endocrinology*, 149:4892–4900.

Roth, T. L., Lubin, F. D., Funk, A. J., & Sweatt, J. D. (2009). Lasting epigenetic influence of early-life adversity on the BDNF gene. *Biological Psychiatry*, 65:760–769.

Roth, T. L., Matt, S., Chen, K., & Blaze, J. (2014). Bdnf DNA methylation modifications in the hippocampus and amygdala of male and female rats exposed to different caregiving environments outside the homecage. *Developmental Psychobiology*, 56: 1755–1763.

Sato, F., Tsuchiya, S., Meltzer, S. J., & Shimizu, K. (2011). MicroRNAs and epigenetics. *FEBS Journal*, 278:1598–1609.

Schmauss, C., Lee-McDermott, Z., & Medina, L. R. (2014). Trans-generational effects of early life stress: the role of maternal behavior. *Scientific Reports*, 4:4873.

Spinelli, S., Chefer, S., Carson, R., E., Jagoda, E., Lang, L., Heilig, M., Barr, C. S., Suomi, S. J., Higley, J. D., & Stein, E. A. (2010). Effects of early-life stress on serotonin(1A) receptors in juvenile Rhesus monkeys measured by positron emission tomography. *Biological Psychiatry*, 67:1146–1153.

Stern, J. M. (1997). Offspring-induced nurturance: Animal-human parallels. *Developmental Psychobiology*, 31:19–37.

Suderman, M., Borghol, N., Pappas, J. J., Pinto Pereira, S. M., Pembrey, M., Hertzman, C., Power, C., & Szyf, M. (2014). Childhood abuse is associated with methylation of multiple loci in adult DNA. *BMC Medical Genomics*, 7:13.

Suomi, S. J. (2006). Risk, resilience, and gene x environment interactions in rhesus monkeys. *Annals of New York Academy of Sciences*, 1094:52–62.

Suri, D., Veenit, V., Sarkar, A., Thiagarajan, D., Kumar, A., Nestler, E. J., Galande, S., & Vaidya, V. A. (2013). Early stress evokes age-dependent biphasic changes in hippocampal neurogenesis, BDNF expression, and cognition. *Biological Psychiatry*, 73:658–666.

Taylor, S. M., & Jones, P. A. (1985). Cellular differentiation. *Int J Obes*, 9 Suppl 1:15–21.

Tottenham, N., Hare, T. A., Millner, A., Gilhooly, T., Zevin, J. D., & Casey, B. J. (2011). Elevated amygdala response to faces following early deprivation. *Developmental Science*, 14:190–204.

Trickett, P., & McBride-Chang, C. (1995). The developmental impact of different forms of child abuse and neglect. *Developmental Reviews*, 15:11–37.

Tyrka, A. R., Price, L. H., Marsit, C., Walters, O. C., & Carpenter, L. L. (2012). Childhood adversity and epigenetic modulation of the leukocyte glucocorticoid receptor: preliminary findings in healthy adults. *PLoS One,* 7:e30148.

Wang, A., Nie, W., Li, H., Hou, Y., Yu, Z., Fan, Q., & Sun, R. (2014). Epigenetic upregulation of corticotrophin-releasing hormone mediates postnatal maternal separation-induced memory deficiency. *PLoS One* 9:e94394.

Weaver, I. C., Meaney, M. J., & Szyf, M. (2006). Maternal care effects on the hippocampal transcriptome and anxiety-mediated behaviors in the offspring that are reversible in adulthood. *Proceedings of the National Academy of Science,* U S A 103:3480–3485.

Weaver, I. C., Cervoni, N., Champagne, F. A., D'Alessio, A. C., Sharma, S., Seckl, J. R., Dymov, S., Szyf, M., & Meaney, M. J. (2004). Epigenetic programming by maternal behavior. *Nature Neuroscience,* 7:847–854.

Chapter 7

Early Context-Dependent Epigenetic Modifications and the Shaping of Brain and Behavior

David Crews and Robert J. Noone

The tendency to succumb to the seduction of dichotomies in lieu of grappling with the reality of complexity is human. This is best seen in the nature/nurture debate that dates at least to the ancient Greeks and is reprised every generation in science under various guises (viz., innate vs. acquired, instinct vs. learned). And with every generation there is a refutation of this false dichotomy as being sterile, yielding no useful offspring in our knowledge base (c.f., Lehrman, 1970; Gottlieb, 2002; Bateson & Gluckman, 2011). This seemingly endless rediscovery is perhaps a good thing as it forces scientists to develop new ways of investigating and illustrating that nothing in biology and psychology is simple. In many ways, the rediscovery of epigenetics refreshes the debate and, perhaps for the first time, offers a solution.

Obviously, suites of genes underlie the fundamental plasticity of an organism, particularly during development or life stage transitions. How do these gene networks interact with the experiences that cumulate during an individual's life history? An important interface between the environment (either internal or external) and the genotype is that of epigenetic modifications. Exactly how these modifications come about is still relatively unknown, but recent studies at both the molecular and molar levels indicate that the origin of such effects may occur in previous generations. That is, experiences of earlier generations can modify regulatory factors affecting gene expression such that the DNA sequence itself is not changed but the individual's physiology and behavior are substantially influenced. Understanding how such modifications actually occur will increase our understanding of how the environment influences the relationship between genotype and behavior during sensitive developmental periods.

The human family is an example of a principal environment influencing the experience and behavior of its members throughout their lives. Later in this chapter it will be suggested that the family likely functions as a significant influence on epigenetic modifications shaping behavior.

An individual's phenotype is influenced by the experiences that accumulate throughout its life (Insel & Fernald, 2004). Early experiences in particular shape how individuals will respond to later experiences, and later experiences modify the effects of earlier experiences (Champagne, 2008; Champagne & Curley, 2010; Curley et al., 2009; Korosi & Baram, 2009; Moriceau et al., 2009; Romeo et al., 2010). Studies of the role of experience in behavioral development can be divided into those that focus on the parental and other social influences versus physical/biotic (e.g., storms that demolish nests early in the reproductive cycle of seasonally breeding birds/appropriate day length and temperature) influences. The former has been well characterized in avian and mammalian species while the latter is best observed in species that depend upon environmental factors to establish gonadal sex or alternative mating strategies within a sex.

Experiences during sensitive periods of development such as embryonic, neonatal, and adolescence can act together or independently to modify the genome without altering DNA structure. These effects, referred to as epigenetic, can lead to an epigenetic inheritance, such that the environment can affect the transcriptome of the individual during its development and potentially that of its descendants. Epigenetic modifications to an individual can either be at the gross or molar level (influencing the individual's interactions with its biotic and physical environment through time) or at the fine or molecular level (altering gene expression at transcriptional and translational levels during development) (Crews, 2008). An example at the molar level would include the emergent properties of progressive changes in development on behavioral outcomes that can be found in precocial birds, where the difference in timing is a major factor in differentiating filial imprinting from sexual imprinting (Bateson, 1991; Gottlieb, 1997). An example of molecular epigenetics would be the finding (see below) that pups of mothers who exhibit high levels of licking and grooming are less reactive to stress as adults as a consequence of increased serotonin tone and DNA methylation within exon 1_7 of the promoter of the glucocorticoid receptor in the hippocampus (Weaver et al., 2004).

Molar and molecular epigenetic modifications interact. Thus, changes at various levels (e.g., pattern of gene expression, physiological systems, and the organization and activation of brain circuits) bring about functional differences in brain and behavior that result in molar epigenetic changes. These then modify how individuals respond to conspecifics and their environment, bringing about changes at higher levels of biological organization. Ultimately these can lead to molecular epigenetic modifications that support the new trajectory in life history.

Epigenetics is a concept, not a technique. Environmentally induced epigenetic modifications can occur at all levels of biological organization, from the molecular to the organism's behavior, and tend to be amplified in their consequences as they ascend through these levels. Individuals vary according to the cumulative experiences they have during their life. It is accepted that cumulative experiences throughout life history interact with genetic predispositions to shape the individual's behavior. However, outside of highly artificial model systems, efforts to understand exactly how this Gene X Environment results in phenotypic change have been singularly unsuccessful. A newly emerging field, known as environmental epigenetics, is the study of how the environment can affect the genome of future generations without changing the DNA sequence, thereby having important and lasting effects.

Put simply, epigenetics applies to traits that are not determined by traditional molecular bases for inheritance. A more precise definition would be that epigenetic effects are changes in the phenotype and/or specific traits that result from the environmental modification of the molecular factors and processes around DNA that regulate genome activity yet are independent of the DNA sequence. Note that the term environment is inclusive of all stimuli that may impinge on the organism during its life cycle. How researchers have interpreted epigenetics reflects its dual origins and the nature of the question being posed. At a basic level it is useful to differentiate *molecular epigenetics* and *molar epigenetics*, or bottom-up vs. top-down epigenetics. The former perspective has emerged within the last 25 years from modern genetics/molecular biology and focuses on molecular levels of analysis. The latter perspective has a deeper history, preceding the re-discovery of Mendel's studies and focuses on questions of evolution and adaptive significance as evident in psychobiology and evolutionary biology. Thus, the object of study in molecular epigenetics is transcriptional and translational control during embryonic development while in molar epigenetics; it is the individual's interactions with its biotic and physical environment through time.

MOLECULAR VERSUS MOLAR EPIGENETICS

Investigators in the field of epigenetics come from one of two distinct lineages. This split history is similar to the origins of the modern study of animal behavior where European ethologists and American comparative psychologists differed in their approach to behavior, both in perspective and substance. Both "molecular" epigenetics and "molar" epigenetics share a common history, namely the sixteenth-/seventeenth-century debates of preformationism versus epigenesis. The central question then was, and continues to be, how a fully integrated multicellular organism develops from a single cell (the fertilized egg). Preformationists believed that adult features were present, fully formed in the egg, and simply unfolded during growth; August Weissman belonged to this group and asserted that the eggs contained all of the elements (later known as genes) to determine the phenotype that would develop. Those believing in epigenesis held that traits emerge as a consequence of the progressive interaction of the constituent parts of the zygote with the environment in which it develops. Although others such as Charles Darwin and Jean-Baptiste Lamarck were believers in epigenesis, the pivotal role of the environment in the developmental process was first demonstrated empirically by Oscar Hertwig (1894) and subsequently by Richard Woltereck (1909), whose early work on *Daphnia*, an organism that can reproduce asexually by cloning, demonstrated that genetically identical individuals would develop very different morphs depending upon their environment.

Molecular Epigenetics

Prior to the 1940s, the gene as the unit of heritable material was a theoretical concept without a physical identity. In 1942 Conrad Waddington proposed the term "epigenotype" as a conceptual model of how genes might interact with their environment and give rise to the phenotype (Waddington, 1942). It is in this sense that the term epigenetics is commonly used in molecular and developmental genetics today, namely, "the study of the mechanisms of temporal and spatial control of gene activity during the development of complex organisms" (Holliday, 1990).

Waddington continues to dominate the way we think of epigenetics and his image of an epigenetic landscape as an emergent process is the defining concept of how epigenetics operates. His structural depiction envisions how the environment shapes phenotypic outcomes and also the importance of timing as well of genes and environment. Although Waddington's formulation conveys the idea that development is irreversible and results in discrete outcomes rather than continuous outcomes, these aspects have now been refuted.

Attendant concepts advocated by Waddington were canalization and genetic assimilation. Canalization connotes the differentiation of the gene/cell type/embryo as development progresses and pathways become more entrenched, thereby making it harder for the canalized development to be dislodged and moved into another pathway. The concept of genetic assimilation emerged in part from his work with *Drosophila*. Waddington speculated that environmentally induced changes in phenotype could become incorporated into the genome, as evidenced by the persistence of the phenotype even after the original selection pressure is relaxed. It is in this manner that natural selection acts on developmental pathways leading to adaptive change in the genome rather than relying on genetic mutation. This dynamic view of development incorporates both homeostasis (the stability of a final steady state) and homeorhesis (the stability of the process of development itself).

Molar Epigenetics

There are two types of molar epigenetics. The first arose from early evolutionists who asked how within a species different phenotypes were shaped by different environments. This area of study fell out of favor for about 60–70 years in European and American science. Interestingly, it continued as a major field of study in Russia and was represented in small part in this country in the work of Theodosius Dobzhansky and his students, most notably Richard C. Lewontin (2000). Today, it has re-emerged as a vigorous area of research among evolutionary biologists and behavioral ecologists. New research on the origins of polymorphisms and polyphenisms has led to a concept now commonly referred to as "phenotypic plasticity," which is considered one of the driving forces in the relatively new union of developmental biologists with evolutionary biologists (Evo-Devo).

The other type of molar epigenetics has an equally old history. In psychology there has long been an interest in behavioral development or behavioral organization. Zing-Yang Kuo, who worked principally in the 1920s and 1930s, created much of the theory. Unfortunately, Kuo returned to China where the political strife interrupted research and, as a consequence, his contributions were marginalized (Greenberg, 2000; Kuo, 1967). The other major figure in the field was Karl S. Lashley and his students, most notable for the purposes of this review, Frank A. Beach (regarded as one of the founders of neuroendocrinology) and Theodore C. Schneirla, (whose approach to the development and display of species-typical behaviors focused on the interaction of the genetic to the environmental levels of biological organization). Examples of this integrative approach are now numerous, but two classic efforts were those of Daniel S. Lehrman and Jay S. Rosenblatt. Lehrman conducted elegant work on the elaborate interaction of parent and offspring that resulted in ringdoves learning to care for their young, and Rosenblatt carried out exquisite research on the physiological and behavioral events that underlie the development of maternal behavior in cats and later rats. Both were students of Schneirla and emphasized the dynamic nature of a process that involves the interaction of the internal milieu and the organism and the interaction of the organism and its environment. Importantly, they defined the environment broadly to include the behavior and physiology of socially important species members. In so doing they laid the foundation for psychobiology, a vibrant field that focuses on how experiences cumulate throughout life to shape the way in which the individual interacts with its social and physical environment (Gottlieb, 2002).

An approach that integrates both molecular and molar epigenetics will be necessary to reveal the mechanisms that underlie behavioral evolution (Bateson & Gluckman, 2011). That is, the continuity between molecular and molar epigenetics are revealed as the constituent elements that interact both positively and negatively in a temporal, spatial, and conditional (internal as well as the social and physical environments) context (Nijhout, 2004). As adaptive responses emerge, they in turn set the stage for future variation. Thus, evolution is a tandem process involving first development, with its built-in flexible responsiveness to both gene products and environment, followed by selection, which dictates which variants are spread and maintained (Stearns, 1989; Lewontin, 2000; West-Eberhard, 2003). In this sense the "genome learns from its experience" (Jaenisch & Bird, 2003).

It is important to consider the issue of life stages. Individuals are particularly sensitive and vulnerable to environmentally induced epigenetic modifications during early life stages or in the period of transition from one stage to another. The time of maximal neuronal plasticity is in the earliest stages of life, beginning before birth and, in mammals, up to weaning. Although the individual's capacity to respond to environmental change or insult with heritable phenotypic variation at a later stage is possible, it is during this early period that hormones and genotype predispose an individual's responses to future experiences throughout the life cycle as well as its susceptibility to developing disorders (Gilbert & Epel, 2008; Bateson & Gluckman, 2011). Although most research has focused on the earliest life stages (fetus and neonate), another period of extreme vulnerability is the period surrounding adrenarche (the increase in activity of the adrenal glands just before puberty) and pubarche (the onset of puberty). It is during adolescence that the body (including the brain) is reshaped by hormones and the individual graduates from dependence to independence, assuming the properties of maturity. Stressors experienced during this period also have enduring effects, including neural remodeling, impaired learning and memory, and altered emotional behaviors in adulthood.

CONTEXT-DEPENDENT VERSUS GERMLINE-DEPENDENT EPIGENETIC MODIFICATIONS

The scope of environmental effects that influence patterns of gene expression in the brain and subsequently behavior is virtually limitless. The extent to which environmentally induced epigenetic modifications can become an inherited trait depends both upon the nature of the stimulus and the mechanism of its action. At a molecular level, CpG sites (regions of DNA where a cytosine nucleotide and a guanine nucleotide are adjacent) are often associated with 5' promoter regions of genes and have a higher probability of undergoing mutation than other regions of the genome. Consequent changes in DNA methylation patterns at CpG islands (DNA regions that contain a high frequency of CpG sites) would persist and, if imprinted in the germline, have the *potential* of becoming heritable.

Context-Dependent Epigenetic Modification

Best studied are the epigenetic modifications that either have an effect early in life, such as exposure to EDCs (endocrine disruptor chemicals) *in utero* or smoking during childhood and adolescence. In the first instance the onset of disease manifests later during the individual's lifetime while in the latter instance, the deleterious effects of smoking decline with time *only if the individual is no longer exposed to the stimulus*. Similarly, an epigenetic modification can be perpetuated across generations by simple persistence of the causal environmental factor such that each generation is exposed to the same conditions.

An excellent example of Context-dependent epigenetic modification and behavior is the work of Meaney and colleagues (Kappeler & Meaney, 2010). In a long series of elegant studies this group has demonstrated that the nature and amount of care a pup receives from the mother modulates its reaction to stress later in life largely through effects on the glucocorticoid receptor (GR) in the hippocampus. This maternal effect can cross generations, but its heritability depends upon the pup's experience in the first week of life. Recently this group has documented that being reared by a high-quality mother results in the expression of the transcription factor A (NGFI-A), a nerve growth factor-inducible protein, that binds to the first exon of the GR gene, resulting in increased expression of GR. High-quality maternal care during this critical period demethylates NGFI-A and the acetylation of histones. Just as cross-fostering can reverse these molecular and behavioral changes, infusion of methionine, a histone deacetylase inhibitor, into the hippocampus can also reverse these events. Other studies demonstrate that the composition of the litter (number of brothers and sisters) also influence anxiety and sociosexual behavior in adulthood (deMederios et al., 2010; Crews et al., 2009).

Germline-Dependent Epigenetic Modification

Germline-dependent epigenetic modifications are fundamentally different than Context-dependent epigenetic modification in that the epigenetic imprint has become independent of the original causative agent. That is, the epigenetic modification is transferred to subsequent generations because the change in the epigenome has been incorporated into the germline. Thus, the effect is manifested in each generation, even in the absence of the causative agent. In such instances the DNA methylation of heritable epialleles (a group of otherwise identical genes that differ in the extent of methylation) are passed through to subsequent generations rather than being erased as occurs normally during gametogenesis and shortly after fertilization.

Transgenerational Inheritance

The defining distinction between Context- and Germline-dependent epigenetic modifications lies in the timing and persistence of the exposure. Exposure to environmental or psychological stressors will bring about change in the epigenome, but the transmission of the effects of that exposure can occur in two basic ways. Context-dependent epigenetic modifications are in direct response to the stimulus. Thus, an endocrine disruptor in the environment will induce changes in all individuals that are exposed to it and, as long as the environment stays contaminated, further generations will also exhibit the modification. On the other hand, Germline-dependent epigenetic modifications can be transmitted to future generations without the requirement of additional exposure. In such instances removal of the contaminant will not result in resumption of the original, nonmodified state because the modification has become part of the germline and will pass to all future generations. Thus, only Germline-dependent epigenetic modifications are truly transgenerational in nature.

By now it should be obvious to the reader that the most important aspect of how one goes about studying behavioral epigenetics is to realize that it is more an issue of perspective or question, and less about the tools and techniques to be implemented. For this reason virtually any aspect of behavior is open to the investigator; tissue differentiation, developmental psychobiology, cognitive development, psychopathology, life history strategies, phenotypic plasticity are just a few examples. The human family is seen as a particularly interesting area for study as it includes a number of levels of interacting processes influencing behavioral epigenetics.

Stress Induces Context-Dependent Epigenetic Modifications

Stress, particularly if sustained, can lead to impaired immunity, disease, and neurological changes characteristic of major depressive illness and particularly chronic anxiety disorders (McEwen, 2010; Romeo et al., 2009). Chronic restraint stress (CRS) in rats has been a standard paradigm for studying such effects on physiology, brain, and behavior. For example, 6 hours daily of immobilization restraint for 3 weeks results initially in elevated corticosterone levels but after 21 days, the hypothalamic-pituitary-adrenal (HPA) axis shows adaptation and levels are back to normal. This however underlies a progressive atrophy of the dendrite length and branching of pyramidal neurons in the CA3 region of the hippocampus, a process mediated by corticosterone potentiating postsynaptic activity and the release of excitatory amino acids from adjacent mossy fiber terminals arising from the granule neurons in the dentate gyrus and acting via NMDA (glutamate) receptors. Conversely, there is an increase in dendritic spine density of neurons in the basolateral amygdala and medial prefrontal cortex (mPFC), and decreased neurogenesis in the dentate gyrus. In addition to these structural changes, stressed rats exhibit a variety of specific cognitive deficits in spatial learning and memory, as well as increased anxiety-like and agonistic behavior.

Integration of Germline- and Context-Dependent Epigenetic Modifications

It is clear that individuals modify, or even recreate, their environment via behavior. Two challenges that must be considered are (i) environmental stressors and (ii) psychological stressors. Both are forced upon the individual, either because they are part of the environment the organism is born into, or are visited upon it during its life. Both induce epigenetic modifications, but of a different sort. The former is dependent upon exposure while the latter can result in alterations to the genome of future generations independently of changes to the DNA sequence through mechanisms that include DNA methylation. There is now clear evidence that an individual's likelihood of developing health problems involves a combination of that individual's own exposures as well as exposures of ancestors in generations past. Another factor that must be considered is the (iii) hormonally induced differentiation of body and brain triggered by genes, resulting in sex differences in physiological and behavioral responsiveness to environmental stimuli. In rodents and humans, males and females differ substantially in reactions to environmental challenges and their propensity to develop illness, disease, and affective disorders.

THE HUMAN FAMILY SYSTEM

The human family provides an interesting example of how Context-dependent epigenetic modifications may shape the neurobiology and behavior of individuals and how such modifications might occur over the course of development and over multiple generations. It also appears likely that the family would entail the interaction of both molecular and molar epigenetic modifications.

The family systems theory developed by Bowen (1978) posits that family interactions over the course of development can be observed to result in individual differences in the degree to which children emotionally separate from their caretakers. This process can further be observed to shape the degree to which higher cortical processes may be involved in regulating the more automatic or instinctual processes at play in behavior, that is, the stress response systems. The degree of emotional separation between parents and offspring over the course of development and the concomitant degree in the capacity to self-regulate emotional reactivity to the social environment (defined in the concept of differentiation of self) results in individual differences in adaptiveness over the life course (Bowen, 1978; Kerr & Bowen, 1988).

Human evolutionary history is marked not only by the rapid expansion of the brain, but by the family network in which development occurs (Flinn, Ward, & Noone, 2005). The family entails prolonged periods of parental and alloparental care and is marked by interdependent attachments among multiple members. Central to the human's adaptive success has been its elaborate brain and a large extended family (Allman, 1999). After birth the brain continues its rapid growth and a significant aspect of its functioning is directed toward the social environment. The development of both emotional autonomy and social connectedness influence neural and hormonal processes affecting behavior which then influence social relationships. In a reciprocal process the relationship environment then influences neural and hormonal processes (Cacioppo & Patrick, 2008). The deep and enduring ties of the family result in stable interactional patterns and become the principal environment influencing brain development and behavior (see Papero, chapter 2).

Siblings can be observed to vary to some degree in the emotional separation they attain in the family by late adolescence/early adulthood. Multiple factors can contribute to this process, but the family can be observed to predictably generate such differences (Kerr & Bowen, 1988; Noone, 2008). The degree to which a child matures and develops emotional autonomy is seen as principally determined by the functioning of the family emotional unit. The position of each child, circumstances around conception and birth, family adaptive patterns, parental levels of maturation occurring in their families of origin, and stressors affecting the family during the child-rearing years, contribute to variation in the maturation of siblings. The degree to which a child moves from complete dependence to relative emotional independence is viewed as determining their overall functioning throughout the life course. The resulting differences in basic adaptiveness are seen as quite stable throughout adulthood, influencing mate selection, and shaping the functioning of the families in the next generation (Noone, chapter 3).

Bowen theory, then, posits that the family system is a distinct environment which differentially influences child development leading to variation in the basic phenotypic adaptiveness of individuals in each generation. The experience and behavior of the preceding generations can be observed to influence the maturational process of individuals. If accurate, it provides an example of how behavioral development might be shaped by family interactions. Given recent discoveries it is not far-fetched to suggest that the family system may entail Context-dependent epigenetic modifications in the brains and behavior of individuals and that these modifications would vary among siblings based on their positions in the family and periods of fortunate and unfortunate events occurring over the course of development.

Epigenetic modifications occurring over the course of development in the family system would be Context-dependent in that the stimuli shaping such modifications would be seen as due to family interactional patterns, such as the nuclear family adaptive patterns described by Bowen (see chapters 2 and 3 in this volume) which are significantly influenced by the previous generation. External environmental stressors as well as intra-family events disturbing a family system's balance, that is births, deaths, etc., might also lead to epigenetic modifications in the brains and behavior of individual members. Theory would predict that the influence of stressors would differentially affect siblings based on their position in the family and the developmental periods in which they occur.

Siblings are differentially influenced by the family environment and this experience not only influences their functioning throughout life, it influences the functioning of the family unit in the next generation. Each family unit, then, can be observed to generate variation in the basic adaptiveness of individuals and families in the following generations. The Context-dependent epigenetic modifications occurring over the course of development would be seen as transmitted into the next generation with some variation.

As mentioned, the work of Meaney and colleagues (Champagne, 2008; Meaney, 2010), in which rodent pups were crossfostered, demonstrated how both molar and molecular epigenetic modifications can result from parental care and influence their behavior into adulthood. The brain and the length and context of development are more complex in the human. Maternal care, for example, is highly influenced by her relationships with other emotionally important members in the family. Likewise both the developing child and the principal caretakers are influenced not only by their direct interactions with other family members, but by the interactions other family members have with each other. While human epigenetic studies are few to date (McGowan et al., 2009), rodent studies demonstrate that variations in the sex ratio of the litter and maternal care can influence neural and brain development. They provide support for the proposition that the human family emotional system can entail epigenetic modifications in the brains and behavior of children. The study of epigenetics may provide evidence that the family emotional system as defined in Bowen theory profoundly influences behavior throughout life and shapes behavior over multiple generations.

SUMMARY

We are at the very beginning of studies of the epigenetics of behavior. Behavioral phenotypes are affected by multiple factors; some beginning in generations past while others originate during sensitive periods or life stages. We now know that genes do not cause behavior, and there is little evidence that, outside of disease and pathology, genotypes predispose individuals to behavior in particular ways. Understanding the development of behavior has yielded more information on the causes of behavior. For example, different "experiences" during sensitive life stages produce variation among individuals that markedly influence how the individual responds to social and sexual cues later in adulthood. This variation is the substrate on which evolution can act. Several studies that deconstruct various confounds inherent in research in developmental psychobiology have been presented. For example, in the ERaKO mouse, we have seen how the sex and genotype ratios of the litter have separate and distinct effects on the nature and quality of the individual's behavior later in adulthood, as well as on the metabolic activity within networks of brain nuclei that underlie these behaviors. The finding that functional neural systems can be re-organized depending upon the composition of the litter in which the individual develops is startling yet yields a deeper understanding of how neural systems are organized early in life.

The recent discovery that the environment can affect the genome of future generations without changing the DNA sequence has particular relevance to understanding brain and behavior. However, it remains to be seen if our increasing understanding of the causes and effects of epigenetic modifications will produce generalizable insights into the causes and functions of behavior. This chapter describes some of the mechanisms by which factors influence adult behavioral responsiveness and their underlying neural substrates; of particular interest in this regard is how the environment can produce significant individual variation in social behaviors. The human family is presented as an example of how a distinct relationship environment might shape such variation. Two distinct epigenetic modifications are described: Context-dependent modifications are similar to proximate environmental effects while Germline-dependent modifications are equivalent to ultimate environmental effects in shaping brain and behavior.

It is clear that ultimate and proximate events interact to influence how an individual responds to events in their own life history and the study of epigenetics may be the method by which these issues can be addressed. To date, only one study has demonstrated that Germline-dependent epigenetic modifications laid down in previous generations alter how individuals respond to a stressor (CRS) experienced during adolescence (Crews, 2011). This result suggests that different types of experiences can result in different epigenetic modifications that are independent of one another, but that together influence the phenotype in novel ways.

REFERENCES

Allman, J. M. (1999). *Evolving brains.* New York: Scientific American Library.

Bateson, P. P. G. (1991). Are there principles in behavioural development? In P. P. G. Bateson (Ed.), *The development and integration of behaviour* (pp. 19–40). Cambridge : Cambridge University Press.

Bateson, P. & Gluckman, P. (2011). *Plasticity, robustness, development and evolution.* Cambridge: Cambridge University Press.

Bowen, M. (1978). *Family therapy in clinical practice.* New York: Jason Aronson.

Cacioppo, J. T. & Patrick, W. (2008). *Loneliness:Human nature and the need for social connection.* New York: W.W. Norton and Company.

Champagne, F. A. (2008). Epigenetic mechanisms and the transgenerational effects of maternal care. *Frontiers in Neuroendocrinology, 29,* 386–397.

Champagne, F. A. & Curley, J. P. (2010). Maternal care as a modulating influence on infant development. In M.S. Blumberg, J.H. Freeman, S.R. Robinson (Eds.), *Oxford handbook of developmental behavioral neuroscience* (pp. 323–341). Oxford: Oxford Library of Neuroscience.

Crews, D. (2008). Epigenetics and its implications for behavioral neuroendocrinology. *Frontiers in Neuroendocrinology, 29,* 344–357.

Crews, D. (2011). Epigenetic modifications of brain and behavior: Theory and practice. *Hormones and Behavior, 59,* 393–398.

Crews, D., Rushworth, D., Gonzalez-Lima, F., & Ogawa, S. (2009). Litter environment affects behavior and brain metabolic activity of adult knockout mice. *Frontiers in Behavioral Neuroscience* 3: 12. doi:10.3389/neuro.08.012.200

Curley, J. P., Davidson, S., Bateson, P., & Champagne, F. A. (2009). Social enrichment during postnatal development induces transgenerational effects on emotional and reproductive behavior in mice. *Frontiers in Behavioral Neuroscience* 29, doi:10.3389/neuro.08.025.2009.

deMedeiros, C. B., Rees, S. L., Llianas, M., Fleming, A., & Crews, D. (2010). Deconstructing early life experiences: Distinguishing the contributions of prenatal and postnatal factors to adult male sexual behavior in the rat. *Psychological Science* 21: 1494–1501. doi:10.1177/0956797610382122

Flinn, M. V., Ward, C. V., & Noone, R. J. (2005). Hormones and the human family. In D. Buss (Ed.), *Handbook of evolutionary psychology* (pp. 552–580). Hoboken, N. J.: John Wiley & Sons, Inc.

Gilbert S. F., & Epel, D. (2008). *Ecological developmental biology: Integrating epigenetics, medicine, and evolution.* Sunderland, ME: Sinauer Associates.

Gottlieb, G. (1997). *Synthesizing nature–nurture: Prenatal roots of instinctive behavior.* Mahwah, NJ: Lawrence Erlbaum.

Gottlieb, G. (2002). Individual development and evolution: The genesis of novel behavior. Mahwah, NJ: Lawrence Erlbaum Associates.

Greenberg, G. (2000). Lessons from Zing-Yang Kuo. *Past to Future, 2,* 13–37.

Holliday, R. (1990). Mechanisms for the control of gene activity during development. *Biological Reviews of the Cambridge Philosophical Society,* 65, 431–471.

Insel, T. R. & Fernald, R. D. (2004). How the brain processes social information: Searching for the social brain. *Annual Review of Neuroscience,* 27, 697–722.

Jaenisch, R., & Bird, B. (2003). Epigenetic regulation of gene expression: How the genome integrates intrinsic and environmental signals. *Nature Genetics,* 33, 245–254.

Kappeler L., & Meaney, M. J. (2010). Epigenetics and parental effects. *Bioessays,* 32, 818–827.

Kerr, M. & Bowen, M. (1988). *Family evaluation.* New York: W. W. Norton.

Korosi, A. & Baram, T. Z. (2009). The pathways from mother's love to baby's future. *Frontiers in Behavioral Neuroscience,* 3, doi:10.3389/neuro.08.027.2009.

Kuo, Z.-Y. (1967). *The dynamics of behavior development.* New York: Random House Press.

Lehrman, D. S. (1970). Semantic and conceptual issues in the nature-nurture problem. In: L. R. Aronson, E. Tobach, D. S. Lehrman, & J. S. Rosenblatt (Eds.) *Development and evolution of behavior* (pp. 17–52). San Francisco: W.H. Freeman.

Lewontin, R. C. (2000). *The triple helix: Gene, organism and environment.* Cambridge, MA: Harvard University Press.

McEwen B. S. (2010). Stress, sex, and neural adaptation to a changing environment: Mechanisms of neuronal remodeling. *Annals of New York Academy of Science.* 1204 Suppl:E38–59.

McGowan, P. O., Sasaki, A., D'Alessio, A. C., Dymov, S., Labonte, B., Szyf, M., Turecki, G., & Meaney, M. J. (2009). Epigenetic regulation of the glucocorticoid receptor in human brain associates with childhood abuse. *Nature Neuroscience,* 12, 342–348.

Meaney, M. J. (2010). Epigenetics and the biological definition of gene x environment interactions. *Child Development,* 81, 41–79.

Moriceau, S., Raineki, C., Holman, J. D., Holman, J. G., & Sullivan, R. M. (2009). Enduring neurobehavioral effects of early life trauma mediated through learning and corticosterone suppression. *Frontiers in Behavioral Neuroscience.* 3, doi:10.3389/neuro.08.022.2009.

Nijhout, H. F. (2004). The importance of context in genetics. *American Scientist,* 91, 416–418.

Noone, R. J. (2008). The multigenerational transmission process and the neurobiology of attachment and stress reactivity. *Family Systems.* 8, 21–34.

Romeo, R. D., Tang, A. C., & Sullivan, R. M. (2009). Early life experiences: Enduring behavioral, neurological, and endocrinological consequences. In D. Pfaff, A.

Arnold, A. Etgen, R. Rubin, & S. Fahrbach (Eds.), *Hormones, brain and behavior, second edition* (pp. 1975–2004). New York: Elsevier Inc.

Romeo, R. D., Tang, A. C., & Sullivan, R. M. (2010). Early life experiences: Enduring behavioral, neurological, and endocrinological consequences. In D. W. Pfaff, A. Arnold, A. Etgen, S. Fahrbach, and R. Rubin (Eds.), *Hormones, brain, and behavior, second edition, volume II.* New York: Academic Press.

Stearns, S. C. (1989). The evolutionary significance of phenotypic plasticity. *BioScience,* 39, 436–445.

Waddington, C. H. (1942). The epigenotype. *Endeavour,* 1, 18–20.

Weaver, I. C., Cervoni, N., Champagne, F. A., D'Alessio, A. C., Sharma, S., Seckl, J. R., Dymov, S., Szyf, M., & Meaney, M. J. (2004). Epigenetic programming by maternal behavior. *Nature Neuroscience*, 7, 847–54.

West-Eberhard, M. J. (2003). *Developmental plasticity and evolution.* New York: Oxford University Press.

Chapter 8

Nonhuman Primate Models of Family Systems

Charles T. Snowdon

What is a good nonhuman animal model for the study of family systems? The simplest answer would be that we should look to our closest primate relatives, the great apes. However, humans differ from our nearest relatives in significant ways. There is a great variety in mating systems among great apes with gorillas living in harems controlled by one or two males, orangutans living by themselves with males and females meeting only rarely to mate. In chimpanzees and bonobos our closest relatives, mating appears to be promiscuous and, in all great apes, mothers provide all of infant care. In none of these species do we find the long-term male-female relationships that characterize most humans. In none of these species is there anything approaching the family life of most human societies.

A good nonhuman animal model of family systems can be of great value in understanding the "natural" basis of family dynamics (independent of culture and religion that affect all of us humans). With a suitable animal model we can study the behavioral, social, hormonal, and developmental aspects of family life under controlled conditions and in species where culture is unlikely to play a role in determining how family behavior "ought" to be.

Where can we find such natural family systems among the primates? Among nonhuman primates there are several species from the Neotropics with family systems similar to humans, the cooperatively breeding marmosets and tamarins. These are small bodied primates (typically weighing 750g or less) but these animals diverged from the evolutionary line that led to humans more than 35 million years ago. How can they help to understanding human family systems?

Most of us are familiar with the notion of divergent evolution (or homologies) whereby species closest to us share features with us and thus are informative about our heritage. However, another approach is through convergent evolution whereby species that are distant from us but share common features are likely to have developed such features to solve similar problems. To study family processes and why family life is important, we must find species that live in families to learn why families are important and how good family dynamics can be maintained.

Humans are cooperative breeders (Hrdy, 2009) and are unlike our closest great ape relatives. The typical interbirth interval for women is shorter than for any of the great apes and yet it takes significantly longer for human infants to reach reproductive maturity than offspring of other great apes. Human mothers need help from multiple helpers to rear children successfully. The only cooperatively breeding primates other than human are the marmosets and tamarins, making them valuable for understanding the biology and behavior of families. Mothers also have shorter interbirth intervals relative to other primates and usually give birth to twins. These twins weigh about 20% of the mother's weight at birth and they need to be carried during the day. Mothers are not only nursing these twins but a few weeks after birth they are pregnant again. It is easy to imagine why helpers are important when mothers face such a burden.

In the field and captivity infant survival is influenced by the number of helpers present (Snowdon, 1996). Only families with a mother and four other helpers reach 100% infant survival. Recent work on human families in hunter-gatherer groups, considered to be our ancestral way of life, shows family members other than the mother are critical to infant survival (Sear & Mace, 2008). Single parent families are on average financially worse off than two parent families (Thompson et al., 1992) and divorce brings disadvantages to children (Hetherington et al., 1998). Infanticide rates are higher for children living with a single genetic parent versus either two genetic parents or a genetic parent and stepparent (Temrin et al., 2000. Father's presence is the major factor influencing whether sons complete college (Buchman & di Prete, 2006).

We have studied the social behavior, development and physiology of tamarins and marmosets for more than 30 years. I will focus on five topics: (1) How do these monkeys develop and maintain a heterosexual relationship? (2) How do parents recruit and maintain nonreproductive helpers to assist with infant care? (3) What are the behavioral and hormonal changes that influence fathers to become devoted and skilled parents who will play the major role in infant care (other than nursing)? (4) How do infants benefit from a cooperative caretaking system? (5) Finally, can these findings help us develop better human family relationships?

DEVELOPING AND MAINTAINING A
RELATIONSHIP WITH A MATE

In contrast to species where fathers play a negligible role or serve primarily as sperm donors, species in which fathers are needed to help infants thrive face problems in forming and maintaining a relationship (or pair-bond). The stereotypical views of sex differences in mating and parenting applied to other species, do not apply here. Due to internal fertilization and pregnancy mammalian mothers incur a high energetic cost which is continued after birth through nursing. In contrast sperm from fathers is much less of an energetic commitment. A mother always can be sure that her infants are her own whereas a male can never be certain of paternity. This has led many to argue that male and female strategies are fundamentally different. A female must carefully choose the best male to provide good genes for her offspring but a male should mate with as many females as possible, since his mating costs are low and his parental uncertainty is high. Males should compete for mates through sexually selected traits that make males much larger and stronger than females. Males have special, often elaborate, ornaments such as horns or brightly colored bodies, and have high rates of fighting or competition. Females are coy and evaluate potential mates, choosing the one with the best genes or best fighting skills.

However, this argument only works so long as a mother can rear her offspring alone without any help from a father. We have already seen that in humans and cooperatively breeding primates, fathers are important for more than just sperm. Instead, the biological differences between parental investment and parental certainty should lead to a confluence of interest between males and females. Males have to develop trust in their partner so that the likelihood of being cuckolded will be relatively low, and the offspring they will care for are likely their own. Females need to develop trust in their male partner to be relatively certain that he will stay to help with child care. For different reasons both males and females in biparental and cooperatively breeding species need to develop trust with each other. This leads to a Mutual Mate Choice Model (Stewart-Williams & Thomas, 2013). Both sexes are choosy of mates and both sexes compete with others of their own sex for access to good mates. Sexually selected traits that attract mates and compete with others of the same sex should appear in both sexes.

This mutual mate choice model can help us explain a really curious fact about humans. Women are very different from great ape females in the development of striking secondary sex characteristics at puberty. When males of other species develop secondary sex characteristics at puberty, we infer that sexual selection is involved and that these characteristics are important in male-male competition and allowing females to make good mate choices.

Secondary sex characteristics in females are evidence of female-female competition which allows males to make a good mate choice. Interestingly, the only other primates where females develop permanent secondary sex characteristics at puberty are tamarins where females develop large, active scent glands in the anogenital and suprapubic regions (French et al., 1984; Heymann, 2003). These scent secretions are important for both female-female competition and male mate choice.

Odors from ovulating females suppress ovulation in cotton-top tamarins (Savage et al., 1988). Daughters never ovulated while living at home with their family, but ovulated within as few as 8 days when transferred to a new environment with a novel male. However, no female whose mother's odors were transferred daily ovulated for the duration of the study. Thus female scents promote female-female competition by suppressing ovulation. These scents are also attractive to males. Transfers of scents from a novel female to paired tamarins led to increased rates of erection and increased mounting behavior by males of their own mates on days when the female scent donor was ovulating, but not on other days (Ziegler et al., 1993). The scent glands of female marmosets and tamarins function as sexually selected traits.

How do these monkeys find mates and develop a relationship? In a field study common marmosets engaged daily in what appeared to be territorial encounters with neighboring groups. They screamed at one another, scent marked vigorously and chased each other. However, in the middle of what seemed to be a contest between groups, a female from one group would slip away and mate with a male from the other group and then quickly return to the territory boundary (Lazaro-Perea, 2001). Animals from each group seemed to be evaluating the opposite sex members of a neighboring group (a Romeo and Juliet romance in the midst of a feud between Capulets and Montagues). When the reproductive female in some groups died, the males joined with the females of a neighboring group and the females joined the males of that group to form new families (Lazaro-Perea et al., 2000). Females who had been reproductively suppressed ovulated quickly and became pregnant within a few weeks of the reproductive female's death. They were already familiar with potential mates from other groups.

In our laboratory new pairs spend a lot of time touching and grooming each other. Grooming increases brain opioid levels in the recipient (Keverne et al., 1989) and reduces levels of the stress hormone, cortisol, in those who do the grooming (Shutt et al., 2007). New pairs also show lots of mating behavior (more than a dozen times a day). The stress hormone, cortisol, was elevated in newly formed pairs (Ziegler et al., 1995) and testosterone levels were elevated in newly paired males (Ginther et al., 2001). Elevated cortisol is not due to stress, but rather the increased activity of being with a new mate.

The pair-bonding hormone, oxytocin, was significantly elevated in the first days after pairing (Snowdon et al., 2010).

How can we evaluate the strength of a pair-bond? When we separated pairs from each other for as short as 30 minutes, both animals gave very plaintive sounding vocalizations and when they were reunited, they showed a high rate of sexual behavior (Porter, 1994). When a novel animal of opposite sex was placed next to a pair, both partners showed aggressive behavior toward intruders and females showed increased rates of scent marking to novel females (French & Snowdon, 1981). Marmosets moved to a novel cage showed lower stress responses when they were moved with their mates (Smith & French, 1997) and even when they just heard the calls of their mates (Ruckstalis & French, 2005). Male tamarins responded to the odors of novel ovulating females by displaying erections and showing increased mounting behavior of their own mates (Ziegler et al., 1993). Females increased the rate of sexual solicitation of their partners when presented with odors of a novel ovulating female (Washabaugh & Snowdon, 1998). When common marmoset males were tested with odors of novel ovulating females, males who were single or mated but without offspring showed an interest in these odors and within 30 minutes, they showed a significant elevation in serum testosterone (Ziegler et al., 2005).

Tamarins and marmosets display frequent sexual behavior throughout the female's ovulation cycle and during pregnancy (Porter & Snowdon, 1997). This is unusual among other primates where females accept mating only around the period of ovulation and rarely mate once they are pregnant. But this pattern is similar to human mating patterns. Why should there be so much sexual activity at times when conception is not possible? The increased sexual activity following a perturbation in the relationship—odor of a novel female, brief separation, start of a new relationship—suggest that non-conceptive sexual behavior may help maintain relationships.

Are there hormonal correlates of relationship quality and attachment? Oxytocin and prolactin are very important in maternal behavior, not only to prepare females for nursing as prolactin does and to control the milk let down response as oxytocin does, but also for maternal infant bonding and infant care. Could these parental hormones also be involved in adult heterosexual bonds? In the monogamous prairie vole when a female forms a pair-bond, there are changes in the distribution of oxytocin receptors in her brain. If one simply infuses some oxytocin into a female's brain, she will form a bond with the first male she encounters (Carter, 1998). Experiments with marmosets showed increased social affiliation with oxytocin and reduced affiliation with oxytocin antagonists (Smith et al., 2010).

Intriguing studies on humans found increased levels of prolactin and oxytocin at orgasm although not during sexual arousal (Krüger et al., 2002).

Massage and even gentle stroking also lead to increased levels of oxytocin and prolactin (Uvnäs-Moberg, 1998). These results suggest that prolactin and oxytocin may be rewards for cuddling and engaging in sexual behavior, helping to strengthen a relationship. Do these hormones predict adult heterosexual relationships? We collected urine samples three times a week from paired tamarins and made behavioral observations. We found a high degree of variation in both hormones and behavior (Snowdon et al., 2010; Snowdon & Ziegler, 2015). Males and females within a pair had similar levels of prolactin and oxytocin, and these levels correlated with the amount of sociosexual behavior that each pair displayed. Variation in male oxytocin was related to how frequently males had sex and variation in female oxytocin was related to how much cuddling and grooming females received (Snowdon et al., 2010). Females in pairs with high oxytocin solicited sex more often than other females and males in the high oxytocin pairs initiated contact and grooming more often than other males. Animals with the highest oxytocin levels were each offering what their partners most needed. There is a striking similarity between male-female relationships in tamarins and the popular caricature of what men and women want.

In summary good relationships in tamarins and marmosets appear to be based on physical contact and non-conceptive sex. Oxytocin and prolactin are released during sex and during physical contact and grooming, and serve as biological rewards for relationships. They may also reinforce other aspects of a partner— the sight, smell, or voice—leading one to recognize and attend to one specific mate rather than responding to anyone of the opposite sex.

HOW DO HELPERS HELP? RECRUITING AND MAINTAINING HELPERS

What makes cooperative breeding special is the involvement of nonbreeding helpers or alloparents. Mothers incur a high energetic cost through nursing and pregnancy and fathers lose up to 10% of their body weight if they have no help with infant care (Achenbach & Snowdon, 2002). Nonreproductive helpers are critical not only for infant survival but for the father's health. With additional helpers, fathers do not lose as much weight. Males, especially subadult and adult sons, share infant carrying with the father and do much more infant care than females (Zahed et al., 2010). Both fathers and helpers play an important role at weaning, by distracting infants from nursing by offering solid food. Young infants learn how to eat solid food, where to find it, and how to process it through interactions with their caretakers (Rapaport & Brown, 2008). But what do helpers gain by sacrificing their reproductive potential to help the breeders?

Recruiting and maintaining helpers is a tricky business. What would motivate an animal to forego its own chance to reproduce and to serve as a nonreproductive helper? Many helpers are related to the infants they care for, and thus they benefit through kin selection. But we have found unrelated helpers. Why are they helping? Helpers may be more likely to impress a female and able to mate with her in the future (Dunbar, 1995). Infant care may be a passport for being in a group. Finally, if there are no other breeding options available (suitable mates or habitat), being a nonreproductive helper may be making the best of a bad lot.

Another explanation is the need for tamarins and marmosets to learn parental skills. When we founded our colony in 1977, the breeding success of captive tamarins was abysmal. Although captive-born animals gave birth as often as wild caught pairs, parents were abusive and seemed unsure of what to do with infants. Most colonies removed infants before weaning and kept them in a nursery, ostensibly to have the mothers ovulate sooner and produce more offspring. These monkeys have to learn parenting skills. If a naïve mother or father were paired with parentally experienced mates, they had some success, but two naïve mates had virtually no chance of reproducing successfully (Epple, 1978; Johnson et al., 1991). The best way to learn these skills is to help parents take care of younger siblings. Sons who had more experience taking care of infants in their family group had a higher infant survival rate when they became parents on their own, although we did not find a similar result for daughters (Zahed et al., 2010). All animals are eager to become involved with infants, but juveniles are excluded from caring for infants in the early months of life (Achenbach & Snowdon, 1998), and subadults and adult males are the main caretakers other than the father (Zahed et al., 2010).

Although there are benefits to being a helper, at some point a helper has learned the skills it needs and might benefit more by reproducing on its own. How do parents control their helpers? A novel male is needed to induce ovulation. When we removed daughters from their mothers, but housed them with their fathers or brothers, they still did not ovulate. Only when the females were away from scents from their mothers and exposed to a novel male did they began to ovulate (Widowski et al., 1990, 1992). As long as females were with their male relatives or were exposed to maternal scent, they remained suppressed.

We found no evidence of reproductive suppression in adult sons living with their families. Testosterone levels in sons are the same as they are in fathers. Sons are also sexually active within the family group, mounting and attempting copulation with their other brothers mainly, but also with their sisters, fathers and even their mothers (Ginther et al., 2001). The Latin name of cotton-top tamarins is *Saguinus oedipus*, but we were surprised to see young males behaving like Oedipus Rex. Adult sons had erections as often

and attempted copulations as often as their fathers, but no one seemed to
mind. We never saw aggression between fathers and sons, and when mothers
were approached sexually by their sons, they simply moved their bodies so
that copulation would be impossible. Immediately after a copulation attempt,
both mother and father sat with the son and groomed him. The tolerance of
son's sexual behavior was remarkable.

Just as grooming is maintaining adult pair-bonds, we found parents used
grooming to reward their helpers. Wild common marmoset parents groomed
offspring much more often than offspring groomed parents (Lazaro Perea
et al., 2004). During the last weeks of the mother's pregnancy in tamarins,
mothers groomed most the sons who had done the most infant care at the
previous birth, whereas fathers groomed most the sons who had done the least
amount of care at the previous birth (Ginther & Snowdon, 2009). What could
explain this sex difference? Each additional helper in the family reduces the
amount of time fathers carry infants (Zahed et al., 2010) and reduces the
amount of weight fathers lose during infant care (Achenbach & Snowdon,
2002). For mothers having only one helper other than the father reduces her
workload to the minimum. Mothers groom sons as a reward for previous
work and to solicit help with the upcoming litter, whereas fathers recruit
new helpers by grooming. In many primates, subordinates are more likely to
groom dominants, but in marmosets and tamarins the reverse is true.

In summary, reproductive suppression of subordinate females and tolerance of the sexual antics of subordinate males leads to only one pair breeding.
In addition to suppressing reproduction, parents actively reward their helpers
by grooming them and differentiate between those who have helped a lot and
those that have helped a little.

What happens when these mechanisms fail? In our tamarin colony, we
infrequently observed severe fights. Fights always occurred when group sizes
became large and always occurred between animals of the same sex—brothers versus brothers and sisters versus sisters or mothers versus daughters
(Snowdon & Pickhard, 1999). Mother-daughter conflict became especially
pronounced when daughters began showing increased levels of estrogen associated with increased scent making. Although these daughters did not ovulate,
they appeared to be on the verge of doing so. We intervened to prevent harm
to either animal.

In the wild two females are often pregnant at the same time, suggesting
that reproductive suppression may not work as well. When two females gave
birth close in time to each other, one female would harass the other female
and her infants often killing them (Digby, 1995, Lazaro-Perea et al., 2000).
When two females bred out of synchrony with each other so that one set of
twins was weaned before the other female's twins were born, there was no
obvious conflict (Digby, 1995). Helpers are the limiting resource for females.

Male infanticide has been described in nonhuman primates, especially in species where one male controls many females. The overthrow of the previous male by a new rival leads the rival to kill all young infants, which induces females to stop nursing and to ovulate more quickly. Thus the new male can sire his own infants sooner. This does not apply to marmosets since females ovulate quickly even while nursing. But it is of interest that infanticide is not unique to males.

BEHAVIORAL AND HORMONAL CHANGES IN FATHERS

How do fathers become good parents? Mothers undergo many physiological and hormonal changes related to pregnancy that are also important in maternal care. Mothers gain weight. Estrogen and progesterone are elevated and drop rapidly at the birth. But estrogen stimulates two hormones associated with birth and nursing. Oxytocin controls uterine contractions during delivery and is involved in the milk let-down response. Prolactin develops mammary tissue to produce milk. These hormones also are responsible for maternal behavior and play a critical role in mother infant bonding (Lévy et al., 2004).

But fathers do not go through pregnancy. Are there changes in fathers' hormones and, if so, when and how do they occur? Prolactin levels are high in fathers measured immediately after they have carried infants (Dixson & George, 1982; Mota et al., 2006). But, experimental manipulations of prolactin levels have led to differing results. In juvenile marmosets with no parental experience, injection of a prolactin blocker reduced response to infants in a subset of juveniles tested (Roberts et al., 2001). However, in experienced marmoset fathers receiving a prolactin blocker, there was no reduction in infant care, but fathers were more interested in being close to infants (Almond et al., 2006).

How can we account for these different findings? One possibility is experience. The studies that found no effect of prolactin blockers used fathers that had experienced multiple births, whereas the study that found an effect of blocking prolactin used immature marmosets without parental experience. Elevated prolactin may be critical for first-time fathers, but not necessary for experienced fathers. Why then is prolactin elevated after males have carried infants? I mentioned that prolactin levels increased in humans after orgasm and that this may serve as a reward to both partners. Prolactin may also reward experienced fathers for infant care.

We were surprised to see elevated prolactin levels in tamarin fathers two weeks before infants were born (Ziegler et al., 1996). How can fathers predict when infants will be born? What stimuli can lead to hormonal changes in fathers? We initiated long-term studies monitoring hormone levels of fathers throughout their mate's pregnancy. Father's hormones began to change well before the end of pregnancy (Ziegler & Snowdon, 2000; Ziegler et al., 2004). Experienced fathers showed more hormonal changes than first-time fathers with significant increases in testosterone, estrogens, and prolactin. Although all first-time fathers had actively participated in caring for younger siblings, their hormones during pregnancy did not change as much as experienced fathers and the changes occurred later in pregnancy (Ziegler et al., 2004).

How do males "know" that their mates are pregnant? We have pregnancy test kits and we talk with our mates, but tamarins and marmosets cannot do that. Halfway through pregnancy, when the fetal adrenal gland begins to secrete glucocorticoids, mothers showed a rapid and sustained increase in glucocorticoid excretion in urine. Within a week, every experienced father showed a transient increase in glucocorticoids followed by increases in testosterone, estrogens and prolactin. The increased glucocorticoids secreted by the mother appeared to be a signal that activated the hormonal system in expectant fathers (Ziegler et al., 2004). Since first-time fathers did not respond in the same way, the response must be learned.

What is the function of all these hormonal changes? And why is testosterone increasing? Studies on parental care in the California mouse (a monogamous species where fathers are important in infant care) provide an answer. Trainor and Marler (2001) hypothesized that testosterone would have a negative effect on parental care and so they castrated males and found that the males were actually worse with infant care than males with intact testes. We know that testosterone can be metabolized to estrogen through an enzyme called aromatase. When they injected castrated males with estrogen, males became great care-takers. When they injected intact male mice with an aromatase inhibitor, the males behaved poorly with infants (Trainor & Marler, 2002). Testosterone is the main source for males to produce estrogen and estrogen, in turn, stimulates the production of both oxytocin and prolactin. Testosterone does not interfere with paternal care, but through its metabolites is important in stimulating infant care hormones.

Male marmosets and tamarins increase body weight during pregnancy just as mothers do, although the trajectories of weight gain differ (Ziegler et al., 2006; Sanchez et al., 2008). The combination of weight gain and hormonal changes closely parallel the couvade syndrome seen in some human men during their partner's pregnancy.

Becoming a father changes the brains of marmosets and tamarins, making them more faithful to their mates and more responsive to their infants. We used functional magnetic resonance imaging to look at brain activity in non-parental males in response to the odors of novel females (Ferris et al., 2001). Female ovulatory odors led to activation of the medial preoptic area and anterior hypothalamus, two brain areas involved in sexual arousal. We tested males with the odor of a novel ovulating female or a control and found that non-parental males showed a great interest in the stimulus, manipulating it, sniffing it and getting erections. We took a blood sample 30 minutes after exposure to the odor and found that testosterone levels were significantly increased. However, fathers with infants were indifferent both behaviorally and hormonally to odors of novel ovulating females. This suggests some mechanism that makes the father faithful to its mate when infants are present (Ziegler et al., 2005).

Family members compete to take care of infants. To measure a male's motivation we developed a two chamber apparatus where a male was placed in one chamber and either a live infant or a recorder playing infant distress calls was placed in the other chamber. An elevated bridge connected the two chambers. Fathers, but not non-fathers, rapidly crossed the bridge when there was a live infant or the playing of distress calls. Furthermore, fathers responded equally to the presence or calls of an unknown infant as to their own infant. Thus, in response to distress calls fathers responded without hesitation and non-fathers were indifferent (Zahed et al., 2008).

Fathers were also more responsive than non-fathers to infant odors as shown by decreasing testosterone levels within 20 minutes of exposure (Prudom et al., 2008). Fathers showed a rapid decrease in testosterone and a rapid increase in estrogen levels in response to the odor of their own infant but not to the odor of an unfamiliar infant. This response disappeared when the infants were old enough to need only minimal parental care. Although fathers did not distinguish between their own and other infants distress calls, they did discriminate between their own and other infants hormonally when odors were presented (Ziegler et al., 2011).

The behavioral evidence that fatherhood changes male brains is indirect. A detailed study of changes in brain structure in father and non-father common marmosets found brain neuroplasticity during parenting as reflected by increase in the density of dendritic spines on pyramidal neurons in the prefrontal cortex similar to mothers (Kozorovitskiy et al., 2006). Brain receptors increased for arginine vasopressin, a hormone similar to oxytocin critical in male parental care in other species. As fathers became less involved in parental care with infant independence, these changes disappeared.

Mother's behavior affects how males will respond to infants. First-time parents are less successful in keeping the infants alive, even with extensive experience as helpers before becoming parents. Mothers are often clumsy and unable to position their infants optimally for nursing. Nursing is the one aspect of parenting that helpers cannot practice in their natal families. First-time mothers are reluctant to share child care with the father. In our field study first-time mothers carried their infants 90% of the time during the first two weeks of life, and the infants did not survive (Savage et al., 1996). Mothers must share infant care with others to be successful.

In summary, the hormones and behaviors of fathers parallel pregnant and nursing mothers. Males undergo significant hormonal changes during the pregnancy of their mate, starting when the fetus produces a high level of glucocorticoids which the mother excretes in her urine. Males convert testosterone into estrogens and these stimulate production of the parental attachment hormones prolactin and oxytocin. Experience is important with first-time fathers lagging behind experienced fathers in these hormonal changes. Fathers are unresponsive to odors of novel ovulating females; fathers are more willing to explore a novel environment to retrieve an infant that is emitting distress calls; fathers appear indifferent to whether it is their own or another infant. Fathers, but not other males, show a rapid decrease in testosterone to the odor of infants, but this response appears to be specific to father's own infants and only during the time when they are dependent upon their parents. First-time fathers react more slowly, and first-time parents have less reproductive success than experienced parents. Mother must let others take care of their infants if cooperative care is to be effective.

BENEFITS TO INFANTS FROM COOPERATIVE REARING

Infants play a central role in the family system of tamarins and marmosets. What benefits do infants gain and how do they respond to cooperative care? Infant survival is a function of having a variety of helpers, but do they gain other benefits? In vervet monkeys where mothers do most of the infant care there four types of parental styles that range along two continua—rejecting versus accepting mothers and permissive versus restrictive mothers (Fairbanks, 1996). Daughters acquire the maternal style that they experienced and apply it to their own infants, perpetuating the type of maternal care they received. In rats the greater amount of maternal licking and grooming an infant receives, the more adaptive it is to stress and the more likely the daughters are to show high levels of licking and grooming of their offspring (Francis et al., 1999). The high levels of licking and grooming lead to greater expression of oxytocin receptors in adult females and of vasopressin receptors in adult males (Francis et al., 2002). Both oxytocin and vasopressin are involved in positive social behavior in many species including humans. Thus variation in a very simple maternal behavior can have profound effects on offspring, and their grandoffspring.

If all mothers treated infants the same with lots of licking and grooming (in the case of rats), or acceptance and permissiveness (in the case of vervet monkeys), we'd have a population of mellow, stress-resistant animals who would behave toward their infants in a similar way. But when there is only one active parent, there will be much variation in care. Cooperative breeding provides a solution to the problem of maternal variation. The actions of multiple caregivers provide a buffer to the variation one would see with a single caregiver. If the mother is restrictive or rejecting, then other family members caring for infants could buffer the effects. This is exactly what we have seen. Across families that varied in experience and group size, infants received the same amount of positive and negative behaviors (Washabaugh et al., 2002). One benefit of cooperative breeding is buffering by multiple caretakers against variation in maternal care.

One finding from tamarins may give human mothers pause about cooperative care. We presented a frightening stimulus to tamarin families. Adult monkeys gave alarm and mobbing calls but the juveniles ran to be comforted by an adult, climbing on their backs. This is as a measure of attachment. We knew for each juvenile how often each family member had carried that individual and which animals had shared food with the juvenile. The juvenile always ran to the family member who had carried it the most and who had shared food most often and, in all but one case, the attachment animal was a brother or father and in no case was the mother the object of attachment (Kostan & Snowdon, 2002). Similar results have been reported for the biparental titi monkey (Mendoza & Mason, 1986; Hoffman et al., 1995). However, titi monkey parents prefer to be with each other rather than with their infants.

Infants learn about food from adults in a way that strongly suggests teaching. Adults regularly share food with infants starting at the time of weaning. This keeps infants occupied and away from nursing on their mothers. Adults use specialized, rapid forms of food calls to attract infants when they share food. Infants who received food sharing at an earlier age moved more rapidly to independent feeding and giving their own food calls than infants who received food later (Joyce & Snowdon, 2007). After infants had become independent and foraged entirely on their own, we introduced a novel foraging apparatus and trained the parents on how to use it. We tested each parent with one juvenile and observed behavior. When food was difficult to get, parents began giving food sharing calls again and rapidly shared food with their juvenile. However, once the juvenile solved the task and found food on its own, the parent immediately stopped calling and sharing food (Humle & Snowdon, 2008). Similar results have been seen in wild lion tamarins. Juveniles quickly learn to feed on fruits but have a hard time catching insects. Adults initially catch an insect, call, and offer it to the juvenile. Later adults call close to where a prey is located, but require the juvenile to catch the prey itself and finally, adults do no coaching (Rapaport & Ruiz-Miranda, 2002; Rapaport, 2006). This progression of food calling and sharing, then not sharing with juveniles before the introduction of the apparatus, then re-initiating calling and sharing with the new apparatus and finally ceasing to call and share when the juvenile solves the new task, appear similar to good teaching— a tutor is sensitive to the skill level and ability of the learner, adjusting its behavior as the learner acquires the skill, setting new goals.

These results contrast greatly with chimpanzees. Chimpanzee mothers don't share food. Wild chimpanzees must learn to forage for dangerous biting ants. In sharp contrast with tamarins, chimpanzee mothers did absolutely nothing to help their infants learn (Humle et al., 2009). Marmosets and tamarins have small brains relative to ape or human brains and yet cooperative care of infants leads to some remarkable abilities not seen in our closest relatives.

WHAT CAN TAMARINS AND MARMOSETS TELL US ABOUT HUMAN FAMILY SYSTEMS?

Tamarins and marmosets have relevance to human family systems. First, it is important to note the value of a trusting relationship between parents. To have a successful family, parents must coordinate their behavior closely, must pay attention to one another and must make some sacrifices for the common good of the family. Both men and women must make careful choices of partners and develop a strong sense of trust. A mother must trust that the father will be committed to help her care for their children after nine months of pregnancy and a father needs to trust that the children he cares for will be his own. A recent intervention study with low-income families found that working on couples' relationships had a greater impact on father's behavior than working on fathers' parenting skills (Cowan et al., 2009).

Our research emphasizes the physical aspects of relationships. Frequent non-conceptive sexual behavior, touch, and grooming all play important roles in relationship maintenance and in response to the inevitable perturbations in relationships. These interactions release rewarding hormones such as prolactin and oxytocin, which in turn may underlie conditioning to a particular mate. This may be an important monogamy maintaining mechanism.

Nonreproductive helpers are critical to tamarin and marmoset family systems. In Africa I was struck by the involvement of children as young as five or six in carrying and looking after younger siblings. In our culture we insulate children from infant care depriving parents of an important source of family help, and ignoring the value of learning child care skills while helping someone else's infants. All monkey males were interested in infants and the critical issue for successful parenting was in knowing what to do. We can help fathers become more engaged by encouraging boys to be interested in babies. Tamarins and marmosets teach us the value of learning infant care skills before becoming parents. In the absence of direct learning in families, we may need effective training programs for expectant parents.

In marmosets and tamarins, fathers and older brothers are willing caretakers of infants. Preparing for infant care involves a fascinating interplay of experience, hormone, and brain changes. Human fathers show decreased testosterone after the birth of infants. Fathers, who are highly involved with their mate during pregnancy and with their infant immediately after birth, develop a stronger attachment to their infants and are more responsive to infant needs than less-engaged fathers (Fleming et al., 2002; Storey et al., 2000).

Active involvement in caring for infants in tamarins and marmosets makes them more faithful to their partners and more sensitive to the needs of their infants. Perhaps if men were more actively involved with their infants and maintained a closer physical relationship with their mates, marriages might be stronger and longer lasting. However, mothers need allow fathers to become involved in infant care from the earliest stages. Men can learn quickly to avoid infant care if mothers reject their initial offers of care.

Being a male does not immunize one against parenting. Observations of who responds to orphan infants in a wide variety of primate species suggest males, even in species that rarely display parental care, are often the first to adopt an orphan infant, and males develop a strong attachment to these infants (Thierrey & Anderson, 1986). Even in chimpanzees where males normally show little interest in infants, over half of adoptions observed were by males (Boesch et al., 2010). Thus male primates, including men, have an intrinsic interest in infants that requires nurturing and direct access to infants for the interest to be expressed.

Cooperative care buffers infants from the variation seen among mothers in species where mothers do all the child care. Instead of perpetuating maternal style across several generations, a cooperative care system leads to high quality care for each generation. Infants receiving higher quality care have more adaptive responses to stressful situations. Early molding of expression of genes that mediate positive social engagement through hormones like oxytocin, vasopressin, and prolactin, can lead to higher quality social relationships with mates, children and others. Socially positive family systems will lead to confident and competent children who will be attractive to mates as adults and will become successful parents themselves.

REFERENCES

Achenbach, G. G. & Snowdon, C. T. (1998). Response to sibling birth in juvenile cotton-top tamarins (*Saguinus oedipus*), *Behaviour*, 135, 845–862.

Achenbach, G. G. & Snowdon, C. T. (2002). Costs of caregiving: Weight loss in captive adult male cotton-top tamarins (*Saguinus oedipus*) following the birth of infants. *International Journal of Primatology*, 23, 179–189.

Almond, R. E. A., Brown, G. R. & Keverne, E. B. (2006). Suppression of prolactin does not reduce infant care by parentally experienced common marmosets (*Callithrix jacchus*). *Hormones and Behavior*, 49, 673–680.

Boesch, C., Bolé, C., Eckhardt, N, & Boesch H. (2010). Altruism in forest chimpanzees: The case of adoption. *PLoS ONE* 5, e8901.

Buchman, C. and Di Prete, T. A. (2006). The growing female advantage in college completion: the role of family background and academic achievement. *American Sociological Review*, 71, 515–541.

Carter, C. S. (1998). Neuroendocrine perspectives on social attachment and love. P*sychoneuroendocrinology*, 23, 779–818.

Cowan, P. A., Cowan, C. P., Pruett, M. K., Pruett, K. & Wong, J. J. (2009). Promoting fathers' engagement with children: Preventative intervention for low-income families. *Journal of Marriage and the Family*, 71, 663–679.

Digby, L., (1995). Infant care, infanticide and female reproductive strategies in polygynous groups of common marmosets (*Callithrix jacchus*) *Behavioral Ecology and Sociobiology*, 37, 51–61.

Dixson, A. F. & George, L. (1982). Prolactin and parental behavior in a male New World primate. *Nature*, 299, 551–553.

Dunbar, R. M. (1995). The mating system of Callitrichid primates: II. The impact of helpers. *Animal Behaviour*, 50, 1071–1089

Epple, G. (1978). Reproductive and social behaviors of marmosets with special reference to captive breeding. *Primates in Medicine*, 10, 50–62.

Fairbanks, L. A. (1996). Individual differences in maternal style: Causes and consequences for mothers and offspring. *Advances in the Study of Behavior*, 25, 579–611.

Ferris, C. F., Snowdon, C. T., King, J. A., Duong, T. Q., Ziegler, T. E., Ugurbil, K., Ludwig, R., Schultz-Darken, N. J., Wu, Z., Olson, D. P, Sullivan, J. M., Jr., Tannenbaum, P. L. & Vaughn, J. T. (2001). Functional imaging of brain activity in conscious monkeys responding to sexually arousing cues. *NeuroReport*, 12, 2231–2236.

Fleming A. S., Corter, C., Stallings, J., & Steiner, M. (2002). Testosterone and prolactin are associated with emotional responses to infant cries in new fathers. *Hormones and Behavior* 42, 399– 413.

Francis, D, Diorio, J., Liu, D, & Meaney, M. J. (1999). Nongenomic transmission across generations of maternal behavior and stress responses in the rat. *Science*, 286, 1155–1158.

Francis, D. D., Young, L. J., Meaney, M. J. & Insel, T. R., (2002). Naturally occurring differences in maternal care are associated with the expression of oxytocin and vasopressin (V1a) receptors: gender differences. *Journal of Neuroendocrinology*. 14, 349–353.

French, J. A. & Snowdon, C. T. (1981). Sexual dimorphism in responses to unfamiliar intruders in the tamarin *(Saguinus oedipus)*. *Animal Behaviour*, 29, 822–829.

French, J. A., Abbott, D. H. & Snowdon, C. T. (1984). The effect of social environment on estrogen secretion, scent marking and sociosexual behavior in tamarins (*Saguinus oedipus*). *American Journal of Primatology*, 6, 155–167.

Ginther, A. J., Ziegler, T. E. & Snowdon, C. T. (2001). Reproductive biology of captive male cotton-top tamarin monkeys as a function of social environment. *Animal Behaviour*, 61, 65–78.

Ginther, A. G. & Snowdon, C. T. (2009). Expectant parents groom adult sons according to previous alloparenting in a biparental cooperatively breeding primate, *Animal Behaviour*, 78, 287–297.

Hetherington, E. M. Bridges, M. & Insabella, G. (1998). What matters? What does not? Five perspectives on the association between marital transitions and children's adjustment. *American Psychologist*, 53, 167–184.

Heymann, E. W. (2003). Scent marking, paternal care, and sexual selection in callitrichines. In: C. B. Jones (ed.), Sexual selection and reproductive competition in primates: New perspectives and directions (pp. 305–325). Norman, OK: American Society of Primatologists.

Hoffman K. A., Mendoza, S. P., Henessy, M. B., & Mason, W. A. (1995). Responses of infant titi monkeys, *Callicebus moloch*, to removal of one or both parents: Evidence for paternal attachment. *Developmental Psychobiology*, 28, 399–407.

Hrdy, S. B. (2009). Mothers and others, Cambridge, MA; Belknapp Press.

Humle, T. & Snowdon, C. T. (2008). Socially biased learning in the acquisition of a complex foraging task in juvenile cottontop tamarins (*Saguinus oedipus*). *Animal Behaviour*, 75: 267–277.

Humle, T., Snowdon, C. T. & Matsuzawa, T. (2009). Social influences on the acquisition of ant dipping among the wild chimpanzees (*Pan troglodytes verus*) of Bossou, Guinea, West Africa. *Animal Cognition*. 12: S37–S48.

Johnson, L. D., Petto, A. J. & Sehgal, P. K. (1991). Factors in the rejection and survival of captive cotton-top tamarins (*Saguinus oedipus*). *American Journal of Primatology*, 25: 91–102.

Joyce, S. M. & Snowdon, C. T. (2007). Developmental changes in food transfers in cotton-top tamarins (*Saguinus oedipus*). *American Journal of Primatology*. 69: 955–965.

Keverne, E. B., Martensz, N. D. & Tuite, B. (1989). Beta-endorphin concentrations in cerebrospinal fluid of monkeys as influenced by grooming relationships. *Psychoneuroendocrinology*, 14, 155–161.

Kostan, K. M. & Snowdon, C. T. (2002). Attachment and social preferences in cooperatively-breeding cotton-top tamarins. *American Journal of Primatology*, 57: 131–139.

Kozorovitskiy, Y., Hughes, M., Lee, K. & Gould, E. (2006). Fatherhood affects dendritic spines and vasopressin V1a receptors in the primate prefrontal cortex. *Nature Neuroscience*, 9, 1094–1095.

Krüger, T., Haake, P., Hartmann, U., Schedlowski, M & Exton, M. S. (2002). Orgasm-induced prolactin secretion: feedback control of sexual drive? *Neuroscience and Biobehavioral Reviews*, 26, 31–44.

Lazaro-Perea, C. (2001). Intergroup interactions in wild common marmosets (*Callithrix jacchus*): territorial defence and assessment of neighbours. *Animal Behaviour*, 62, 11–21

Lazaro-Perea, C., Castro, C. S. S., Harrison, R., Araujo, A., Arruda, M. F. & Snowdon, C. T. (2000). Behavioral and demographic changes following the loss of the breeding female in cooperatively breeding marmosets. *Behavioral Ecology and Sociobiology*. 48, 137–146.

Lazaro-Perea, C., Arruda, M. F. & Snowdon, C. T. (2004). Grooming as reward? Social functions of grooming in cooperatively breeding marmosets. *Animal Behaviour*, 67, 627–636.

Levy, F., Keller, M. & Poindron, P. (2004). Olfactory regulation of maternal behavior in mammals. *Hormones and Behavior*, 46, 284–302.

Mendoza, S. P. & Mason, W. A. (1986). Parental division of labor and differentiation of attachments in a monogamous primate (*Callicebus moloch*), *Animal Behaviour* 34, 1336–1347.

Mota, M. T., Franci, C. R. & Sousa, M. B. (2006). Hormonal changes related to paternal and alloparental care in common marmosets (*Callithrix jacchus*). *Hormones and Behavior*, 49, 293–302.

Porter, T. A. (1994). The development and maintenance of heterosexual pair associations in cotton-top tamarins (*Saguinus oedipus*). Unpublished dissertation, University of Wisconsin.

Porter, T. A. & Snowdon, C. T. (1997). Female reproductive status and male pairmate behavior in cotton-top tamarins. *Annals of the New York Academy of Sciences*, 807, 556–558.

Prudom, S. L., Broz, C. A., Schultz-Darken, N.J., Ferris, C. T., Snowdon, C. T. & Ziegler, T. E. (2008). Exposure to infant scent lowers serum testosterone in father common marmosets (*Callithrix jacchus*). *Biology Letters*, 6, 603–605.

Rapaport, L. G. (2006). Provisioning in wild golden lion tamarins (*Leontopithecus rosalia*): Benefits to omnivorous young. *Behavioral Ecology*, 17, 212–221.

Rapaport, L. G. & Ruiz-Miranda, C. R. (2002). Tutoring in wild golden lion tamarins. *International Journal of Primatology*, 23, 1063–1070.

Rapaport L. G. & Brown G. R. (2008). Social influences on foraging behavior in young nonhuman primates: Learning what, where, and how to eat. *Evolutionary Anthropology*. 17, 189–201.

Roberts, R. L., Jenkins, K. T., Lawler, T., Wegner, F. H. & Newman, J. D. (2001). Bromocriptine administration lowers serum prolactin and disrupts parental responsiveness in common marmosets (*Callithrix jacchus*). *Hormones and Behavior*, 39, 106–112.

Rukstalis, M. & French, J. A. (2005). Vocal buffering of the stress response: exposure to conspecific vocalizations moderates urinary cortisol excretion in isolated marmosets. *Hormones and Behavior*, 47, 1–7.

Sánchez, S., Peláez, F., Fidalgo, A., Morcillo, A. & Caperos, J. (2008). Changes in body mass of expectant male cotton-top tamarins (*Saguinus oedipus*). *Folia Primatologica*, 79, 458–462.

Savage, A., Ziegler, T. E. & Snowdon, C. T. (1988). Sociosexual development, pair-bond formation and mechanisms of fertility suppression in female cotton-top tamarins (*Saguinus oedipus oedipus*). *American Journal of Primatology*, 14, 345–359.

Savage, A., Snowdon, C. T., Giraldo, H & Soto, H. (1996). Parental care patterns and vigilance in wild cotton-top tamarins (*Saguinus oedipus*). In M. Norconk, A.

Rosenberger & P. A. Garber (Eds.), *Adaptive radiations of neotropical primates* (pp. 187–199). New York: Plenum.

Sear, R. & Mace, R. (2008). Who keeps children alive? A review of the effects of kin on child survival. *Evolution and Human Behavior,* 29, 1–18.

Shutt, K., MacLarnon, A. Heistermann, M. & Semple S. (2007). Grooming in Barbary macaques: Better to give than to receive? *Biology Letters,* 3, 231–233.

Smith, A. S., Agmo, A., Birnie, A. K., & French, J. A. (2010). Manipulation of the oxytocin system alters social behavior and attraction in pair-bonding primates, *Callithrix penicillata. Hormones and Behavior,* 57, 255–262.

Smith, T. E. & French, J. A. (1997). Social and reproduction conditions modulate urinary cortisol excretion in black tufted-ear marmosets (*Callithrix kuhli*). *American Journal of Primatology,* 42, 253–267.

Snowdon, C. T. (1996). Parental care in cooperatively breeding species. In: J. S. Rosenblatt & C. T. Snowdon (Eds.), *Parental care: Evolution, mechanisms and adaptive significance* (pp. 643–689). San Diego: Academic Press.

Snowdon, C. T. & Pickhard, J. J. (1999). Family feuds severe aggression among cooperatively breeding cotton-top tamarins. *International Journal of Primatology,* 20, 651–663.

Snowdon, C. T., Pieper, B. A., Boe, C. Y., Cronin, K. A. Kurian, A. V. & Ziegler, T. E. (2010). Variation in oxytocin levels is associated with variation in affiliative behavior in monogamous pairbonded tamarins, *Hormones and Behavior,* 58, 614–618.

Snowdon, C. T. & Ziegler, T. E. (2015). Variation in prolactin is related to variation in sexual behavior and contact affiliation. *PLoS ONE,* 10, e0120650.

Stewart-Williams, S. and Thomas, A. G. (2013). The ape that thought it was a peacock: Does evolutionary psychology exaggerate human sex differences? *Psychological Inquiry,* 24, 137–168.

Storey, A. E., Walsh, C. J., Quinton, R., & Wynne-Edwards, K. E. (2000). Hormonal correlates of paternal responsiveness in new and expectant fathers. *Evolutionary Human Behavior,* 21, 79–95.

Temrin, H., Buchmayer, S. & Enquist, M. (2000). Step-parents and infanticide: New data contradict evolutionary predictions. *Proceedings of the Royal Society, London, Series B.* 267, 943–945.

Thierry, B. & Anderson J. R, (1986). Adoption in anthropoid primates. *International Journal of Primatology,* 7, 191–216.

Thompson, E., McLanahan, S, & Curtin, R. B. (1992). Family structure, gender and parental socialization. *Journal of Marriage and the Family,* 54, 368–378.

Trainor, B. C. & Marler, C. A. (2001). Testosterone, paternal behavior and aggression in the monogamous California mouse. *Hormones and Behavior,* 40, 32–42.

Trainor, B. C. & Marler, C. A. 2002. Testosterone promotes paternal behavior in a monogamous mammal via conversion to oestrogen, *Proceedings of the Royal Society of London, Series B. Biological Sciences,* 269, 823–829.

Uvnäs-Moberg, K., (1998). Oxytocin may mediate the benefits of positive social interaction and emotion. *Psychoneuroendocrinology,* 23, 819–836.

Washabaugh, K. & Snowdon, C. T. (1998). Chemical communication of reproductive status in female cotton-top tamarins (*Saguinus oedipus*). *American Journal of Primatology*, 45, 337–349.

Washabaugh, K. F., Ziegler, T. E. & Snowdon, C. T. (2002). Variations in care for cotton-top tamarin (*Saguinus oedipus*) infants as a function of parental experience and group size. *Animal Behaviour*, 63, 1163–1174.

Widowski, T. M., Ziegler, T. E., Elowson, A. M. & Snowdon, C. T. (1990). The role of males in stimulation of reproductive function in female cotton-top tamarins, (*Saguinus oedipus*). *Animal Behaviour*, 40, 731–741.

Widowski, T. M., Porter, T. A., Ziegler, T. E. & Snowdon, C. T. (1992). The stimulatory effect of males on the initiation, but not the maintenance, of ovarian cycling in cotton-top tamarins (*Saguinus oedipus*) *American Journal of Primatology*, 26, 97–108.

Zahed, S. R., Prudom, S. L., Snowdon, C. T. & Ziegler, T. E. (2008). Male parenting and response to infant stimuli in the common marmoset (*Callithrix jacchus*). *American Journal of Primatology*. 70, 84–92.

Zahed, S. K., Kurian, A. V. and Snowdon, C. T. (2010). Social dynamics and individual plasticity of infant care behavior in cooperatively breeding cotton-top tamarins. *American Journal of Primatology*, 72, 296–306.

Ziegler, T. E., Epple, G., Snowdon, C. T., Porter, T. A., Belcher, A., & Kuederling, I. (1993). Detection of the chemical signals of ovulation in the cotton-top tamarin, *Saguinus oedipus*, *Animal Behaviour*, 45: 313–322.

Ziegler, T.E., Scheffler, G., & Snowdon, C.T. (1995). The relationship of cortisol levels to social environment and reproductive functioning in female cotton-top tamarins, *Saguinus oedipus*. *Hormones and Behavior*, 29, 407–424.

Ziegler, T. E., Wegner, F. H., & Snowdon, C. T. (1996). A hormonal role for male parental care in a New World primate, the cotton-top tamarin (*Saguinus oedipus*). *Hormones and Behavior*, 30, 287–297.

Ziegler, T. E. & Snowdon, C. T. (2000). Preparental hormone levels and parenting experience in male cotton-top tamarins (*Saguinus oedipus*). *Hormones and Behavior*, 38: 159–167.

Ziegler, T. E., Washabaugh, K. F. & Snowdon, C. T. (2004). Responsiveness of expectant male cotton-top tamarins (*Saguinus oedipus*) to mate's pregnancy. *Hormones and Behavior*, 45, 84–92.

Ziegler, T. E., Schultz-Darken, N. J., Scott, J. J., Snowdon, C. T., & Ferris, C. F. (2005). Neuroendocrine response to female ovulatory odors depends upon social condition in male common marmosets, *Callithrix jacchus*. *Hormones and Behavior* 47, 56–64.

Ziegler, T. E., Prudom, S. L., Schultz-Darken, N. J., Kurian, A. V. & Snowdon, C. T. (2006). Pregnancy weight gain: Marmoset and tamarin dads show it too. *Biological Letters*. 2, 181–183.

Ziegler, T. E., Peterson, L. J., Sosa, M. E., & Barnard, A. M. (2011). Differential endocrine responses to infant odors in common marmoset (*Callithrix jacchus*) fathers. *Hormones and Behavior*, 59, 265–270.

Chapter 9

The Instinctual Foundations
of Infant Minds

How Primary Affects Guide the Construction of Their Higher Cognitive Proclivities and Abilities

Jaak Panksepp and Marina Farinelli

Human infants are born with affective minds that surely allow them to promptly experience themselves as coherent entities, as they receive diverse sensory inputs from their bodies and the world. These primal aspects of consciousness, with a variety of intrinsic emotional, homeostatic, and sensory systems, coursing through their old mammalian (subcortical) brains, are essential for the growth of all the other mental abilities. Although we know little about their primal affective selves, which provide a center of coherence for all important future life activities, we can finally be confident that such powers of the mind emerge from subcortical brain regions (Damasio, 2012; Denton, 2006; Merker, 2007; Panksepp, 1998a,b; Solms & Panksepp, 2012) There are good reasons to believe that both human and animal possess coreselves that are heavily intermeshed with the primal emotional, homeostatic, and exteroceptive systems of their brains—which engender diverse affective powers of the mind that are finally beginning to be understood neuroscientifically. This kind of knowledge will eventually help clarify not only how the upper mind matures in healthy ways, but should also provide novel ideas for alleviating psychiatric problems that are so common in our species, perhaps others also. Here, we will reflect on these developmental issues as they may impact child development.

The cross-species analyses of fundamental mental processes (e.g., emotional and homeostatic feelings) are newcomers on the landscape of psychological science. The name of the most relevant bridge discipline is *affective neuroscience.* It offers empirical strategies to cross between animal emotional behaviors and their valenced (positive and negative) states of mind, as models for our own, based on demonstrable evolutionary homologies. Such foundations of mammalian minds are of foremost importance in understanding how we can promote better "family values" where children have social environments in which they can thrive. Admittedly, we are only at the beginning of a long journey to understand how affective feelings are constructed within mammalian brains. A critical aspect of this journey is that at the most fundamental psychological level (called "primary-processes" here), all mammals share the same basic emotional tool kits, among which the most important for mental health are *emotional* feelings. Of course, the influence of *homeostatic* feelings such as HUNGER and THIRST, and of course the many *sensory* feelings (e.g., pleasant and aversive tastes and smells) that can feel good or bad in various ways, surely impact the qualities of mental life. In general, the labeling convention for primary-processes (evolutionarily ingrained tools for living) that we use is full capitalization—for instance, SEEKING, RAGE, FEAR, LUST, CARE, PANIC and PLAY for the primary-process emotional systems that control distinct affective (valenced feeling) forms of arousal.

The positive and negative feeling states are regulated by diverse neuro-chemistries, with specificity provided by various neuropeptides (brain opioids, oxytocin, orexin, choleocystokin, corticotropin realeasing factor, and so forth). The overall arousal dimension of experience, which may be shared by all affective and cognitive systems, are heavily dependent on more general purpose acetylcholine, norepinephrine and serotonin activities (Panksepp, 1986; Pfaff, 2006), but here we will only focus on the emotional feelings that are most important for understanding psychiatric disorders and the overall quality of existence.

One prominent investigator of fear-learning in rat brain has recently claimed that "We will never know what an animal feels" (LeDoux, 2012, p. 666). This was a common view throughout the twentieth century, even though since 1954 we have been able to empirically determine that the shifting arousals of certain brain systems (with directed electrical Deep Brain Stimulation (DBS) can be "rewarding" and/or "punishing" (see the seminal work Olds & Milner's and Delgado & Miller's group, both published in 1954). Since we humans have no "rewarding" nor "punishing" events in our lives without accompanying affective feelings, it is reasonable, as a working hypothesis, to argue that brain rewards and punishments are experienced by other animals when their emotional systems are stimulated, especially if that knowledge can illuminate and even predict affective state shifts that humans experience (Panksepp, 1982; 1985; 1998a; 2005). If the animal work predicts the efficacy of new psychiatric treatments in humans (e.g., Panksepp et al., 2014; Panksepp & Yovell, 2014), we should have even more confidence that our science is on the right track.

Now the data for affective states in animals is abundant, and our cardinal thesis is that certain human feelings can finally be understood by studying the homologous processes in animal brains. Here we will summarize why such cross-species emotional-affective investigations are critically important for understanding our deeper (i.e., primary-process) affective nature, and why it may even illuminate issues that may guide understanding of the emotional values upon which affectively positive and negative family structures are built.

The DBS evidence-based thesis is that animals feel their emotional system arousals intensely, and their brain-feelings (indeed key aspects of their "family values" emerging from the CARE system) have a strong evolutionary relationship to our own, with remarkable neuroanatomical, neurophysiological and neurochemical homologies. Can we be *certain*? Of course, we can't, because science never provides proofs, only the weight-of-evidence to differentiate views. At the same time, we have no comparable scientific evidence that animals think or experience cognitive ideas about their feelings and the environmental events that surround them in the deeply thinking-feeling ways that we do. The probability is high that they have diverse sensory experiences, surely those of touch, hearing and vision, which probably evolved in that order (e.g., that conclusion can based on the ventral to dorsal sensory layering within the superior colliculi—see Figure 16.1, p. 312, in *Affective Neuroscience* (Panksepp et al., 1998a). They also surely smell and taste the world in both valenced (sensory-affective) as well as cognitive (exteroceptive) ways, and there is a distinct possibility that the evolution of affects was a critical evolutionary passage for many cognitive developments, especially programming of higher cortical functions. In any event, animals surely also have primal *homeostatic* affects (e.g., HUNGER and THIRST), whose satisfactions guide behavioral strategies—see Denton (2006) for a fine discussion of those "bodily" *homeostatic* feelings.

The evolutionary value of all such valenced states of mind is surely related to the predictive value of such feelings for survival. In complex organisms, behavior-only mechanisms may be less precise guides to where one stands in terms of the many survival-relevant states that are needed in order to sustain life. It is likely that the fluctuations of affective-states control learning process. This linkage is probable since the unconditional (primary-process) states of the nervous system cannot respond rapidly in optimal (behaviorally complex) ways to environmental changes. Only through learning and memory, based on past affective shifts that accompany behaviors, can adaptive survival-promoting behavior patterns be optimized.

Surprisingly, more concerted effort has been devoted to the study of learning and memory than the affects that accompany unconditional emotional and other affective response patterns. The fact that the study of affect, until quite recently in human psychology, has remained an unembraced orphan as a topic of research (see Miskovic et al., 2015), is partly because causal brain-research (not just correlative—i.e., EEG and brain imaging) is needed for in-depth understanding (and the discipline of psychology has never developed a solid foundation in neuroscience, especially subcortically focused animal neuroscience where the best causal work on emotions comes from). In any event, valenced experiences—the varieties of desirable (rewarding) and undesirable (punishing) affective consciousness—remain pervasive, life-supportive brain process that psychology and psychiatry ignore at their peril. Here we will focus on child development where abundant conceptual and empirical wisdom has already been shared by many others (e.g., Narvaez et al., 2012; 2014; Reddy, 2008; Trevarthen, 2009).

THE EMOTIONAL DIMENSIONS OF EARLY CHILDHOOD DEVELOPMENT

What are the implications of the affective neurosciences for understanding the minds of human infants, and the family dynamics that are needed to support healthy mental growth and happiness as opposed to decline and misery? Of course human babies can't talk any more than most other species. But based on animal research we can be *confident* that our babies, during their first years of life, have comparable feelings to most of the ones identified in animal models. The most important finding that allows this bold statement is that animals can "tell" us they have feelings by the consistently rewarding and punishing properties of deep brain stimulations (DBS) that evoke coherent emotional responses, and corresponding affective experiences are consistently reported by humans receiving such brain stimulations (Panksepp, 1985). There are at least seven primal emotions: In animals we can evoke behavior patterns that reflect (i) SEEKING/exploration-curiosity urges, (ii) RAGE/anger, (iii) FEAR/anxiety, (iv) LUST/sexual eagerness, (v) CARE/ maternal-nurturance, (vi) PANIC/separation-distress, and (vii) PLAY/social-joy. None of these evoked states is affectively neutral!

DEVELOPMENTAL TRAJECTORIES OF HIGHER MENTAL PROCESSES (COGNITIONS)

Although the above facts allow us to understand human affective sentience through the study of evolutionarily related brain mechanisms of animals, we have no comparably robust (*causal*) ways to study the experiential aspects of cognitive decision making, although great progress is being made in studying neural *correlates* (Rolls, 2014). While considering these primal-evolved sub-cortical affective functions of mammalian brains, it is important to recognize that the tops of our infants' brains, their neocortices (aka "thinking caps"), although evolutionarily structured as predictably interconnected neural networks (almost like un-programmed RAM chips in one's newly purchased computer), are basically cognitively empty at birth. There may be some very interesting cognitive capacities in the brains of our infants before birth, but we have no experimental way to determine whether they arise from their neo-cortices or from lower brain regions. This is a critical issue, for we do know that infants born without their "thinking caps"—eventually programmed by experiences, from early family life to cultural expectations–are mentally alive and emotionally vibrant creatures (Merker, 2007; Solms & Panksepp, 2012).

To the best of our knowledge, all neocortical functions emerge through the auspices of learning and memory, which are most robustly guided by affective shifts. This makes the social-affective qualities of early family life critical for optimal socio-cognitive-emotional development. Indeed, even though this is not the place to dwell on such details, modern epigenetic mechanisms have been revealed—namely changes in gene expression patterns without a change in nucleotide sequences of DNA (e.g., through gene methylation, histone modifications, etc), whereby life experiences can have life long changes in gene expression patterns with massive implications for bodily and mental health (see Weaver et al., 2004 and chapter 6 in this book by Champagne and Curley). The science is not sufficient for mental health prescriptions, but some future possibilities will be along the lines we will discuss here—minimize negative affects, without eliminating them completely (having just enough for resilience), and maximize positive affects, which intrinsically maximize resilience and thereby minimize the development of life long psychiatric problems that compromise the overall quality of life (for those interested in the abundant details, see the Fall issue of *Dialogues in Clinical Neuroscience* (Vol 16, No 3) for up-to-date information.)

Thus while evolution provided the raw affective tools for mental life, whose neural circuits probably guide adaptive learning, with the associated memory formation, it enriched the neocortex with diverse cognitive capacities. Many of those cognitive superstructures, built on affective foundations, are acquired through the emotional qualities of interpersonal interaction. A wonderful clinically oriented guidebook on how that can be achieved during early child development has been provided by Margot Sunderland (2006), (and for diverse psychological as well as diverse and important neuroscience perspectives, see Narvaez et al., 2012). The qualities of family environments, with their interblending of affective realities and cognitive potentials, are decisive in the emerging qualities of children's personalities and intellectual potentials.

This conceptual issue bears repeating: With regard to the cognitive side of infant development, we need to recognize how fundamentally empty of cognitive riches the neocortex of infants is at birth. In a sense, philosophers such as John Locke (1632–1704) were partly correct in their vision of the newborn mind being a *tabula rasa*. Indeed, we are born with higher brain (neocortical) brains regions that are essentially empty of thoughts and memories. As far as cognitive/knowing skills are concerned, newborn cortices are more akin to "blank-slates" than "beehives" of evolutionarily specialized "modular" specializations. Once we realize this, the outstanding importance of high quality family emotional lives, full of enthusiasms and joys, along with well-attuned social sensitivities, can be seen as critical for the development of the higher mental apparatus, with its various cognitive strengths and weaknesses.

THE NEUROSCIENCE OF CORTICAL DEVELOPMENT

Many evolutionary psychologists still believe our cognitive apparatus has been programmed by evolution. There is little to support that contention (Panksepp & Panksepp, 2000; Panksepp, 2007a). Life experiences modularize the tops of our brains. Even the capacity of the visual cortex to see the world is learned. The first definitive lines of evidence came with the Nobel Prize winning work of Hubel and Wiesel (1962) on the visual systems of cats. It became clear that "normal" early experiences with vision were essential for normal visual abilities to develop in the cortex. For instance, if one eye of a newborn kitten was prevented from seeing, then the visual cortex for that eye was monopolized by the one intact eye, which prevented normal stereoscopic (depth) vision from developing. Eyes unused for a certain amount of time after birth (e.g., with one eye being covered) would forever remain visually deficient. The uncovered eye would take up too much of the territory in the visual cortex that would normally be programmed by the uncovered eye.

Across the years this developmental lesson has been solidified with additional remarkable findings: (i) If we surgically excise (eliminate) the visual cortices in fetuses (of rodents, that is), and ask if those animals, when mature, have major visual deficits, the surprising and resounding answer is "no they do not" (Sur & Rubinstein, 2006). Although the subcortical visual networks do have a neurochemical urge to innervate the cortex (normally the occipital lobe), if the closest tissue is removed, the neurons simply lay down roots in the closest remaining cortex, and program it to be visually skilled.

We will not dwell on other such remarkable facts, but simply reiterate: All the specializations of the neocortex that have been closely studied are developmentally rather than evolutionarily programmed. This contrasts with the abundant evidence that our subcortically generated primary emotions and

other primal affective capacities are more definitively evolutionarily programmed than our cognitive tendencies. After a brief synopsis of the substan-
tive progress that has been achieved about mammalian emotional networks,
we will move on to consider how such knowledge can help optimize family
dynamics to help assure that children have excellent opportunities to grow
into richly empathic, self-actualizing adults, who are optimally situated to
construct positive social worlds down through the generations.

THE INSTINCTUAL FOUNDATIONS OF OUR
PRIMAL AFFECTS: THE ANIMALIAN AFFECTIVE/
EVOLUTIONARY FOUNDATIONS OF HUMAN MINDS

Here is a synopsis of basic emotion systems (archival-worthy details can
be found in Panksepp, 1998a and Panksepp & Biven, 2012). The following
seven primary emotional networks have been delineated through animal brain
research and they are abundantly corroborated by both human brain research
and psychological experiences. We focus first on the four affectively positive
primal emotions, and then the three negative ones:

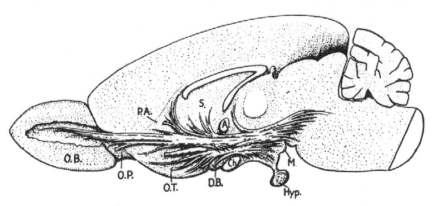

**Figure 9.1   A drawing of the Medial Forebrain Bundle (MFB), which illustrates the main
trajectory of the SEEKING system (classically referred to as "the brain reward system").**
It runs up from the midbrain, through the lateral hypothalamus (LH), into more rostral
neural regions, with abundant descending connections as well as local control (such
as specific hormonal fields (e.g., sex and stress steroids), as well as neuropeptides such
as those that control male and female LUST (vasopressin & oxytocin respectively) and
CARE (especially oxytocin and prolactin). Other neural regions pictured: optic chiasm
(Ch), olfactory bulbs (O.B.), olfactory peduncle (O.P.), paraolfactory area (P.A.), olfactory
tract (O.T.), diagonal band of Broca (D.B.), anterior commissure (A), pituitary gland/the
hypophysis (Hyp.), septum (S.), and mammillary bodies (M). *Source*: Figure from Le Gros
Clark, 1938

1. Highly motivated SEEKING behaviors (mainly, exploration, foraging and inquisitiveness), along with positive feelings of enthusiasm and exhilaration, can be engendered by a massive neural system called the Medial Forebrain Bundle (see Figure 1) which has only recently been characterized in humans (Coenen et al., 2012), and many are beginning to envision that stress (especially PANIC) induced depletion of this system can promote depression (Panksepp et al., 2014) and suicide (Panksepp & Yovell, 2014). This complex system is the bedrock for three more specific enthusiasms—LUST, CARE, and PLAY. It motivates us to pursue all things needed for survival, and it can promote all kinds of addictions from drugs to all the other excessive appetites. Thus, an early parental focus to channel this psychic energy (of enthusiasm and curiosity) toward an engagement with the better values of the world is an essential nurturant responsibility.
2. LUST, which comes in male and female varieties, and takes advantage of regions of the SEEKING system that are especially enriched in gonadal hormone receptors (especially testosterone in males and estrogen and progesterone in females); this focuses the SEEKING system toward passionate feelings of sexual desire, that get dramatically magnified by puberty. Wise parental guidance through such development passages is possible, especially if it recognized that transsexual brain and body organizations have always been with us, where feminized brains can developmentally emerge in male-typical bodies and masculinized brains in female ones. The acceptance of such natural variations should be part of the learned wisdom of parenthood. Other key aspects are part of our inherited adult wisdom.
3. A natural consequence of reproduction is the sensitization of the SEEKING system toward maternal CARE. This kind of sensitization occurs especially in MFB regions that have abundant prolactin and oxytocin receptors, which are commonly more enriched in female than male brains. The CARE system is also surely an important contributor to empathic tendencies. There are gender differences in this system, but not, as far as we know, in early childhood. Female brains generally come to be more adept at CAREing, but the potential is there in males, and can be cultivated by reinforcing so many opportunities that are available, especially with pets. Boys that want to play with dolls should not be discouraged, for fear of influencing their gender identities. There is no evidence that can occur, although when it has occurred biologically, wise parents should recognize and cherish the differences.
4. Finally, young animals, whether human or other mammals, have robust (indeed "rough-and-tumble") PLAY urges, characterized by delightful physical engagements full of running, chasing, wrestling, and laughter (indeed, we discovered a simple way to study this in rats by tickling them). The underlying brain circuits for the last three variants of SEEKING are

probably the fundamental source of "social joys", with many brain benefits (Burgdorf et al., 2011; Moskal et al., 2011), especially against depression (Panksepp et al., 2014; Panksepp & Yovell, 2014). Children that do not get adequate social play may gradually become impulsive and thereby be diagnosed with Attention Deficit Hyperactivity Disorders (ADHD). Most medicines given to ADHD-type children tend to reduce playfulness. The first line of defense against ADHD should be abundant daily play. In single child families, making this a daily routine, twice a day (especially by fathers), can benefit children in many ways (Panksepp & Scott, 2013).

5. Among the three negative systems, the aversive feeling of FEAR was the first to be studied. This system coaxes animals to recoil from potential harm, and is probably one the major sources of the feeling that accompany anxiety disorders. A child that has too many such feelings may not be able to take full advantage of its many manifestations of SEEKING urges. Excessive sensitivity of the FEAR system surely participates in the genesis of anxiety disorders, partly because the system can become sensitized—namely, more susceptible to being aroused (Adamec & Young, 2000).

6. The intense feeling of RAGE is quite a different negative feeling, commonly called anger, which emerges when one's desires are thwarted. Thus psychological frustrations and bodily irritations lead one to reach out and strike someone. This system can surely be *sensitized*, so that the more a child has experienced anger, the more likely this system will become excessively responsive, just like the FEAR system.

7. Finally, there is a PANIC system that engenders a distinct negative type of feelings that arise from the severance of social bonds—basically the negative feelings of grief and loneliness that arise from the deprivation of social support. Thus, this system also figures prominently in the quality of social bonds. Brain opioids, which are normally activated by social contacts (Keverne et al., 1989; Panksepp & Bishop, 1981), powerfully soothe this type of psychological pain, providing one reason that people, especially those who are lonely and in psychological pain, get attracted to opioid drugs. Depression and even suicidal tendencies induced by excessive PANIC can be effectively reversed with safe opioids that have long been known to reduce feelings of PANIC (separation-distress)—(for a synopsis of those clinical findings, see Panksepp & Yovell, 2014).

THE "LAWS OF AFFECT" THAT GUIDE LEARNING AND MEMORY

Enormous advances have been made in the last few decades in understanding how primal emotions are organized in the brain, and how *primary-process* emotions control *secondary-process* learning and memory, which provide the essential ingredients for *tertiary-process* higher-order mental activities (Panksepp & Biven, 2012). This hierarchical organization of the BrainMind in terms of nested hierarchies, allows us to better conceptualize the bottom-up development of human mind. In sum, mammalian brains contain a fundamental emotional substrate for positive and negative feelings and behaviors that accompany the energetic, positively motivated life activities that subserve all our emotional and bodily needs.

This knowledge is helping us re-conceptualize the scientific foundations of psychiatry and psychotherapy, which may eventually lead to major advances in the treatment of emotional disturbances that control the development and expression of mental illnesses. The affective neuroscience approach allows us to focus more directly and effectively on the emotional problems of people (hence we developed the Affective Neuroscience Personality Scales (ANPS)— see Davis & Panksepp, 2011 for most recent version), and it provides new insights on how to reestablish positive affective balance, using the natural plasticity of the human MindBrain. The importance of focusing on the neural dynamics of SEEKING, PANIC and PLAY systems in emotional homeostasis and development of new antidepressant treatments has been recently extensively discussed (Watt & Panksepp, 2009; Panksepp et al., 2014).

At the same time a focus on how our neuroscientific understanding of the various primary-process positive emotions, especially PLAY and social solidarity, can strengthen positive attitudes has received considerable attention (Burgdorf et al., 2011; Gruber et al., 2014; Sheldon et al., 2011). Also, the Affective Neuroscience Personality Scales (ANPS) will be introduced as a tool to provide better objective measure of clients' specific primary-process emotional strengths and weaknesses. Some recent applications of ANPS (Farinelli et al., 2013; 2015) in stroke patients put in evidence the impact of specific brain lesions on basic emotion (SEEKING, in particular) and depression. Observed abnormalities concerning mainly basic emotions also indicate that the effect of brain lesions may enhance the interrelation between basic emotions and attachment. Main findings of the mentioned studies shed light on the possible relationships between emotions and attachment that are subserved by distinct and segregated underlying neural systems.

Basic emotions are associated with different neural systems in subcortical networks, while social attachment (based on learning) is assumed to be related to neural activity in more cortical regions such as some regions of the cortical midline structure and, in particular, the medial orbital prefrontal cortex or the ventromedial prefrontal cortex. ANPS could be a useful instrument in the follow-up of patients during the different phases of the reorganization of the self, following brain lesions and to choose specific rehabilitative and psychotherapeutic techniques.

IMPLICATIONS FOR FAMILY DYNAMICS AND CHILD DEVELOPMENT AND RELATED PSYCHIATRIC PROBLEMS

Although infants of no species are born with cognitively rich lives—minds full of perceptually based knowledge, ideas and intuitions—they have basic learning and memory mechanisms to acquire those capacities, but those require various affects, attention and lots of neocortex. Thus basic emotions are a substantial part of the neuro-mental engines that motivate children to learn and remember. In short, a child's instinctual emotional life is a critical foundation upon which their memories and cognitive styles are formed. Thereby the affective qualities of early development, and the resulting memories, have a lasting influence on the cognitive channels that control how one thinks about the world and their role in the greater social order (or disorder!). Surely the family dynamics can cast both sunny light and abysmal darkness on these processes. By fusing the realities of the past with the possibilities of the future, one's character is formed. So let us briefly consider some very general advice one might offer from this perspective, especially for the first years of life, as one considers a select group of emotional primes.

SEEKING: This system is the foundation for enthusiasm, curiosity, and ultimately creativity, and under the worst conditions, diverse addictions. Parents are well advised to provide environments where a variety of opportunities are provided for engaging this system in ways that can broaden children's interest both in social and nonsocial domains. Obviously, this will require remaining attuned to the activities that engage a child, while at the same time providing opportunities for broadening interests, especially in activities that have strong social components that require shared attention. Obviously, the computer revolution has provided many creative options, but also activities that promote autistic aloneness. In this, we should remember that when a human engages youngsters in the learning of new languages, the most progress is made with real CAREing human beings. Infants looking at a video rendition of the same person, obtain few benefits (Kuhl, 2009); infants are designed for social engagements (Reddy, 2010; Trevarthen, 2009) and everything that maximizes those opportunities are bound to yield more lasting life benefits than those that are pursued in "autistic" aloneness.

LUST: Infantile sexuality has been a contentious topic in psychoanalysis, and there is insufficient space here to weave through that contentious topic. What affective neuroscience can add is clarity about the simple fact that bodily gender and brain gender are controlled by different developmental programs. Thus, wise parents should recognize that a male brain organization in a male-typical body is the norm, as is a female brain organization in a female-typical body. However, as many cultures have recognized, without much worry, that cross body-brain variations are normal as far as our neuroscientific under-standing of sexual variation is concerned. The hormonal patterns that lead to the masculinization and feminization of brain organization—most of which is expressed at the subcortical primary-process emotional levels (admittedly, in the minority of children)—should be deemed normal variants of human developmental trajectories. Children's gender-identity and resulting devel-opmental trajectories, whatever they are, should be allowed to be manifested with consistent parental support and care, channeled as much as possible toward consistent pro-social values.

CARE: Obviously the care-giving urges, typically stronger in mothers than fathers (indeed, more in girls than boys), need to be a blessing for each child's life. There should be a consistent sense of security that is affirmed in the earliest interactions. Perhaps the most compelling short image we have is of a mother holding her baby, with caresses and hugs, accompanied by the whispering or singing of 'sweet somethings' in the baby's ears. These affirm the solidity of parent-infant bonds, which provide ideal affective jumping-off points for the essential playful interactions that enrich a child's life from the very beginning, promoting the likelihood of become caring adults. Both affective qualities allow children to grow up into warm and engaging people who have a seemingly natural capacity to make others feel good and welcome.

PLAY: The whole social developmental trajectory is guided by the qualities of social PLAY—one of the greatest pro-social forces of the brain, much underutilized, even misunderstood and marginalized in modern life, perhaps contributing to the current epidemic of childhood psychiatric disorder. All children should be allowed to freely engage with each other in joyous games of their own making, allowing them to grow up to be superb parents. The fin-est parental indicator that one is on the right path with young children is the abundance of the laughter, and desire to engage in physical tickle games with parents, that evolve into a diversity of fun social activities. We were shocked to discover a primal form of laughter in laboratory rats twenty years ago, but that is another story, starting with (Panksepp & Burgdorf, 1999; 2000; Panksepp et al., 2001), and now progressing well for a long time without much funding or scientific interest, but remarkable enthusiasm from animal lovers (for summaries, see Burgdorf & Panksepp, 2006; Panksepp, 2007b).

Obviously most early play should be among children, but in a one-child family, the father is well advised to take up the slack, for a play-starved child is liable to act out in troublesome ways, that may be seen by professionals (especially those untutored in ludic behaviors) as an ADHD. One of the shocking affective neuroscience facts found first through animal research is that the medications that are commonly given to ADHD children are agents that consistently reduce playfulness in animals. There are good reasons to believe that abundant childhood play can provide prophylaxis for the development of such disorders (Panksepp, 2008; Panksepp & Scott, 2013).

PANIC: Although all of the above systems have a role in social bonding, there are reasons to believe that feelings of separation distress, and especially their alleviation, are key factors in early social attachment bonds (Panksepp, Herman et al., 1980: Panksepp, Siviy & Normansell, 1985 and many other reviews). Children without secure attachments are likely to have emotional problems throughout life. This has been obvious ever since the work of John Bowlby (1980). However modest doses of separation distress can surely be used by parents effectively as a way of instructing children in the value of basic human relations. There are many safe situations where secure children may challenge the need of parents to shift priorities from, let's say, outdoor play at a playground where there are no other children to other activities/responsibilities. And if their child gets grumpy and doesn't cooperate, a willingness to walk away, perhaps around a corner, and wait for the child to get a bit distressed, followed promptly by a comforting reunion, may be a useful lesson that can facilitate future cooperation and development of pro-social values.

In any event, separation-distress needs to be seen as a useful index of the pro-social qualities of a child. There is considerable evidence that autistic children may have a deficit in social bonding by their failure to show any distress upon separation, perhaps in some caused by elevated brain opioid activity which can markedly dampen activity in separation distress systems. We have often seen such children to exhibit more pro-social behaviors after their levels of endogenous opioid activity have been reduced with very modest dose of the opiate-receptor anatagonist naltrexone (for overview, see Panksepp & Sahley, 1987, with our best double-blind study being Bouvard et al., 1995).

It would be interesting to study with tools like the ANPS, basic emotional profiles and attachment styles of parents of children suffering from ADHD and other behavioral, mental and psychosomatic disorders aimed at characterizing the developmental context and the benefits of interventions and therapies. Furthermore, the emotional and attachment-style assessment of parents would contribute to focus psychological interventions not only on symptoms shown by children but on the structure and functioning of the whole family. Psychotherapeutic practice shows that family members very often need to be actively involved during the psychotherapeutic process to make possible lasting changes at very basic levels. Family members along with various psychological and psychopharmacological treatments can positively contribute to improved child mental health. Variants of the ANPS (e.g., comparable *state* measures) could also be used to monitor changes in family dynamics during complex psychotherapeutic processes to help assure that children are exhibiting positive affective rebalancing of the family relational system.

These are just modest examples of the types of thinking that affective neuroscience perspectives suggest in terms of child development issues. Clearly, a book could be written about child development issues based on an understanding of the fundamental emotional systems of mammalian brains. Indeed, a superlative one has been written (Sunderland, 2006). And this chapter is just a brief sampler of the brain-mind issues that taking primal emotional systems seriously suggest in their roles as major barometers and guides of our lives.

DENOUMENT

In sum, we are finally able to weave a coherent web of evidence concerning the affective foundations of the human mind, shared with many other mammals because the underlying ancestral solutions to living are the shared genetic birthrights of all mammals, as Darwin surmised in his last two books—the *Descent of Man* (1871) and *Expression of Emotions in Man and Animals* (1872). Of course, our capacity to understand, or even accept the evidence for the existence of the internal feelings of other animals, has long been denied by prominent scientists (see Panksepp, 1998, 1999), even to this day (e.g., LeDoux, 2012; Rolls, 2014). We scientists share three fundamental values: Beside our primal values of (i) skepticism and (ii) the fact that scientific conclusions always need to be based on the weight-of-evidence, not "proof" (which does not exist in deep science) we also recognize (if adequately philosophically trained) that (iii) there is no absolutely perfect scientific understanding, namely "proof," in our fragile (always open to modification) attempts to understand nature.

For the past half century, abundant lines of evidence have supported the conclusion that other animals do feel their emotions (for overviews, see Panksepp, 1981; 1982; 1998a; Panksepp & Biven, 2012), and because of the remarkable anatomical and neurochemical homologies that exist among the most ancient (subcortical) brain area, we can provisionally conclude, based on the weight-of-evidence, that all mammals have a diversity of evolutionarily/genetically endowed brain emotional systems that are rewarding or punishing, and hence they also have homologous (evolutionarily *related*, albeit surely not *identical*) affective experiences. We are almost at the point where we can reach the same conclusions with respect to homeostatic affects like HUNGER, THIRST, and DISGUST (Denton, 2006).

In short, the neuroscientific study of all mammals (at least those that share evolutionarily related brain sensory, homeostatic, and emotional affective systems) can provide important evidence concerning our own affective lives. That such evolved survival indicators help jump-start and consolidate the acquisition of new knowledge, based on the brain's intrinsic capacities for learning and memory, allows us to entertain new "Laws of Affect" (Panksepp, 2012) as opposed to the behavioristic "Law of Effect" that still encourages some to talk about "negative reinforcement" processes (i.e., that translates to "elimination of punishments") as opposed to affectively meaningful psychological concepts such as "relief." If anyone still has trouble believing animals have feelings akin to "relief" when given "safety signals" indicating that shock will be withheld for a while (during commonly used classical fear-conditioning paradigms), they need to explain why their animals so consistently exhibit "double-respirations" (also known as "sighing") when safety signals periodically come on to relieve their emotional agony (Soltysik & Jelen, 2005). Conversely, from a feeling perspective, if we tickle rats, as we have now been doing for a quarter century as a measure of positive social affect, we were recently pleased by the work of Polish colleagues that such animals become "optimistic" based on solid behavioral observations (Rygula et al., 2012).

Still the evidence-based conclusion that animals do experience diverse affects (Panksepp, 1998; 2005; 2011a,b) does *not* permit us to jump to the conclusion that there is sufficient evidence to conclude that animals "think" about their dilemmas in ways that resemble our *ideas*. We cannot go there with any scientific confidence, albeit there are impressive lines of evidence that they also may experience complex emotions, even some as subtle as "regret" (Steiner & Redish, 2014). The fact that animals experience survival values affectively, does not yet allow us to conclude that they think about their place in the world in any way that resembles the cognitive activities that our massive neocortical regions permit.

The implications of our growing understanding of the neuroscience of cross-mammalian affective processes, has profound implications for understanding the maturing minds of our babies, and the importance of family dynamics in providing a secure base for healthy psychological growth. We have only touched upon a few simple implications of this knowledge: Perhaps the most important being that sufficiently rich storehouses of positive affective memories allow growing children to become adults who naturally promote positive human relationships and values that nourish healthy societies. The simple fact that diverse positive and negative affects emerge neurodynamically in humans at subcortical primary-process levels, where all mammals share brain emotional and homeostatic mechanisms that affectively encode for survival trajectories, provides for a psychologically satisfying understanding of the kinds of creatures we are, and how we can become better in the midst of supportive families and cultural dynamics.

In sum, affects are the neuropsychological representatives of survival values—all good/desirable feelings statistically predict survival trajectories; all bad/undesirable feelings indicate animals need to take certain actions to maximize survival. Because of a shared ancestral past, we share basic affective feelings with all the other mammals, as well as diverse other organisms. To our astonishment, even crayfish return to places where they received drugs that are highly addictive in humans—amphetamine, cocaine and morphine—presumably because they engender desirable feelings (Huber et al., 2011), but of a kind that is hard for us to understand with any precision. But the lack of precision at the psychological level does not preclude confidence in the conclusion that they also experience the world in ways indicative of survival & thriving versus likelihood of destruction. Family dynamics that favor the former are to be cherished and culturally promoted. Those that favor the latter are not worthy of our admiration.

An understanding of the neurobiology of human affective sentience, so important for understanding ourselves and helping people in psychiatric distress, has long been delayed by too many prominent scientists claiming we cannot know anything about the emotional feelings of other animals. We can. And that is a solid pathway to understanding our own primal emotional feelings scientifically.

REFERENCES

Bouvard, M. P., Leboyer, M., Launay, J. M., Recasens, C., Plumet, M. H., Waller-Perotte, D., Tabuteau, F., Bondoux, D., Dugas, M., Lensing, P., & Panksepp, J. (1995). Low-dose naltrexone effects on plasma chemistries and clinical symptoms in autism: A double-blind, placebo-controlled study. *Psychiatry Research, 58,* 191–201.

Bowlby, J. (1980). *Attachment and loss, Vol. 3. Loss: Sadness and depression.* New York, NY: Basic Books.

Burgdorf, J. & Panksepp, J (2006). The neurobiology of positive emotions. *Neuroscience and Biobehavioral Reviews, 30,* 173–187.

Burgdorf, J., Wood, P. L., Kroes, R. A., Moskal, J. R., & Panksepp, J. (2007). Neurobiology of 50-kHz ultrasonic vocalizations in rats: Electrode mapping, lesion, and pharmacology studies. *Behavioral Brain Research. 182,* 274–283.

Burgdorf, J., Panksepp, J., & Moskal, J. R. (2011). Frequency-modulated 50kHz ultrasonic vocalizations: A tool for uncovering the molecular substrates of positive affect. *Neuroscience & Biobehavioral Reviews, 35,* 1831–1836.

Coenen, V. A., Panksepp, J., Hurwitz, T. A., Urbach, H., & Mädler, B. (2012). Human medial forebrain bundle (MFB) and anterior thalamic radiation (ATR):

Diffusion tensor imaging of two major subcortical pathways that may promote a dynamic balance of opposite affects relevant for understanding depression. *The Journal of Neuropsychiatry and Clinical Neurosciences.* 24, 223–236.

Damasio, A. R. (2010). *Self comes to mind: Constructing the conscious brain.* New York, NY: Pantheon Books.

Davis, K. L., & Panksepp, J. (2011). The brain's emotional foundations of human personality and the Affective Neuroscience Personality Scales. *Neuroscience & Biobehaviooral Reviews*, 35, 1946–1958.

Delgado, J. M., Roberts, W. W., & Miller, N. E. (1954). Learning motivated by electrical stimulation of the brain. *American Journal of Physiology*, 179, 587–593.

Denton, D. (2006). *The primordial emotions: The dawning of consciousness.* New York, NY: Oxford University Press, New York.

Farinelli M., Panksepp, J., Gestieri L., Leo M. R., Agati, R., Maffei, M., Leonardi, M. & Northoff, G. (2013). SEEKING and depression in stroke patients: An exploratory study, *Journal of Clinical and Experimental Neuropsychology*, doi:10.1080/13803395.2013.776009.

Farinelli, M., Panksepp, J., Cevolani, D., Gestieri, L., Maffei, M., Agati, R., Pedone, V. & Northoff, G. (2015). Do brain lesions in stroke affect basic emotions and attachment? *Journal of Clinical and Experimental Neuropsychology*, doi: 10.1080/13803395.2014.991279.

Gruber, J., & Moskowitz, J. D. (2014). *Positive Emotion: Integrating the Light Sides and Dark Sides.* Oxford University Press, New York

Hubel, D. H. & T. N. Wiesel. (1962). Receptive fields, binocular interaction And functional architecture in the cat's visual cortex, *Journal of Physiology,* 160, 106–154.

Keverne, E. B., Martensz, N., & Tuite, B. (1989). B-Endorphin concentrations in CSF of monkeys are influenced by grooming relationships. *Psychoneuroendocrinology*, 14, 155–161.

Kuhl, P. K. (2009). Early language acquisition: Neural substrates and theoretical models. In M. S. Gazzaniga (Ed.), *The Cognitive Neurosciences, 4th Edition* (pp. 837–854). Cambridge, MA, MIT Press.

LeDoux, J. (2012). Rethinking the emotional brain. *Neuron*, 73, 653–676.

LeDoux, J. (2014). Coming to terms with fear. *Proceedings of the National Academy of Sciences USA, 111*, 2871–2878.

Le Gros Clark, W. E. (1938). *The Hypothalamus.* Edinburgh: Oliver & Boyd.

Merker, B. (2007). Consciousness without a cerebral cortex: A challenge for neuroscience and medicine. *Behavioral and Brain Sciences, 30*, 63–134.

Miskovic, V. Kuntzelman K., & Fletcheret, N. (2015). Searching for affect in affective neuroscience: Challenges and opportunities. *Psychology of Consciousness: Theory, Research, and Practice, 2*(1), 1–18.

Moskal, J. R., Burgdorf, J., Kroes, R. A., Brudzynski, S. M., & Panksepp, J. (2011). A novel NMDA receptor glycine-site partial agonist, GLYX-13, has therapeutic potential for the treatment of autism. *Neuroscience & Biobehavioral Reviews, 35*, 1982–1988.

Narvaez, D. (2014). *Neurobiology and the development of human morality.* New York: Norton.

Narvaez, D., Panksepp, J., Schore, A., & Gleason, T. (Eds.). (2012). *Human nature, early experience and the environment of evolutionary adaptedness.* New York, NY: Oxford University Press.

Olds, J., & Milner, P. (1954). Positive reinforcement produced by electrical stimulation of the septal area and other regions of rat brain. *Journal of Comparative and Physiological Psychology,* 47, 419–427.

Panksepp, J. (1981). Hypothalamic integration of behavior: Rewards, punishments, and related psychobiological process. In *Handbook of the hypothalamus, Vol. 3, Part A. Behavioral studies of the hypothalamus.* P. J. Morgane and J. Panksepp (Eds.). (pp, 289–487). Marcel Dekker, New York.

Panksepp, J. (1982). Toward a general psychobiological theory of emotions. *The Behavioral and Brain Sciences,* 5, 407–467.

Panksepp, J. (1985). Mood changes. In P. J. Vinken, G. W. Bruyn, & H. L. Klawans (Eds.). *Handbook of Clinical Neurology* (Revised Series). Vol. 1. (45): *Clinical Neuropsychology.* Amsterdam: Elsevier Science Publishers, pp. 271–285.

Panksepp, J. (1986). The neurochemistry of behavior. *Annual Review of Psychology,* 37, 77–107.

Panksepp, J. (1990). Can "mind" and behavior be understood without understanding the brain? A response to Bunge. *New Ideas in Psychology,* 8, 139–149.

Panksepp, J. (1998a). *Affective neuroscience: The foundations of human and animal emotions.* New York: Oxford University Press.

Panksepp, J. (1998b). The periconscious substrates of consciousness: Affective states and the evolutionary origins of the SELF. *Journal of Consciousness Studies,* 5, 566–582.

Panksepp, J. (1999). Emotions as viewed by psychoanalysis and neuroscience: An exercise in consilience, and accompanying commentaries. *Neuro-Psychoanalysis.* 1, 15–89.

Panksepp, J. (2005). Affective consciousness: Core emotional feelings in animals and humans. *Consciousness & Cognition,* 14, 19–69.

Panksepp J. (2007a). The neuroevolutionary and neuroaffective psychobiology of the prosocial brain. In R.I.M. Dunbar and L. Barrett (eds.) *The Oxford handbook of evolutionary psychology* (pp. 145–162) Oxford, UK: Oxford University Press.

Panksepp J. (2007b). Neuroevolutionary sources of laughter and social joy: Modeling primal human laughter in laboratory rats. *Behavioral Brain Research.* 182, 231–44.

Panksepp, J., (2008). PLAY, ADHD and the construction of the social brain: Should the first class each day be recess? *American Journal of Play,* 1, 55–79.

Panksepp, J. (2011a). Cross-species affective neuroscience decoding of the primal affective experiences of humans and related animals. *PLoS One,* 6(8), e21236. doi:10.1371/journal.pone.0021236.

Panksepp, J. (2011b). The basic emotional circuits of mammalian brains: Do animals have affective lives? *Neurosciences & Biobehavioral Reviews,* 35, 1791–1804.

Panksepp, J. (2012). Empathy and the Laws of Affect. *Science,* 334, 1359–1359.

Panksepp, J. & Bishop, P. (1981). An autoradiographic map of ^{3}H diprenorphine binding in the rat brain: Effects of social interaction. *Brain Research Bulletin,* 7, 405–410.

Panksepp, J. & Biven, L. (2012). *Archaeology of Mind: The Neuroevolutionary Origins of Human Emotions.* New York: Norton.

Panksepp, J. & Burgdorf, J. (1999). Laughing rats? Playful tickling arouses high frequency ultrasonic chirping in young rodents. In S. Hameroff, D. Chalmers & A. Kazniak, pp. 231–244, *Toward a science of consciousness III,* Cambridge, Mass.: MIT Press.

Panksepp, J. & Burgdorf, J. (2000). 50k-Hz chirping (laughter?) in response to conditioned and unconditioned tickle-induced reward in rats: Effects of social housing and genetic variables. *Behavioral Brain Research,* 115, pp. 25–38.

Panksepp, J., Burgdorf, J. & Gordon, N. (2001). Toward a genetics of joy: Breeding rats for "laughter." In A. Kazniak (ed.) *Emotion, qualia, and consciousness.* pp. 124–136, World Scientific: Singapore.

Panksepp, J., Herman, B. H., Vilberg, T., Bishop, P., & DeEskinazi, F. G. (1980). Endogenous opioids and social behavior. *Neuroscience and Biobehavioral Reviews,* 4, 473–487.

Panksepp, J. (1986). The psychobiology of prosocial behaviors: Separation distress, play, and altruism. In *Altruism and Aggression, Biological and Social Origins,* C. Zahn-Waxler, E. M. Cummings & R. Iannotti (Eds.). Cambridge, Cambridge University Press, 19–57.

Panksepp, J. & Panksepp, J. B. (2000). The seven sins of evolutionary psychology. *Evolution & Cognition,* 6, 108–131.

Panksepp, J., & Sahley, T. (1987). Possible brain opioid involvement in disrupted social intent and language development of autism. *In Neurobiological issues in autism,* E. Schopler & G. Mesibov (Eds.). (pp. 357–382). New York: Plenum Press.

Panksepp, J. & Scott, E. L. (2013). Reflections on rough and tumble play, social development, and Attention-Deficit Hyperactivity Disorders. In A. L. Meyer and T. P. Gullotta (eds.), *Physical Activity Across the Lifespan,* (pp. 23–38). Springer Science+Business Media New York.

Panksepp, J., Siviy, S. M., & Normansell, L.A. (1985). Brain opioids and social emotions. In *The psychobiology of attachment and separation.* In M. Reite and T. Fields (Eds.). New York: Academic press, 3–49.

Panksepp, J., Wright, J. S., Döbrössy, M. D., Schlaepfer, T. E., & Coenen, V. A. (2014). Affective neuroscience strategies for understanding and treating depressions: from preclinical models to novel therapeutics. *Clinical Psychological Science,* 2, 472–494.

Panksepp, J. & Yovell, Y. (2014). Preclinical Modeling of Primal Emotional Affects (SEEKING, PANIC and PLAY): Gateways to the Development of New Treatments for Depression. *Psychopathology,* 47, 383–93.

Panksepp, J. & Panksepp, J. B. (2000). The seven sins of evolutionary psychology. *Evolution & Cognition:* 6, 108–131.

Pfaff, D. (2006). *Brain arousal and information theory.* Cambridge, MA: Harvard University Press.

Reddy, V. (2010). *How infants know minds.* Cambridge, MA: Harvard University Press.

Rolls, E.T. (2014). *Emotion and decision making explained,* Oxford University Press, Oxford, UK.

Rygula, R., Pluta, H., & Popik, P. (2012). Laughing rats are optimistic. *PLoS ONE* 7(12), e51959.

Sheldon, K. M., Kashdan, T. B., & Steger, M. F. (Eds.) (2011) *Designing positive psychology: Taking stock and moving forward.* New York: Oxford University Press.

Solms, M. & Panksepp, J. (2012). The "Id" knows more than the "Ego" admits: Neuropsychoanalytic and primal consciousness perspectives on the interface between affective and cognitive neuroscience. *Brain Science, 2,* 147–175.

Soltysik, S. & Jelen, P. (2005). In rats, sighs correlate with relief. *Physiology & Behavior, 85,* 598 – 602.

Steiner, A. P. & Redish, A.D. (2014). Behavioral and neurophysiological correlates of regret in rat decision-making on a neuroeconomic task. *Nature Neuroscience,* 17, 995–1002.

Sunderland, M. (2006). *The science of parenting.* New York: Dorling Kindersley.

Sur, M., & Rubinstein, J. L. (2005). Patterning and plasticity of the cerebral cortex. *Science,* 310, 805–810.

Trevarthen, C. (2009). The functions of emotion in infancy: The regulation and communication of rhythm, sympathy, and meaning in human development. In Diana Fosha, Daniel J. Siegel, and Marion F. Solomon, eds. *The Healing Power of Emotion: Affective Neuroscience, Development, and Clinical Practice.* New York: Norton, 55–85.

Watt, D. F. & Panksepp, J. (2009). Depression: An evolutionarily conserved mechanism to terminate separation-distress? A review of aminergic, peptidergic, and neural network perspectives. *Neuropsychoanalysis,* 11, 5–104.

Weaver, I. C., Cervoni, N., Champagne, F. A., Alessio, A. C., Sharma, S., Seckl, J. R., Dymov, S., & Meaney, M. J. (2004). Epigenetic programming by maternal behavior. *Nature Neuroscience,* 7/8, 847–854.

Chapter 10

Evolution of Psychological Mechanisms for Human Family Relationships

Mark V. Flinn

The human family seems to follow a typical mammalian pattern: intense maternal care including breastfeeding of an altricial (helpless) offspring, with some support from an assortment of other relatives–fathers, siblings, aunts, and the like. Beyond the shared mammal/primate commonality, however, humans exhibit a suite of highly unusual traits. We are the only species characterized by the combination of: stable breeding bonds, extensive paternal effort in a multi-male group, lengthy childhood, extended bilateral kin recognition, grandparenting, and controlled exchange of mates among kin groups (Alexander, 1990b; Chapais, 2008). These characteristics are important for theoretical and pragmatic understanding of family relationships and the supporting cognitive, emotional, and physiological mechanisms; they also provide critical insights into the puzzle of human evolution.

In this chapter I first review a general model for the evolution of human mating, parenting, and kinship patterns based on a process of runaway social selection (Alexander, 2006; Flinn & Alexander, 2007; Flinn et al., 2007). I then briefly evaluate the physiological mechanisms that underpin these central aspects of our sociality. My objectives include providing important information and ideas from biological and cultural anthropology that contribute to understanding the evolutionary psychology of the human family, with insights for clinical practice.

BRAIN, CHILDHOOD, AND FAMILY

Evolution of Mind in the Family Crèche

Information processing (intelligence) and social communication (language) are core human adaptations. By all measures the human brain that enables these abilities is an astonishing organ. Its cortex comprises about 30 billion neurons of 200 different types, each of which are interlinked by about a thousand synapses, resulting in $>10^{15}$ connections working at rates of up to 10^{10} interactions per second (Edelman, 2006). Quantifying the transduction of these biophysical actions into specific mental activities—that is, thoughts and emotional feelings—is difficult, but it is likely that humans have more information processing capacity than any other species (Roth & Dicke, 2005).

The human brain evolved at a rapid pace: hominin cranial capacity tripled (from an average of about 450cc to 1350 cc) in less than two million years (Lee & Wolpoff, 2003)—roughly 100,000 neurons and supportive cells per generation. Structural changes such as increased convolutions, thickly myelinated cortical neurons, lateral asymmetries, increased von Economo neurons, expansion of the neocortex, and enhanced integration of the cerebellum also were significant (Schoenemann, 2006). In comparison with most other parts of the human genome, selection on genes involved with brain development was especially intense (Gilbert et al., 2005).

The human brain has high metabolic costs: about 50% of an infant's, and 20% of an adult's, energetic resources are used to support neurological activity (Elia, 1992). Thoughts are not free; the high levels of glucose and other energetic nutrients required to fuel human cognition involve significant trade-offs (Campbell, 2010). Although the increase in energetic resources allocated to the brain was accompanied by a corresponding decrease in digestive tissue (Aiello & Wheeler, 1995), this does not explain what the selective pressures for enhanced information processing were, nor why the resources were not reallocated to direct reproductive function. The obstetric difficulties associated with birthing a large-headed infant generate additional problems (Rosenberg & Trevathan, 2002). The selective advantages of increased intelligence must have been high to overcome these costs.

The human brain, in short, is a big evolutionary puzzle. It is developmentally and metabolically expensive. It evolved rapidly and consistently. And it enables unusual human cognitive abilities such as language, empathy, foresight, consciousness, mental time-travel, creativity, and theory of mind (ToM). Advantages of a larger brain may include enhanced information processing capacities to contend with ecological pressures that involve sexually dimorphic activities such as hunting and complex foraging (Kaplan & Robson, 2002). There is little evidence, however, of sufficient domain-specific enlargement of those parts of the brain associated with selective pressures from the physical environment, including subsistence activities (Geary & Huffman, 2002; Adolphs, 2003). Indeed, human cognition has little to distinguish itself in the way of specialized ecological talents. Our remarkable aptitudes for tool use and other technological behaviors depend primarily on general aptitudes for social learning and fluid intelligence (Geary, 2005). A large brain may have been sexually selected because intelligence was an attractive trait for mate choice (Miller, 2000). However, there is little sexual dimorphism in encephalization quotient or intelligence psychometrics (Geary, 2010), nor is there a clear reason why brains would have been a target for sexual selection driven by mate choice uniquely and consistently among hominins.

The human brain did not evolve as an isolated trait. Concomitant changes in other traits provide clues to what selective pressures were important during hominin evolution. Changes in life history patterns accompanied the evident increases in information processing and communication during the Pleistocene (Dean et al., 2001). Gestation (pregnancy) was lengthened, but the resultant infant was even more altricial (Rosenberg, 2004). Human infants must be carried, fed, and protected for a long period in comparison with those of other primates. And yet humans have shorter interbirth intervals than other hominoids (Robson & Wood, 2008). Human childhood and adolescence are also exceptionally lengthy (Del Giudice, 2009). This extension of the juvenile period appears costly in evolutionary terms. The delay of reproduction past fifteen years of age or older involves prolonged exposure to extrinsic causes of mortality and longer generation intervals. Parental and other kin investment continues for an unusually long time, often well into adulthood and perhaps even after the death of the parents. Like the big brain, human life history is an evolutionary puzzle (Muehlenbein & Flinn, 2010).

Of course the child must accumulate energetic resources necessary for physical somatic growth. Whether the lengthening of the human juvenile period was an unavoidable response to an increasing shortage of calories, however, is uncertain. Other hominoids (chimpanzees, gorillas, and orangutans) grow at similar overall rates, but mature earlier (Leigh, 2004). Increased body fat is associated with earlier puberty for girls, although psychological and genetic factors are also important, and the relation is not significant for boys (Lee et al., 2010). Moreover, low birth weight is associated with earlier puberty in some conditions (Karaolis-Danckert et al., 2009). The peculiarities of the human growth curve are also difficult to explain from a simple model of food scarcity—the general timing of growth spurts do not appear linked to a pattern of caloric surpluses. Hence although it is clear that human female growth and reproductive maturation are sensitive to fat accumulation (Ellison, 2001; Sloboda et al., 2007), the lengthening of the juvenile period during human evolution seems likely to have involved more than simple energetic constraints on growth.

The life history stage of human childhood appears to be an adaptation enabling cognitive development, including complex social skills and emotional regulation (Alexander, 1990a; Bjorklund & Pelligrini, 2002; Del Giudice, 2009; Flinn, 2004; Konner, 2010). The human child is an extraordinarily social creature, motivated by and highly sensitive to interpersonal relationships. Learning, practice, and experience are imperative for social success. The information processing capacity used for human social interactions is considerable, and perhaps significantly greater than that involved with foraging, locomotion, tool-making, and other subsistence skills (Schoenemann, 2006).

The child needs to master complex dynamic social tasks such as developing appropriate cognitive and emotional responses during interactions with peers and adults in the local community. The learning environments that facilitate and channel these aspects of human mental phenotypic plasticity appear to take on a special importance. Much of the data required for the social behavior necessary to be successful as a human cannot be "preprogrammed" into specific, detailed, fixed responses. Social cleverness in a fast-paced, cumulative cultural environment must contend with dynamic, constantly shifting strategies of friends and enemies, and hence needs information from experiential social learning and creative scenario-building (Flinn, 1997; 2006; Del Giudice, 2009).

To summarize my argument to this point, human childhood may be viewed as a life history stage that is necessary for acquiring the information and practice to build and refine the mental algorithms critical for negotiating the social relationships that are key to success in our species (Geary & Flinn, 2001). Mastering the social environment presents special challenges for the human child. Social competence is difficult because the targets (other children and adults) are constantly changing and similarly equipped with theory of mind and other cognitive abilities. Selection for flexible cognitive problem solving would also enhance complementary development of more sophisticated ecological skills such as hunting and complex extractive foraging (Kaplan et al., 2000).

Human social relationships are especially complex because they involve extensive coalitions. We are extraordinarily cooperative, most exceptionally and importantly in regard to competition with other groups (Alexander, 1990b: 2006; Bowles, 2009; Flinn et al., 2005). Humans are unique in being the only species that engages in group-against-group play including team sports. This trait is cross-culturally universal, emerges early in child development, and often is the object of tremendous collective effort.

The family environment is a primary source and mediator of the ontogeny of information processing abilities, including social competencies and group cooperation. Human biology has been profoundly affected by our evolutionary history as unusually social creatures, immersed in networks of family, kin, and dynamic, intercommunity coalitions.

THE HUMAN FAMILY

All human societies recognize kinship as a key organizational principle (Brown, 1991). All languages have kinship terminologies and concomitant expectations of obligations and reciprocity (Murdock, 1949; Fortes, 1969). Human kinship systems appear unique in the universal recognition of both bilateral (maternal and paternal) and multigenerational structure, with a general trend for co-residence of male kin, but a dozen or more major variants (Flinn & Low, 1986; Murdock, 1949). These aspects of human kinship link families into broader cooperative systems, and provide additional opportunities for alloparental care during the long social childhood. Three species-distinctive characteristics stand out as unusually important in this regard: (1) fathering, that is, extensive and specific investment by males, (2) grandparenting, and (3) networks of kinship that extend among communities and involve affinal (ties by marriage) and consanguineal (ties by blood) relationships (Walker et al., 2013; Macfarlan et al., 2014).

Fathers

Mammals that live in groups with multiple males—such as chimpanzees *(Pan troglodytes)*—usually have little or no paternal care, because the non-exclusivity of mating relationships obscures paternity (Alexander, 1990b; Clutton-Brock, 1991). In contrast, it is common for human fathers to provide protection, information, food, and social status for their children (Gray & Anderson, 2010). Paternal care in humans appears to be facilitated by relatively stable pair-bonds, which not only involves cooperation between mates that often endures over the lifespan, but which requires an unusual type of cooperation among co-residing males—respect for each other's mating relationships.

The relatively exclusive mating relationships that are characteristic of most human societies (Flinn & Low, 1986) generate natural factions within the group. Mating relationships also can create alliances in human groups, linking two families or clans together (e.g., Macfarlan et al., 2014). By way of comparison, in chimpanzee communities it is difficult for even the most dominant male to monopolize an estrous female; usually most of the males in a community mate with most of the females (Goodall, 1986; Mitani et al., 2010). Chimpanzee males in effect "share" a common interest in the community's females and their offspring. Human groups, in contrast, are composed of family units, each with distinct reproductive interests. Human males do not typically share mating access to the entire group's females; consequently, there are usually reliable cues identifying which children are their genetic offspring, and which are those of other males (for exceptions, see Walker,

Hill & Flinn, 2010). Because humans live in multi-male groups, yet often maintain stable and exclusive mating relationships, the potential for fission along family lines is high. Still, human groups overcome this inherent conflict between family units to form large, stable coalitions—a "federation of families" (Chapais, 2013).

This unusual tolerance among co-residential males and their families stands in contrast to the norm of polygamous mate competition in group-living non-human primates. Selection pressures favoring such tolerance are uncertain, but likely involve the importance of both male parental investment and male coalitions for intra-specific conflict (Alexander, 1990b; Wrangham, 1999).

The advantages of intensive parenting, including paternal protection and other care, require a most unusual pattern of mating relationships: moderately exclusive pair-bonding in multiple-male groups. No other primate (or mammal) that lives in large, cooperative multiple-reproductive-male groups has such extensive male parental care targeted at specific offspring. Competition for females in multiple-male groups usually results in low confidence of paternity (e.g., bonobos & chimpanzees). Males forming exclusive "pair-bonds" in multiple-male groups would provide cues of non-paternity to other males, and hence place their offspring in great danger of infanticide (Hrdy, 1999). Paternal care is most likely to be favored by natural selection in conditions where males can identify their offspring with sufficient probability to offset the costs of investment, although reciprocity with mates is also likely to be involved (Geary & Flinn, 2001). Humans exhibit a unique "nested family" social structure, involving complex reciprocity among males and females to restrict direct competition for mates among group members.

It is difficult to imagine how this system could be maintained in the absence of another unusual human trait: concealed or "cryptic" ovulation (Alexander & Noonan, 1979). Human groups tend to be male philopatric (males tending to remain in their natal groups), resulting in extensive male kin alliances, useful for competing against other groups of male kin (LeBlanc, 2003; Wrangham & Peterson, 1996). Females also have complex alliances, but usually are not involved directly in the overt physical aggression characteristic of intergroup relations (Campbell, 2002; Geary & Flinn, 2002). Relationships among human brothers and sisters are lifelong even where residence is in different communities, in contrast with the absence of significant ties or apparent kin recognition after emigration in other hominoids. Parents, grandparents, and other kin may be especially important for the child's mental development of social and cultural maps because they can be relied upon as landmarks who provide relatively honest information. From this perspective, the evolutionary significance of the human family in regard to child development is viewed more as a nest from which social skills may be acquired than just as an economic unit centered on the sexual division of labor (Flinn & Ward, 2005).

In summary, the care-providing roles of fathers are unusually important in humans, particularly in regard to protection and social power, but are flexible components of the human family, and are linked with the roles of other relatives, including grandparents. In addition to the effects of direct parental care, paternity provides the basis for critical bilateral kinship links that extend across communities and generations. The neuroendocrine mechanisms that underpin human paternal and grandparental psychology are not well studied, but likely involve the common mammalian affilative hormones oxytocin and arginine vasopressin, with additional influence from the hypothalamic-pituitary-gonadal and hypothalamic-pituitary-adrenal (HPA) systems (Gray & Campbell, 2009).

Grandparents

Grandparents and grandoffspring share 25% of their genes identical by descent, a significant opportunity for kin selection. Few species, however, live in groups with multiple overlapping generations of kin. Fewer still have significant social relationships among individuals two or more generations apart. Humans appear rather exceptional in this regard. Grandparenting is cross-culturally ubiquitous and pervasive (Murdock, 1967; Sear & Mace, 2005; Voland et al., 2005). Our life histories allow for significant generational overlaps, including an apparent extended post-reproductive stage facilitated by the unique human physiological adaptation of menopause (Alexander, 1990b; Hawkes, 2003).

The significance of emotional bonding between grandparents and grandchildren is beyond doubt. The evolved functions are uncertain, but likely involve the exceptional importance of long-term extensive and intensive investment for the human child. The emotional and cognitive processes that guide grand-relationships must have evolved because they enhanced survival and eventual reproductive success of grandchildren. Leaving children with grandparents and other alloparental care providers allows parents to pursue productive activities that would otherwise be risky or difficult when encumbered with child care. In addition to the physical basics of food, protection, and hygienic care, psychological development of the human child is strongly influenced by the dynamics of the social environment (Konner, 2010). Grandparents may have knowledge and experience that are important and useful for helping grandchildren and other relatives survive and succeed in social competition (Coe, 2003; Hrdy, 2009). Humans are unusual in the critical role of kin in alloparental care and group coalitions.

Extended Kinship and Control of Mating Relationships

The direct application of theory from evolutionary biology to human marriage
behavior and mating strategies is. . .not possible until the theory is modified
to take into consideration the interdependency of individuals. . .and how their
interdependency—coalition alliances—structures human mating behavior.
Chagnon, 1979, p. 88.

Human communities are composed of families embedded in complex kin
networks. The importance of kinship in traditional societies is paramount;
social power is primarily contingent upon support from relatives. Complex
kinship alliances are arguably the most distinguishing social behavioral
characteristic of humans in preindustrial cultures, and yet it is rarely discussed in evolutionary psychology or evolutionary economics. Reciprocity
in all its various guises (for review, see Alexander, 2006) is inextricably
bound up with kinship in traditional societies, perhaps most importantly
in regard to the control of mating in the institution of marriage. The vast
majority of nonindustrial cultures in the Ethnographic Atlas (Murdock,
1967) have rules and preferences specifying what categories of relatives
are appropriate for mating/marriage; these rules and preferences involve
issues of resultant kin ties in addition to inbreeding avoidance. It is worth
emphasizing that humans are unique in the regulation of mating relationships by kin groups. The reason for controlling who mates with who is
that humans are unique in the great importance of kinship-ties for alliances
among groups (e.g., Macfarlan et al., 2014). Mates are usually obtained via
strategic negotiation between kin groups. No other species exhibits systematic preferences and prohibitions for mating relationships between specific
types of cousins.

If human ancestors had intergroup relations similar to that of chimpanzees
(see Mitani et al., 2010; Wrangham, 1999; Wrangham & Peterson, 1996),
it would have been difficult to make even the first steps toward cooperative
alliances among males (and females) in different communities. An adult
male attempting to establish a relationship with another group likely would
be killed as he entered their range. Somehow our ancestors overcame such
obstacles to the first steps towards the core human adaptation of intercommunity alliances. It is possible that our ancestors did not have hostile intergroup relations; this seems unlikely, however, on both empirical (LeBlanc,
2003) and theoretical (Alexander, 1990b) grounds. Surely the most potent
factor driving the evolution of the psychological, social, and cultural mechanisms enabling the formation of increasingly large and complex coalitions
was competition with other such coalitions (Alexander, 1990b; Flinn et al.,
2005).

Recognition of kinship among individuals residing in different communities is key to intergroup cooperation. Humans are different from other hominoids in the coevolutionary development of (a) stable and moderately exclusive breeding bonds, (b) bilateral kin recognition and relationships, and (c) reciprocity and kin links among coresident families (Alexander, 1990b; Chapais, 2013; Flinn et al., 2007). In short, the family was a critical building block for the evolution of more complex communities, with flexible residence choice with kin in multiple communities and apparent intentional cultivation of ties with relatives in multiple locations.

Hard evidence for the evolutionary trajectory of human family, kinship, and intergroup relations is scarce and indirect; neurobiology and physiology, however, provide some important clues.

NEUROLOGICAL AND PHYSIOLOGICAL MECHANISMS

Neuroendocrine systems may be viewed as complex sets of mechanisms designed by natural selection to communicate information among cells and tissues. Steroid and peptide hormones, associated neurotransmitters, and other chemical messengers guide behaviors of mammals in many important ways (Ellison, 2001; Lee et al., 2009; Panksepp, 1998). For example, analysis of patterns of hormone levels in naturalistic contexts can provide important insights into the evolutionary functions of the neuroendocrine mechanisms that guide human behaviors (e.g., Ponzi et al., 2014). Here I focus on the neuroendocrine mechanisms that facilitate human family relationships.

Hormonal Basis for Attachment and Family Love

Some of the most precious human feelings are stimulated by close social relationships: a mother holding her newborn infant; brothers reunited after a long absence; lovers entangled in each other's arms. Natural selection has designed our neurobiological mechanisms, in concert with our endocrine systems, to generate potent sensations in our interactions with these most evolutionarily significant individuals. We share with our primate relatives the same basic hormones and neurotransmitters that underlie these mental gifts. But our unique evolutionary history has modified us to respond to different circumstances and situations; we are rewarded and punished for somewhat different stimuli than our phylogenetic cousins. Chimpanzees and humans share the delight—the sensational reward—when biting into a ripe, juicy mango. But the endocrine, neurological, and associated emotional responses of a human father to the birth of his child (e.g., Storey et al., 2000) are likely to be quite different from those of a chimpanzee male. Happiness for a human has many unique designs, such as romantic love (Fisher et al., 2006), that involve modification of the neurological receptors and processors of shared endogenous messengers from our phylogenetic heritage.

Attachments or bonding are central in the lives of the social mammals. Basic to survival and reproduction, these interdependent relationships are the fabric of the social networks that permit individuals to maintain cooperative relationships over time. Although attachments can provide security and relief from stress, close relationships also exert pressures on individuals to which they continuously respond. It should not be surprising, therefore, that the neuroendocrine mechanisms underlying attachment and stress are intimately related to one another. And although more is known about the stress response systems than the affiliative systems, we are beginning to get some important insights into the neuroendocrine mechanisms that underpin human relationships (Lee et al., 2009; Rilling, 2013).

The mother-offspring relationship is at the core of mammalian life, and it appears that some of the biochemistry at play in the regulation of this intimate bond was also selected to serve in primary mechanisms regulating bonds between mates, paternal care, the family group, and even larger social networks. Although a number of hormones and neurotransmitters are involved in attachment and other components of relationships, the two peptide hormones, oxytocin (OT) and arginine-vasopressin (AVP), appear to be primary (Heinrichs, Dawans, & Domes, 2009; Lee et al., 2009; Seltzer, Ziegler, & Pollak, 2010), with dopamine, cortisol, and other hormones and neurotransmitters having mediating effects.

Experience affects the neuroendocrine systems involved in the expression of parental care. The HPA system of offspring during development is influenced by variation in maternal care, which then influences their maternal behavior as adults. Such changes involve the production of, and receptor density for, stress hormones and OT (Champagne & Meaney, 2001; Fleming et al., 1999). HPA-modulated hormones and maternal behavior are related in humans during the postpartum period (Fleming et al., 2002). During this time, cortisol appears to have an arousal effect, focusing attention on infant bonding. Mothers with higher cortisol levels were found to be more affectionate, more attracted to their infant's odor, and better at recognizing their infant's cry during the postpartum period.

fMRI studies of brain activity involved in maternal attachment in humans indicate that the activated regions are part of the reward system and contain a high density of receptors for OT and AVP (Bartels & Zeki, 2004; Fisher et al., 2006). These studies also demonstrate that the neural regions involved in attachment activated in humans are similar to those activated in nonhuman animals. Among humans, however, neural regions associated with social judgment and assessment of the intentions and emotions of others exhibited some deactivation during attachment activities, suggesting possible links between psychological mechanisms for attachment and management of social relationships. Falling in love with a mate and affective bonds with offspring may involve temporary deactivation of psychological mechanisms for maintaining an individual's social "guard" in the complex reciprocity of human social networks. Dopamine levels are likely to be important for both types of relationship but may involve some distinct neural sites. It will be interesting to see what fMRI studies of attachment in human males indicate because that is where the most substantial differences from other mammals would be expected. Similarly, fMRI studies of attachment to mothers, fathers, and alloparental care providers in human children may provide important insights into the other side of parent-offspring bonding (Swain, 2011).

Androgens including testosterone also appear to be involved in the regulation of paternal behavior. For example, human fathers tend to have lower testosterone levels when they are involved in childcare activities (Berg and Wynne-Edwards, 2002; Fleming et al., 2002; Gray & Campbell, 2009; Kuzawa et al., 2009), although the relation with the key paternal role of offspring protection is uncertain. Human males stand out as very different from our closest relatives the chimpanzees in the areas of paternal attachment and investment in offspring. Investigation of the neuroendocrine mechanisms that underpin male parental behavior may provide important insights into these critical evolutionary changes.

The receptor density for OT and AVP in specific brain regions might provide the basis for mechanisms underlying other social behaviors. Other neurotransmitters, hormones, and social cues also are likely to be involved, but slight changes in gene expression for receptor density, such as those found between the meadow and prairie voles in the ventral palladium (located near the nucleus accumbens, an important component of the brain's reward system), might demonstrate how such mechanisms could be modified by selection (Lim et al., 2004). The dopamine D2 receptors in the nucleus accumbens appear to link the affiliative OT and AVP pair-bonding mechanisms with positive rewarding mental states (Aragona et al., 2006; Curtis and Wang, 2003). The combination results in the powerful addiction that parents have for their offspring (Love, 2014).

Given the adaptive value of extensive biparental care and prolonged attachment found in the mating pair and larger family network, it is not surprising that similar neurohormonal mechanisms active in the maternal-offspring bond would also be selected to underlie these other attachments. Though there is some variation among species and between males and females, the same general neurohormonal systems active in pair-bonding in other species are found in the human (Wynne-Edwards, 2003; Panksepp, 1998; Lee et al., 2009).

Androgen response to pair-bonding appears complex (e.g., van der Meij et al., 2008), but similar to parent-offspring attachment in that pair-bonded males tend to have lower testosterone levels in non-challenging conditions (Alvergne et al., 2009; Gray & Campbell, 2009). Moreover, males actively involved in caretaking behavior appear to have temporarily diminished testosterone levels and neurobiological changes (e.g., Abraham et al., 2014).

Hormonal mechanisms for another key human adaptation, bonding among adult males forming coalitions—"band of brothers"—is less well studied. Social effects such as victories against outsiders produce elevations in testosterone, but defeating friends does not. Changes in oxytocin are also contingent on relationships (De Dreu, 2012). Human males, moreover, may differentially respond to females contingent on whether the females are in a stable breeding bond with a close friend; males have lower testosterone after interacting with wives of their relatives and friends (Flinn et al., 2012). Involvement of the affiliative neuropeptides (OT and AVP) in relationships among adult males is unknown, and should be a key target for research efforts.

The challenge before human evolutionary biologists and psychologists is to understand how these general neuroendocrine systems have been modified and linked with other special human cognitive systems to produce the unique suite of human family behaviors. Analysis of hormonal responses to social stimuli may provide important insights into the selective pressures that guided the evolution of these key aspects of the human mind.

SUMMARY AND CONCLUDING REMARKS

Human childhood is a life history stage that appears necessary and useful for acquiring the information and practice to build and refine the mental algorithms critical for negotiating the social coalitions that are key to success in our species. Mastering the social environment presents special challenges for the human child. Social competence is difficult because the target is constantly changing and similarly equipped with theory of mind and other cognitive abilities. Family environment, including care from fathers and grandparents, is a primary source and mediator of the ontogeny of social competencies.

Social competence is developmentally expensive in time, instruction and parental care. Costs are not equally justified for all expected adult environments. The human family may help children adjust development in response to environmental exigencies for appropriate trades-offs in life history strategies. An evolutionary developmental perspective of the family can be useful in these efforts to understand this critical aspect of a child's world by integrating knowledge of physiological causes with the logic of adaptive design by natural selection. Human biology has been profoundly affected by our evolutionary history as unusually social creatures, including, perhaps, a special reliance upon cooperative fathers, grandparents, and kin residing in other groups. Indeed, the mind of the human child may have design features that enable its development as a group project, guided by the multitudinous informational contributions of its ancestors and co-descendants.

Understanding the coevolution of the core human adaptations of stable breeding bonds, biparental care, altricial infancy, prolonged childhood, complex social intelligence, extended kinship networks, and intergroup alliances, presents difficult challenges for evolutionary psychology and family therapy. The inclusion of ideas and methods from anthropology and the life sciences may prove helpful, and hopefully make the task merrier.

REFERENCES

Abraham, E., Hendler, T., Shapira-Lichter, I., Kanat-Maymon, Y., Zagoory-Sharon, O., Feldman, R. (2014). Father's brain is sensitive to childcare experiences. *Proceedings of the National Academy of Sciences,* 111(27), 9792–9797.

Adolphs, R. (2003). Cognitive neuroscience of human social behavior. *Nature Reviews, Neuroscience,* 4(3), 165–178.

Aiello, L. C., & Wheeler, P. (1995). The expensive-tissue hypothesis: The brain and the digestive system in human and primate evolution. *Current Anthropology, 36,* 199–221.

Alexander, R. D. (1990a). Epigenetic rules and Darwinian algorithms: The adaptive study of learning and development. *Ethology and Sociobiology,* 11, 1–63.

Alexander, R. D. (1990b). *How humans evolved: Reflections on the uniquely unique species.* Museum of Zoology (Special Publication No. 1). Ann Arbor: The University of Michigan.

Alexander, R. D. (2006). The challenge of human social behavior. *Evolutionary Psychology, 4,* 1–32.

Alexander, R. D. & Noonan, K. L. (1979). Concealment of ovulation, parental care and human social evolution. In N. A. Chagnon & W. G. Irons (Eds.), *Evolutionary biology and human social behavior: An anthropological perspective* (pp. 436–453). North Scituate, MA: Duxbury Press.

Alvergne, A., Faurie, C., & Raymond, M. (2009). Variation in testosterone levels and male reproductive effort: Insight from a polygynous human population. *Hormones and Behavior,* 56(5), 491-497.

Aragona, B. J., Liu, Y., Yu, Y. J., Curtis, J. T., Detwiler, J. M., Insel, T. R., et al., (2006). Nucleus accumbens dopamine differentially mediates the formation and maintenance of monogamous pair bonds. *Nature Neuroscience,* 9, 133–139.

Bartels, A. & Zeki, S. (2004). The neural correlates of maternal and romantic love. *NeuroImage,* 21, 1155–1166.

Berg, S. J. & Wynne-Edwards, K. E. (2002). Changes in testosterone, cortisol, and estradiol levels in men becoming fathers. *Mayo Clin. Proc.* 76, 582–592.

Bjorklund, D. F. & Pellegrini, A. D. (2002). *The origins of human nature: Evolutionary developmental psychology.* Washington, DC: APA Press.

Bowles, S. (2009). Did warfare among ancestral hunter-gatherers affect the evolution of human social behaviors? *Science,* 324, 1293–1298.

Brown, D.E. (1991). *Human universals.* Philadelphia: Temple University Press.

Campbell, A. (2002). *A mind of her own: The evolutionary psychology of women.* London: Oxford University Press.

Campbell, B. C. (2010). Energetics and the human brain. In M. Muhlenbein, (ed). *Human evolutionary biology,* pp. 425–438. Cambridge: Cambridge University Press.

Champagne, F. A. & Meaney, M. J. (2001). Like mother, like daughter: Evidence for non-genomic transmission of parental behavior and stress responsivity. *Progress in Brain Research,* 133, 287–302.

Chapais, B. (2008). *Primeval kinship: How pair-bonding gave birth to human society.* Cambridge, MA: Harvard University Press.

Chapais, B. (2013). Monogamy, strongly bonded groups, and the evolution of human social structure. *Evolutionary Anthropology,* 22, 52–65.

Clutton-Brock, T. H. (1991). *The evolution of parental care.* Princeton, NJ: Princeton U. Press.

Coe, K. (2003). *The ancestress hypothesis: Visual art as adaptation.* New Brunswick: Rutgers University Press.

Curtis, T. J. & Wang, Z. (2003). The neurochemistry of pair bonding. *Current Directions in Psychological Science,* 12(2), 49–53.

Dean, C., Leakey, M.G., Reid, D., Schrenk, F., Schwartz, G.T., Stringer, C., & Walker, A. (2001). Growth processes in teeth distinguish modern humans from *Homo erectus* and earlier hominins. *Nature,* 414, 628–631.

De Dreu, C. K. W. (2012). Oxytocin modulates cooperation within and competition between groups: an integrative review and research agenda. *Hormones and Behavior,* 61(3), 419-428.

Del Giudice, M., 2009. Sex, attachment, and the development of reproductive strategies. *Behav. Brain Sci.* 32, 1–21.

Del Giudice, M., Angeleri, R., Manera, V., 2009. The juvenile transition: A developmental switch point in human life history. *Dev. Rev.* 29, 1–31.

Edelman, G. M. (2006). *Second nature: brain science and human knowledge.* New Haven: Yale University Press.

Elia, M. (1992). Organ and tissue contribution to metabolic rate. In J. M. Kinner & H. N. Tucker (eds.), *Energy Metabolism: Tissue Determinants and Cellular Corollaries,* pp. 61–79. New York: Raven Press.

Ellison, P. T. (2001). *On Fertile Ground, a Natural History of Human Reproduction.* Cambridge, MA: Harvard.

Fisher, H., Aron, A., & Brown, L. L. (2006). Romantic love: A mammalian system for mate choice. *Phil. Trans. R. Soc. B* 361, 2173–2186.

Fleming, A. S., Corter, C., Stallings, J., & Steiner, M. (2002). Testosterone and prolactin are associated with emotional responses to infant cries in new fathers. *Hormones and Behavior,* 42, 399–413.

Fleming, A. S., O'Day, D. H., & Kraemer, G. W. (1999). Neurobiology of mother-infant interactions: Experience and central nervous system plasticity across development and generations. *Neuroscience and Biobehavioral Reviews, 23,* 673–685.

Flinn, M. V. (1997). Culture and the evolution of social learning. *Evolution and Human Behavior,* 18(1), 23–67.

Flinn, M. V. (2004). Culture and developmental plasticity: Evolution of the social brain. In K. MacDonald & R. L. Burgess (Eds.), *Evolutionary perspectives on child development* (pp. 73–98). Thousand Oaks, CA: Sage.

Flinn, M.V. (2006). Evolution and ontogeny of stress response to social challenge in the human child. *Developmental Review 26,* 138–174.

Flinn, M. V. & Alexander, R. D. (2007). Runaway social selection. In S. W. Gangestad & J. A. Simpson (Eds.), *The evolution of mind* (pp. 249–255). New York: Guilford press.

Flinn, M. V., Geary, D. C., & Ward, C. V. (2005). Ecological dominance, social competition, and coalitionary arms races: Why humans evolved extraordinary intelligence. *Evolution and Human Behavior,* 26(1), 10–46.

Flinn, M. V. & Low, B. S. (1986). Resource distribution, social competition, and mating patterns in human societies. In D. Rubenstein & R. Wrangham (Eds.), *Ecological aspects of social evolution,* pp. 217–243. Princeton NJ: Princeton University Press.

Flinn, M. V., Duncan, C., Quinlan, R. L., Leone, D. V., Decker, S. A. & Ponzi, D. (2012). Hormones in the wild: Monitoring the endocrinology of family relationships. *Parenting: Science and Practice,* 12(2), 124–133.

Flinn, M. V., Nepomnaschy, P., Muehlenbein, M. P., & Ponzi, D. (2011). Evolutionary functions of early social modulation of hypothalamic-pituitary-adrenal axis development in humans. *Neuroscience and Biobehavioral Reviews,* 35(7), 1611–1629.

Flinn, M. V., Ponzi, D., & Muehlenbein, M. P. (2012). Hormonal mechanisms for regulation of aggression in human coalitions. *Human Nature,* 22(1), 68–88.

Flinn, M. V., Quinlan, R. J., Ward, C. V., & Coe, M. K., 2007. Evolution of the human family: Cooperative males, long social childhoods, smart mothers, and extended kin networks. In Salmon, C. & Shackelford, T., (Eds.), Family Relationships. Oxford University Press, Oxford, chapter 2, pp. 16–38.

Flinn, M. V. & Ward, C. V. (2005). Evolution of the social child. In B. Ellis & D. Bjorklund (Eds.), *Origins of the social mind: Evolutionary psychology and child development,* chapter 2, pp. 19–44. London: Guilford Press.

Flinn, M. V. & Ward, C. V. (2015). Hormones and the evolution of human sociality. In: *Handbook of Evolutionary Psychology, 2nd edition,* D. Buss (Ed.). chapter 24. New York: Wiley.

Fortes, M. (1969). *Kinship and the social order.* Chicago, IL: Aldine.

Geary, D. C. (2005). *The origin of mind: Evolution of brain, cognition, and general intelligence.* Washington, DC: American Psychological Association.

Geary, D. C. (2010). *Male, female: The evolution of human sex differences* (2nd edition). Washington, DC: American Psychological Association.

Geary, D. C. & Flinn, M. V. (2001). Evolution of human parental behavior and the human family. *Parenting: Science and Practice,* 1, 5–61.

Geary, D. C. & Flinn, M. V. (2002). Sex differences in behavioral and hormonal response to social threat. *Psychological Review,* 109(4), 745–750.

Geary, D. C. & Huffman, K. J. (2002). Brain and cognitive evolution: Forms of modularity and functions of mind. *Psychological Bulletin,* 128(5), 667–698.

Gilbert, S. L., Dobyns, W. B., & Lahn, B. T. (2005). Genetic links between brain development and brain evolution. *Nature Reviews Genetics,* 6(7), 581–590.

Goodall, J. (1986). *The chimpanzees of Gombe: Patterns of behavior.* Cambridge, MA: Belknap Press of Harvard University Press.

Gray, P. B. & Anderson, K. G. (2010). *Fatherhood: Evolution and Human Paternal Behavior.* Cambridge, MA: Harvard University Press.

Gray, P. B. & Campbell, B. C. (2009). Human male testosterone, pair bonding and fatherhood. In P. T. Ellison & P. B. Gray (eds.), *Endocrinology of Social Relationships.* Cambridge: Harvard University Press.

Hawkes, K. (2003). Grandmothers and the evolution of human longevity. *American Journal of Human Biology,* 15, 380-400.

Heinrichs, M., Dawans, B. V., & Domes, G. (2009). Oxytocin, vasopressin, and human social behavior. *Frontiers in Neuroendocrinology,* 30(4), 548–557.

Hrdy, S. B. (1999). *Mother nature: A history of mothers, infants, and natural selection.* New York: Pantheon.

Hrdy, S. B. (2009). *Mothers and others: The evolutionary origins of mutual understanding.* Cambridge: Harvard University Press.

Kaplan, H. S. & Robson, A. J. (2002). The emergence of humans: The coevolution of intelligence and longevity with intergenerational transfers. *Proceedings of the National Academy of Sciences,* 99(15), 10221–10226.

Karaolis-Danckert N., Buyken, A.E., Sonntag, A., & Kroke, A. (2009). Birth and early life influences on the timing of puberty onset: results from the DONALD (DOrtmund Nutritional and Anthropometric Longitudinally Designed) Study. American Journal of Clinical Nutrition 90(6), 1559–1565.

Konner, M. (2010). *The evolution of childhood: Relationships, emotion, mind.* Cambridge, MA: Harvard University Press.

Kuzawa, C. W., Gettler, L. T., Muller, M. N., McDade, T. W., & Feranil, A. B. (2009). Fatherhood, pairbonding and testosterone in the Philippines. *Hormones and Behavior,* 56(4), 429-435.

Leblanc, S. A. (2003). *Constant battles: The myth of the peaceful, noble savage.* New York: St. Martin's Press.

Lee, H.-J., Macbeth, A. H., Pagani, J., & Young 3rd, W. S. (2009). Oxytocin: The great facilitator of life. *Progress in Neurobiology,* 88(2), 127–151.

Lee, J. M., Kaciroti, N., Appugliese, D., Corwyn, R. F., Bradley, R. H., & Lumeng, J. C. (2010). Body mass index and timing of pubertal initiation in boys. *Archives of Pediatrics and Adolescent Medicine,* 164(2), 116–123.

Lee, S. H. & Wolpoff, M. H. (2003). The pattern of evolution in Pleistocene human brain size. *Paleobiology,* 29, 186–196.

Leigh, S. R. (2004). Brain growth, cognition, and life history in primate and human evolution. *American Journal of Primatology,* 62, 139–164.

Love, T. M. (2014). Oxytocin, motivation and the role of dopamine. *Pharmacology Biochemistry and Behavior,* 119, 49–60.

Macfarlan, S. J., Walker, R. S., Flinn, M. V. & Chagnon, N. A. (2014). Lethal coalitionary aggression and long-term alliances among Yanomamö men. *Proceedings of the National Academy of Sciences,* 111(52), 16662–16669.

Miller, G. E. (2000). *The mating mind: How sexual choice shaped the evolution of human nature.* New York: Doubleday.

Mitani, J. C., Watts, D. P., & Amsler, S. J. (2010). Lethal intergroup aggression leads to territorial expansion in wild chimpanzees. *Current Biology* 20(12), R507–R508.

Muehlenbein, M. & Flinn, M. V. (2011). Pattern and process of human life history evolution. In T. Flatt & A. Heyland (Eds.), *Oxford handbook of life history,* chapter 23, pp. 153–168. Oxford: Oxford University Press.

Murdock, G. P. (1949). *Social structure.* New York: Macmillan.

Murdock, G. P. (1967). *Ethnographic atlas.* Pittsburgh, PA: University of Pittsburgh Press.

Panksepp, J. (2004). *Affective neuroscience: the foundations of human and animal emotions.* New York: Oxford University Press.

Ponzi, D., Muehlenbein, M. P., Sgoifo, A., Geary, D. C., & Flinn, M. V. (2014). Day-to-day variation of salivary cortisol and dehydroepiandrosterone (DHEA) in children from a rural Dominican community. *Adaptive Human Behavior and Physiology,* 1, 12–24.

Rilling, J. K. (2013). The neural and hormonal bases of human parental care. *Neuropsychologia,* 51(4), 731–747.

Robson, S. L. & Wood, B. (2008). Hominin life history: Reconstruction and evolution. *Journal of Anatomy,* 212(4), 394–425.

Rosenberg, K. (2004). Living longer: Information revolution, population expansion, and modern human origins. *Proceedings of the National Academy of Sciences* 101(30), 10847–10848.

Rosenberg, K. & Trevathan, W. (2002). Birth, obstetrics and human evolution. *BJOG: An International Journal of Obstetrics & Gynecology,* 109(11), 1199–1206.

Roth, G. & Dicke, U. (2005). Evolution of the brain and intelligence. *TRENDS in Cognitive Sciences,* 9(5), 250–257.

Schoenemann, P. T. (2006). Evolution of the size and functional areas of the human brain. *Annual Review of Anthropology,* 35, 379–406.

Sear, R. & Mace, R. (2008). Who keeps children alive? A review of the effects of kin on child survival. *Evolution and Human Behavior,* 29(1), 1–18.

Seltzer, L. J., Ziegler, T. E., & Pollak, S. D. (2010). Social vocalizations can release oxytocin in humans. *Proc. R. Soc. B,* doi:10.1098/rspb.2010.0567.

Sloboda, D. M., Hart, R., Doherty, D. A., Pennell, C. E., & Hickey, M. (2007). Age at menarche: Influences of prenatal and postnatal growth. *Journal of Clinical Endocrinology and Metabolism,* 92, 46–50.

Storey, A. E., Walsh, C. J., Quinton, R. L., & Wynne-Edwards, K. E. (2000). Hormonal correlates of paternal responsiveness in new and expectant fathers. *Evolution and Human Behavior* 21, 79–95.

Swain, J. E. (2011). The human parental brain: In vivo neuroimaging. *Progress in Neuro-Psychopharmacology & Biological Psychiatry,* 35, 1242–1254.

van der Meij, L., Buunk, A. P., van de Sande, J. P., & Salvador, A. (2008). The presence of a woman increases testosterone in aggressive dominant men. *Hormones and Behavior,* 54, 640–644.

Voland, E., Chasiotis, A., & Schiefenhövel, W. (2005). *Grandmotherhood: The evolutionary significance of the second half of female life.* New Brunswick, NJ: Rutgers University Press.

Walker, R. S., Beckerman, S., Flinn, M. V., Gurven, M., von Reuden, C. R., Kramer, K. L., Greaves, R. D., Córdoba, L., Hagen, E. H., Koster, J. M., Sugiyama, L., Hunter, T. E., & Hill, K. R. (2013). Living with kin in lowland horticultural societies. *Current Anthropology,* 54(1), 96–103.

Walker, R. S., Flinn, M. V., & Hill, K. (2010). The evolutionary history of partible paternity in lowland South America. *Proceedings of the National Academy of Sciences,* 107(45), 19195–19200.

Wrangham, R. W. (1999). Evolution of coalitionary killing. *Yearbook of Physical Anthropology,* 42, 1–30.

Wrangham, R. W. & Peterson, D. (1996). *Demonic males.* New York: Houghton Mifflin Company.

Wynne-Edwards, K. E. (2003). From dwarf hamster to daddy: The intersection of ecology, evolution, and physiology that produces paternal behavior. In *Advances in the study of behavior,* ed. P. J. B. Slater, J. S. Rosenblatt, C. T. Snowden, & T. J. Roper, 32, 207–261. San Diego, CA: Academic Press.

Chapter 11

The Family System of a Social Wasp

Raghavendra Gadagkar

In many species of insects individuals organize themselves into societies that parallel, and in many respects surpass, our own societies. They live in colonies, which are essentially families, ranging from nuclear families to extended joint families and sometimes, even clans. The best examples of these are to be found in the insect orders Hymenoptera (ants, bees, and wasps) and Isoptera (termites). In the termites, both males and females are involved in family life. In the ants, bees and wasps however, only females participate in family life and they have therefore been dubbed 'feminine monarchies' (Sarton, 1943). We, as humans, cannot help but be curious about how these families function and perhaps dysfunction. How do insects that diverged from us hundreds of millions of years ago, deal with what must be very similar opportunities and challenges afforded by family life? (Wilson, 1971).

My students and I spend most of our time pondering over these questions and seeking answers through observation and experimentation. We have chosen the social wasp *Ropalidia marginata*, which occurs abundantly all over peninsular India and indeed, in and around our homes and offices, (Gadagkar, 2001). We study these wasps wherever they occur in nature but we have also learnt to bring them to our laboratory and keep them in cages of different sizes and stack them up in the vespiary (the house of wasps). Here I will attempt to describe our current understanding of the family system of *R. marginata*, deliberately using, to the extent possible, the same language that we normally use to describe human families and societies. I will deliberately use the terms colony and family interchangeably (Figure 11.1).

Figure 11.1   The Family System of the Social Wasp, *Ropalidia marginata*. A typical nest showing the nest, adult wasps, and brood. *Photo credits:* Dr. Thresiamma Varghese

THE FATHER

The father is always absent in any *R. marginata* family. He is only represented by his sperm, which now reside in and are nourished by his mate, inside of her body (in a gland called the "spermatheca"), to be used when needed. Adult males spend only about a week in the family of their birth and then leave to lead a nomadic life, never to return. They may mate with females (usually from other colonies) whom they may encounter while the latter are away from their own homes, in search of food. After thus donating sperm to one or more females in such chance encounters, they simply die. But as an evolutionary biologist would not fail to note, they have passed on their genes (through their sperm) for potential transmission to future generations, via the females they have mated with (Gadagkar, 2001).

There is also something peculiar about how they were born. Their mother produces them by laying unfertilized eggs, even though she may well have had a supply of sperm in her spermatheca. Those sperm she would reserve for producing daughters. Sons are always produced through the parthenogenetic development of unfertilized eggs. This, of course, means that the unfertilized eggs carry only one set of chromosomes, namely those of the mother. Thus the adult males also have only one set of chromosomes. This condition is referred to as "haploidy" as opposed to "diploidy," which is the normal condition (two sets of chromosomes) in all of us (males and females), as also in the females of *R. marginata*. An amusing consequence of this is that males in *R. marginata* (and of course also in all species of ants, bees and wasps) have neither fathers nor sons—they only have grandfathers and grandsons (Wilson, 1971).

THE MOTHER

The mother is obviously a pivotal figure in this feminine monarchy. Every family (which we usually call a 'colony'), is headed by a single adult reproducing female and we respectfully call her the 'queen'. I will call her mother and queen interchangeably. Unlike in the advanced insect societies such as those of honey bees, ants, and some wasps, the queen of *R. marginata* are morphologically indistinguishable from everybody else in the family. She is not consistently smaller, bigger, or shaped differently from anybody else. So we have to watch her in the act of laying eggs before we can identify her among all the other similar-looking females (Gadagkar, 2001). Of course if we dissect her abdomen we can see that she has very well-developed ovaries unlike any worker. Based on what was known in the literature from studies of other social wasps, we expected the mother queen to be an exceptionally active, interactive, and aggressive individual, preventing everyone else from reproducing and making them all work for the welfare of the family, by sheer physical harassment (Gamboa et al., 1990; Reeve & Gamboa, 1987). However, we were in for a big surprise. It turns out that an *R. marginata* queen is exceptionally meek and docile—inactive, noninteractive, and unaggressive (Premnath, Sinha, & Gadagkar, 1995). *R. marginata* families frequently lose their mother—she dies, is overthrown as the queen, or driven away. In our observations over the years we have seen queens with life spans as short as a week all the way to as long as almost a year. From long-term observations of many families, we have computed the life span of mothers to be about 80 ± 72 days (Gadagkar et al., 1993). Once they leave or are driven away from their family, as far as we know, they have no further life. But as long as they are healthy and in control, they are treated with respect—no one bites them or chases them around, as is the normal treatment for the rest of the family members.

THE CHILDREN

The adult children of the family consist of the mother's sons and daughters. Sons and daughters can easily be distinguished from each other by the relatively paler faces of the sons. As mentioned already, the sons stay only for a week or so after birth and leave after that. Many fewer sons are produced than daughters. This must certainly have to do with the fact that daughters work as helpers (usually called 'workers') in addition to, or instead of, becoming future queens while sons never work as helpers. Sons are also produced mainly in the summer (although some sons may be produced in some nests at any given time) while daughters are produced throughout the year. We have also observed that mothers in newly founded colonies first produce at least one batch of daughters before producing sons, and many mothers may die before they ever produce any sons. On the other hand, mothers who have failed to mate can at least produce sons, by laying unfertilized eggs. So in most families, most of the time, we see only daughters and no sons. We have observed daughters to stay in the nests of their birth for very variable periods of time—from just a few days all the way to several months (mean ± S.D. = 27 ± 23 days; Gadagkar, 2001).

While sons have only one option open to them, namely to leave and lead a nomadic life, daughters have at least six options open to them (Figure 11.2). One option is to leave their mother's family and start their own new family, all by themselves, that is, to mate, gather sperm and become single mothers. Daughters taking this option build a nest, lay eggs, forage for food, feed their larvae, guard their nest and bring their offspring to adulthood, all by themselves, without the aid of any helpers. This, of course, is the typical lifestyle of most solitary insects and must have been the lifestyle of the evolutionary ancestors of *R. marginata*. It is remarkable that in spite of millions of years of evolutionary history as a social species, the solitary lifestyle has not been forgotten. A second option for the daughters is to leave as a small group and co-found a new family where only one of them reproduces (becomes the queen) while the rest act as helpers, at least in the beginning. A third option is to join a newly founded family as a nonreproducing helper. A fourth option is to invade a small family, drive away the existing queen, take charge as the new queen and start reproducing, with support of the helpers of the previous queen, who generally seem willing to help the new invading queen just as they did for the old queen. A fifth option, and by far the most commonly chosen option, is to stay back in their mother's nest, and spend their entire lives as nonreproductive helpers. As evident from the fourth option described above, such helpers will usually continue to work as helpers even when their mother dies and someone else takes the position of the queen of their colony. The sixth option is to stay back, work as

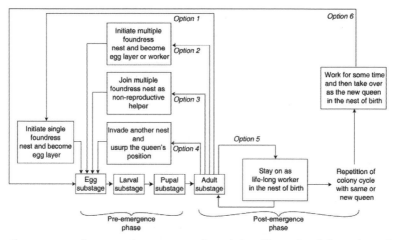

Figure 11.2 Diagrammatic Representation of the Life Cycle of the Colony showing the different options open to adult female wasps. Males are not shown. For schematic convenience, the egg, larval, and pupal stages are shown as being distinct. In reality, there is considerable overlap between them, especially when several colony cycles are repeated on the same nest. Similarly, change of queens can take place at any time of the colony cycle. Note also that new colonies may be initiated at any time of the year and may also be abandoned at any time of the year and at any stage in the colony cycle. *Source*: Redrawn from p. 256, Fig. 15.1 from ch. 15: "The evolution of eusociality, including a review of the social status of *Ropalidia marginata*" by Raghavendra Gadagkar from *Natural History and Evolution of PaperWasps* edited by Turillazzi, Stefano & West-Eberhard, Mary Jane (1996). By permission of Oxford University Press

helpers for some time and at an opportune moment, drive away their mother (or wait till their mother dies on her own) and take over as the new queen of the colony of their birth. It is perhaps not so surprising that the option of staying on as lifelong nonreproducing helpers is the most commonly adopted one, as it is the safest one. Starting a family on one's own is prone to failure, usurping the position of another queen in another family is risky, and to be able to drive away your mother or have her die on her own in your lifetime is a very rare chance (mother queens live much longer than helpers) (Gadagkar, 2001).

RELATIVES

Most *R. marginata* families consist not merely of a mother and her daughters and some occasional sons but also of many kinds of close and distant relatives, all living together and acting as helpers, assisting a single fertile queen to reproduce. By long-term observations of several colonies where every egg, larva, pupa, and adult wasp was tagged and censused three times a week, we have constructed pedigrees of queens in colonies of *R. marginata,* the most complex of which (Figure 11.3) shows that a queen may be replaced by her daughters, sisters, nieces, or cousins and that helpers may share their nests with their mother, brothers, sisters, nieces, nephews, cousins, mother's cousins, mother's cousin's children and even mother's cousin's grandchildren (Gadagkar et al., 1993). I am very fond of saying that an *R. marginata* family will put any Indian joint family to shame. There are reasons why the members of the family can be a mixture of close and distant relatives. When new colonies are founded, wasps from two or more different colonies may come together and jointly start a new colony (Shakarad & Gadagkar, 1995). Queens may mate with more than one

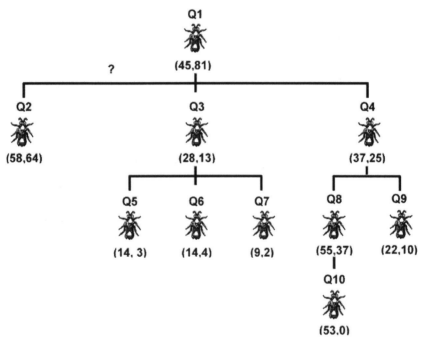

Figure 11.3   A Pedigree of Queens in a Colony of the Social Wasp, *Ropalidia marginata*. This means that Q2, Q3 and Q4 were daughters of Q1, and Q5, Q6 and Q7 were daughters Q3 and so on. The question mark indicates that the relationship of Q2 alone to Q1 was somewhat doubtful. Of the two numbers in parentheses the first one indicates the tenure in days of each queen and the second one indicates the number of offspring she produced during her tenure. *Source:* Reprinted by permission of the publisher from *Survival Strategies: Cooperation and Conflict in Animal Societies.* "A pedigree of queens in a colony of the social wasp *Ropalidia marginata*", by Raghavendra Gadagkar, p. 117, Cambridge, Mass.: Harvard University Press, Copyright © 1997 by the President and Fellows of Harvard College

male, resulting in the queen's daughters sometimes being half-sisters (step-sisters) (Muralidharan, Shaila, & Gadagkar, 1986). And as discussed above, offspring of successive queens may coexist in a colony.

The obvious question that arises is whether the members of nuclear family treat the members of the extended family—the relatives—differently. We have spent a great deal of time investigating this question. And again we were in for a big surprise. First, we asked whether the wasps could tell their nestmates (family members and relatives living together) apart from any non-nestmates, when they possibly encounter each other outside the context of their nest. To answer this question we put three female wasps in a little plastic box and observed their interactions. Two of the three wasps were chosen such that they were nestmates and the third was a non-nestmate of the other two. We found that nestmate-nestmate interactions were more tolerant than nestmate-nonnestmate interactions. This was true not only when the nestmates were previously familiar with each other by virtue of having shared the same nest, but even when they had never previously encountered each other, by virtue of being born on two experimentally separated fragments of the same nest. They were unable to recognize their nestmates from their non-nestmates only when they were removed from their nests before birth and hatched in an incubator. We concluded from this that wasps carry, on their body and in their brains, a label and template respectively, of their nest identity. They then compare the label on the bodies of an encountered wasp (on or away from the nest) with the template stored in their brain and decide whether the encountered individual is a nestmate or non-nestmate. However wasps are not born with their colony-specific labels and templates; both labels and templates are acquired after birth, from their nest and/or nestmates. This explains why nestmates born on different fragments of the same nest can recognise each other while wasps born in an incubator cannot. Thus all wasps living together in the same family, including the mother and her offspring as well as any other relatives acquire the same labels and templates. Hence they have no way of telling apart close from distant relatives and no way therefore of treating anybody differently—they all live as one (happy?—see above) family (Venkataraman et al., 1988).

THE NURSERY

A typical family consists of many more immature stages than adults. The immature stages are comprised of eggs, larvae of five distinct stages of development (Figure 11.4), and pupae. The eggs and pupae need no care other than to be guarded against being eaten by predatory ants or other species of wasps. But the larvae need to be fed several times everyday for 3–4 weeks after

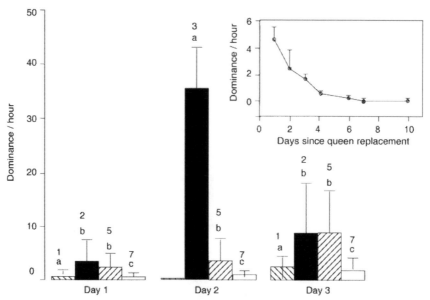

Figure 11.4   **A typical Queen Removal Experiment showing the frequencies per hour of dominance behaviour shown by the queen (left hatched bars), potential queen (black bars), max worker (the individual who showed maximum behavioral dominance in the colony apart from the queen and the PQ) (right shaded), and mean worker (open bars) on days 1, 2 and 3.** Inset: Dominance acts per nest-mate per hour shown by replacement queens from the day of takeover up to 10 days after queen replacement. Means and 1 S.D. are shown for nine nests for days 1–7 and six nests on day 10. *Source*: Redrawn with permission from Sudha Premnath, Anindya Sinha, Raghavendra Gadagkar, "Regulation of worker activity in a primitively eusocial wasp, *Ropalidia marginata*", *Behavioral Ecology*, 1995, 6, 2, by permission of Oxford University Press

which they pupate. This is a major task for the whole family, although the mother does very little of it. In a large active colony, there may be hundreds of hungry larvae being fed constantly by dozens of adults and this is fascinating to watch. Generally adults working outdoors bring food and hand it over to those working indoors who then feed the larvae. It makes you wonder how each of the hundreds of larvae of different ages and sizes and hunger levels are fed as per their need (and none forgotten), not to mention how those working outside know what, when, and how much to bring. It must be mentioned that when there is a real shortage of food, the adults will cannibalize the larvae before they themselves die of hunger. There is one fascinating quirk that I cannot help mentioning. One might imagine that the family must face serious problems associated with toilet training for the young ones. The adults conveniently defecate while hanging on to their nests and dangling their abdomens away from the surface of the nest, but what about the larvae that are essentially sedentary? No problem, because the larvae do not defecate. Their faecal matter accumulates at the end of the digestive tract and is finally removed once and for all, by the adults who chew a hole at the bottom of the larval chamber and extract it out of the bottom end of the fully grown larvae! (Gadagkar, 1991).

THE HOUSE

The wasp family constructs a house for itself. This is called a nest and it is an exquisitely elaborate structure made from paper—hence social wasps are often called paper wasps. And of course they manufacture their own paper by scraping cellulose fibres from plants, adding some secretions and chewing it up into pulp before spreading it into a thin layer. The nest is a two dimensional array of nearly perfect hexagonal cells with a depth of about 5–10 mm. One egg is laid in each cell and that individual stays in that cell through larval and pupal development. The nest surface is periodically cleaned and coated with some secretions making it both water proof and unsuitable for the growth of unwanted bacteria and fungi. The whole structure is attached to a rock, wall or leaf, by means of one or more pedicels. These pedicels are regularly coated with an ant-repellent dark substance also secreted by the adults. This secretion exudes from an opening in their abdomen making it easy for them to rub their abdomens around the pedicels. In the absence of this active defence, ants would quickly find the nest and consume the eggs, larvae, and pupae. And yet, this does not protect the brood from flying enemies. Tiny parasitic wasps (belonging to the Hymenopteran family Ichneumonidae) literally inject their eggs using long and thin ovipositors into the larvae of *R. marginata* wasps. Certain kinds of parasitic flies (belonging to the Dipteran family Tachinidae) "air-drop" their own tiny larvae onto the nest. In both cases the parasite larvae consume the host larvae and complete their development and fly away to attack other *R. marginata* nests. And finally and most devastatingly, adults of a large predatory wasp called *Vespa* alight on *R. marginata* nests and consume the larvae and pupae. Adult *R. marginata* wasps are entirely defenceless and watch helplessly while the predator feasts on the brood they have been ceaselessly caring for. *Vespa* never takes adult *R. marginata* and this may be the reason why the adults avoid the risk of injury of attempting to defend their brood and prefer instead to stay alive and produce more brood. The nest is a well-adapted dwelling place for the family, with the eggs, larvae and pupae being inside the cells and the adults sitting on the surface of the nests. The nest of a large colony, covered on the surface by adult wasps is surely a frightening sight for many other predators including humans (Gadagkar, 2001).

REPRODUCTION

As mentioned before, only one member of the family reproduces and we call her the queen. She is usually (but not always) the oldest member of the family and usually (but not always) the mother of the rest of the family. The rest of the family does not reproduce and labours instead to rear the queen's offspring. This is an act of altruism and a great evolutionary paradox. Why does evolution by natural selection not eliminate such altruism and promote only selfish behaviour. The phenomenon becomes even more paradoxical when we realize that most or all the members of the family are potentially capable of reproducing—they are merely suppressed in the presence of the queen. I shall return to the evolutionary paradox of altruism later. Here I wish to dwell on the mechanism of suppression of reproduction by the rest of the family. Since *R. marginata* queens are meek and docile, physical aggression cannot be the mechanism of suppression. We have found instead that the queen seems to suppress reproduction by the rest of the family by means of chemicals that she secretes from her body and rubs on the nest surface. Such chemicals are called pheromones but the exact mechanism of how they suppress ovarian development of the wasps is not understood (Sumana et al., 2008; Bhadra et al., 2010).

Whatever the mode of suppression, we know that it is reversible. If the queen dies or is experimentally removed by us, one of the hitherto non-reproducing individual becomes the next queen. When we had first discovered that the queen is a meek and docile individual, we had wondered why the rest of the family accepts her as their queen. In other species where the queen is active, interactive and aggressive, it is not so difficult to see that everybody else accepts her. Not so in this species. To solve this paradox, we conducted experiments in which we removed the queen and continued to observe the rest of the family. Incidentally, we mark all wasps uniquely with spots of coloured paints and can therefore follow changes in their behaviour over time. A great surprise awaited us when we first experimentally removed a queen from a colony. The *R. marginata* family is normally fairly peaceful with just an occasional act of aggression by some of the members toward others. These infrequent acts of aggression involve one wasp biting, pecking at, or chasing another, and are called dominance-subordinate interactions, the biter, pecker, or chaser being referred to as the dominant wasp and the bitten, pecked, or chased wasp being referred to as the subordinate wasp (Gadagkar, 2001). Upon removal of the queen, the normally peaceful colony immediately became extremely aggressive, increasing the normal low levels of dominance-subordinate behaviours manyfold. Even more surprisingly, all of the new aggression was shown by a single member of the family. We discovered later that this individual could be the daughter, sister, niece or cousin of the original removed queen. We also found out soon that if we replaced the original queen within 24 hours, the newly aggressive individual lost her aggression and went back to her normal behaviour. If we did not replace the original queen, the newly aggressive individual went on to become the next queen, but of course only after she lost her aggression, so that she could be a truly meek and docile queen. We labelled this hyperaggressive member of the family as 'potential queen' (PQ) (Figure 11.4). Thus we solved the problem of why the rest of the members of the family accept a meek and docile individual as their queen—the queen starts her career as a hyperaggressive individual and only after she is accepted does she become meek and docile (Premnath, Sinha, & Gadagkar, 1995; Sumana et al., 2008; Kardile & Gadagkar, 2002). Although this experiment helped solve one outstanding problem, it opened up several new problems, but then that is the joy of science.

Perhaps the most important new question was which of the family members is chosen or allowed to become the potential queen and eventually the new queen. As humans this question is one of obvious interest to us but as evolutionary biologists, it was truly fundamental. Reproduction after all is the currency of evolutionary fitness—those who reproduce stay in the race and those who don't are eliminated by natural selection. So there must be a great deal of competition about which member of the family replaces the old queen and becomes the new queen of the colony. We have set ourselves the goal of predicting the queen's successor before removing the original queen. To achieve this goal we have tried every possible experimental strategy and worked very hard for many years but we have utterly failed. To this day we cannot predict the queen's successor before removing her. The potential queen seems not to be special in any way. She is not the biggest or smallest, oldest or youngest, laziest or most hardworking, the most dominant or least dominant, not even the one with the best or least developed ovaries (Deshpande et al., 2006). Although we did not achieve our goal, we discovered two other remarkable features about the working of the *R. marginata* family.

The first of these remarkable features is that there is not just one potential queen, but a whole series of them. Since the potential queen can be detected by her hyperaggressive behaviour, we asked what would happen if we also removed the hyperaggressive potential queen before she had the chance to drop her aggression and start laying eggs. Thus we removed the potential queen within an hour of removing the original queen. To our great surprise we found that upon removing the potential queen, another member of the family immediately became hyperaggressive and would go on to lose her aggression and lay eggs if neither the queen nor the previous potential queen was returned. This meant that there were two potential queens in waiting even before the loss of the queen. And it did not stop there. We could remove potential queen number two and get potential queen number three, remove number three and get potential queen number four, remove number four and get potential queen number five (Figures 11.5 and 11.6). Thus there appears to be a long queue of potential queens each waiting for their turn to succeed their predecessor queens (Bang & Gadagkar, 2012).

The second remarkable feature is that the entire family seems to know who their next queen is going to be. Remarkable as it is, it is made even more remarkable by the fact that we ourselves cannot predict the queen's successor, in spite of all our experimentation. We had a strong suspicion that the wasps may know their successor because in the long queue of PQs, each PQ seemed to know her place in the queue and did not break the queue. Put in another way, none of the potential queens were challenged when they became hyper-aggressive; two or more individuals did not appear to compete when there is a vacancy for the queen's position. We then conducted a more direct test of the hypothesis that the wasps know who their successor is, that is, that there is a previously decided heir designate.

The experiment involved cutting the nest in half, separating the two halves with a wire mesh screen so that the wasps cannot go through. We then randomly reintroduced all the wasps, including the queen, half of them on each side. This of course meant that there was a queen-right side (with queen) and a queen-less side (without queen). We already knew that in such a situation, the wasps on the queen-less side cannot detect the queen on the queen-right side and will therefore behave as if they have lost their queen, that is, a potential queen will become hyperaggressive (Sumana et al., 2008). Now we argued that if the heir designate happens by chance to be in the queen-less side, she will be the unchallenged PQ on her side and of course there will be no PQ on the queen-right side. Once we saw a PQ on the queen-less side, we swapped the positions of the queen and PQ. Now the PQ has been brought to the other side but since she is the heir designate for the whole colony she should not be challenged by the wasps on the new side either. However, only in half the experiments would the heir designate end up in the queen-less side by chance alone. In the other half of the experiments, the heir designate would be in the queen-right side where she will have no opportunity to take over. On the queen-less side however, there is no queen and we expect the 'best' individual in this side to become the PQ. We now swap the positions of this non-heir designate PQ and the queen. Here the outcome of the swapping should be different. The non-heir designate PQ may have been the 'best' in the queen-less side but not on the queen-right side. Here she comes face-to-face with the true heir designate of the whole colony and should be challenged, resulting in the true heir designate now becoming the PQ. Thus we predicted that the new heir designate PQ should be unchallenged on both sides. Thus in about half the experiments, the first individual to become PQ should be accepted on both sides, but in the remaining half of the experiments

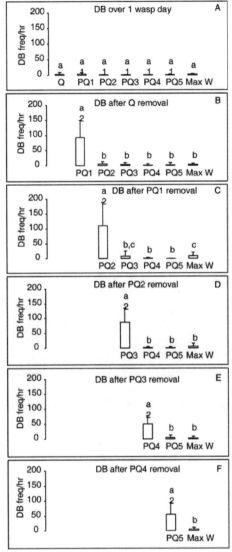

Figure 11.5   Evidence for a Reproductive Queue in *R. marginata*. Means and standard deviations of frequencies per hour of behavioral dominance of (A) the queen, five PQs and the max worker (the individual who showed maximum behavioral dominance in the colony apart from the queen and the five PQs) in normal queen-right colonies, and (B–F) the PQs and the max workers in the absence of the queen and the preceding PQs (n = 19 colonies). Note that each PQ showed higher aggression after the queen and the previous PQs were removed than what she showed in the queen-right colony and also compared to any other individual in the queen-less colony. DB = behavioral dominance; Q = queen; PQ1...PQ5 = potential queens 1–5; Max W = max worker. *Source:* Redrawn with permission from Bang and Gadagkar 2012

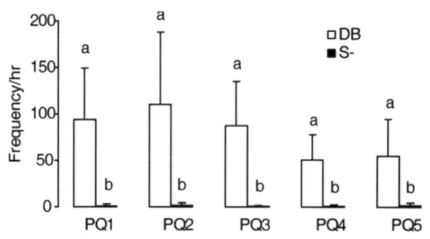

Figure 11.6   **Behavioural Dominance Shown and Received (mean ± s.d.)** by different PQs in the absence of the queen and previous PQs. Note that each PQ showed significantly higher behavioural dominance than what she received. On an average, dominance shown by each PQ was ~40–180 fold higher than the dominance she received. DB = behavioural dominance shown; S- = behavioural dominance received; PQ1...PQ5 = potential queens 1–5. *Source*: Redrawn with permission from Bang and Gadagkar 2012

the first individual to become PQ should be unacceptable on the opposite side and a new PQ acceptable to both sides should emerge. This is exactly what we found (Figure 11.7), but with one unexpected twist. When the PQ was unacceptable on the opposite side, she was not challenged. Instead she on her own dropped her aggression, as if she knew that it was not her turn yet. And she did not challenge the second individual (the true heir designate) when the latter became hyperaggressive. Hence we concluded that all the wasps knew who their next successor would be, and let it not be forgotten, even though we ourselves could not identify her. In other words, there was a heir designate but she was cryptic to us (Bhadra & Gadagkar, 2008).

THE ORGANIZATION OF WORK

Another new question arose in our minds when we found that the new queen is aggressive only for about a week and then becomes meek and docile. How does a meek and docile queen ensure that the rest of the family worked hard to care for her brood? In other species where the queen is aggressive throughout her career, she is known to use physical aggression (dominance-subordinate interactions) to ensure that everybody does their respective jobs. For instance, if a worker (all non-reproducing female members of the colony

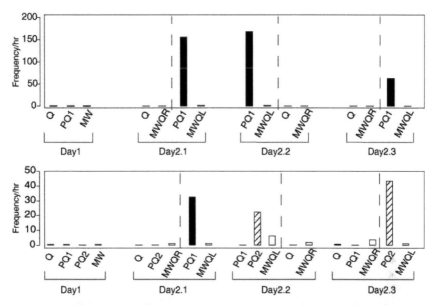

Figure 11.7 The Q-PQ Exchange Experiment. Upper panel: A typical experiment in which the PQ1 was the cryptic successor. The frequency per hour of dominance behavior exhibited by the Queen, PQ1 and Max worker (defined as the worker showing maximum aggression) on day 1 in the normal colony, and on the queen-right and queen-less fragments in the three sessions on day 2 are shown. Lower panel: A typical experiment in which the PQ2 was the cryptic successor. The frequency per hour of dominance behaviour exhibited by the Queen, PQ1, PQ2 and Max worker on day 1 in the normal colony, and on the queen-right and queen-less fragments in the three sessions on day 2 are shown. *Source*: Redrawn with permission from (Bhadra & Gadagkar 2008)

are referred to as workers) began to rest after she brought some food and distributed it, the queen in other species would go and bite, peck or chase the lazy member of her family (show dominance behaviour) as a result of which the latter would leave to work again. But how does the queen ensure that her workers work hard in *R. marginata*? In an attempt to answer this question, we conducted another experiment. We compared the working habits of all family members before and after removal of the queen, that is, in a queen-right and a queen-less colony. We chose two important kinds of work for our study, namely, bringing food and feeding the larvae. We found to our surprise that the presence or absence of the queen made no difference to the workers—they worked anyway. There was no difference between the queen-right and queen-less conditions in the rates at which food was brought to the colony and the rates at which the larvae were fed. In other words, the queen does not regulate the work of the rest of the family and can therefore afford to be meek and docile, especially since she uses pheromones (and not aggression) to maintain her reproductive monopoly in the family (Premnath, Sinha, & Gadagkar ,1996).

But somebody should regulate the work of the family. Even if the wasps are intrinsically hardworking, somebody should tell when to bring more food and when to stop. In particular, those members of the family working outside should be told about the hunger levels of the family. We have investigated this question and found that the workers self-organize their work in a decentralized, bottom-up manner without the need for centralized, top-down control. How do they manage to do this? We hypothesized that workers use the low levels of dominance-subordinate behaviour seen in normal queen-right colonies to regulate each other's work. More specifically, we hypothesized that dominance behaviour shown to workers signalled the need for work. Thus family members working inside and who have information about the hunger levels of the colony can communicate this information to those working outside by means of dominance behaviour. We obtained three lines of evidence in support of this hypothesis. First, we found a positive correlation between the amounts of dominance behaviour a member of the family receives and her relative contribution to the family's foraging effort (Premnath, Sinha, & Gadagkar, 1995). Second, we found that giving excess food to the whole family reduced not only the levels of dominance-subordinate behaviour in the family as a whole, but also the levels of dominance behaviour received by habitual foragers (Bruyndonckx, Kardile, & Gadagkar, 2006). Conversely, by starving a colony we were able to increase the rates of dominance-subordinate behaviour in the colony. This increase was not simply an expression of general stress or unrest. Habitual foragers were the specific targets of such increased dominance behaviour (Lamba, Chandrasekhar, & Gadagkar, 2008).

There are two other aspects of division of labour within the family that I should mention. One has to do with the fact that the wasps gradually change their behavioural profiles as they age. This phenomenon is called age polyethism. Typically wasps first work inside, beginning with feeding the larvae and graduate to building the nest as they get a bit older, and then they work outside the nest, beginning with bringing fibre and finally becoming food foragers (Figures 11.8 and 11.9) (Naug & Gadagkar, 1998). The other has to be the fact that males do not do any work in the family. This is true for all ants, bees and wasps and is a curiosity that is not fully understood. In our species, males, of course, leave their family of birth and lead a nomadic life. But even their laziness during the week they live with the family is striking because females of that age begin to work. We have specifically focused some of our studies on male laziness. Using feeding of the larvae as an example of work, we reasoned that the males might not work for one or more of the following three reasons. One, they do not know how to feed the larvae. Two, they do not forage by themselves and depend on the females to supply even the food

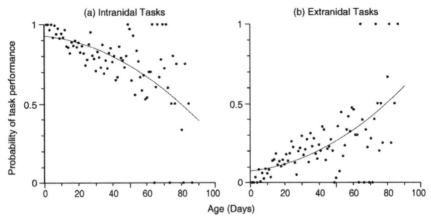

Figure 11.8 Young Wasps Work inside the Nest (intranidal work) and older wasps work outside the nest (extranidal work). Probability of task performance is plotted as a function of the age of the wasps fitted with 2-degree polynomial regression lines. Data points represent the mean value for all individuals in that age class in five colonies. (a) Intranidal tasks and (b) Extranidal tasks. *Source*: With kind permission from Springer Science+Business Media: *Behavioral Ecology and Sociobiology*, 42, 1998, page 39, Dhruba Naug and Raghavendra Gadagkar, figure number 2

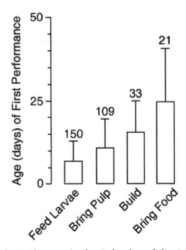

Figure 11.9 Age Dependent Changes in the Behavior of the Adult Female Wasps. Mean (± s.d.) of age of first performance of feed larva, build nest, bring pulp [for building the nest] and bring food. Number of wasps observed is given above the respective bars. *Source*: With kind permission from Springer Science+Business Media: *Behavioral Ecology and Sociobiology*, 42, 1998, page 39, Dhruba Naug and Raghavendra Gadagkar, figure number 3

they need for themselves; therefore they never have any leftover food to offer to the larvae. Three, because the females do a good and adequate job of feeding the larvae, they see no scope for them to add to the labour of the females, especially since they have to depend entirely on the females to get the food in the first place. To test these hypotheses, we first hand-fed the males to satiation and offered them even more food. Sure enough they began to feed the larvae showing that they were not incapable of doing so. However, they did rather too little of it. Then we hand-fed the males to satiation and simultaneously removed all the females and thus left the hungry larvae entirely under the care of well-fed males. Now the males indeed began to feed the larvae at rates comparable to those of the females. Thus males can and do feed larvae given an opportunity. In fairness to the females, it must be said however that the larvae did not do very well under the care of the males! (Sen & Gadagkar, 2006).

THE BALANCE BETWEEN COOPERATION AND CONFLICT

Perhaps the most striking feature of the wasp family is the extreme cooperation within the family. As we have seen, only one member of the family, the queen, reproduces and the rest of the family labours for her reproductive success. Besides, the rest of the family need no top-down orders from the queen—they work whether or not she is present and self-regulate their work in a decentralized manner. Even more impressively, they deal with the death or loss of their queen, in what we humans would consider a most civilized manner. The members of the family seem to queue up in an orderly manner to replace the queen, even before the death of the queen and implement the queue without overt conflict upon the actual loss of the queen. As far as we can tell, there is little overt conflict even when the queue is being established in the presence of the queen. Why should there be so much cooperation, so much peace? And, is there no conflict at all in their lives? It turns out that the extreme cooperation within a family is matched by extreme conflict between families. I have already mentioned that the wasps have a well-developed ability for nestmate discrimination. So far I have pointed out how this helps maintain peace inside the family, because all family members carry the same labels and templates used in nestmate discrimination. The flip side of this is of course that it also makes possible and indeed promotes war with outsiders. We have seen direct evidence of this.

In one experiment, we introduced all the members of one nest, without their nest and brood, into another cage containing a different resident colony. The resident wasps showed a very nuanced response to the 'invading' aliens. The very young aliens were permitted to join the resident nest. The older workers (nonreproductives) were permitted to live in the cage but were not permitted to get close to the resident nest. The alien queen, who obviously constitutes the greatest reproductive threat to the resident colony, was attacked and torn to pieces, even when she was away from the resident nest (Venkataraman & Gadagkar, 1992). We seldom see non-nestmates land on natural colonies but when they do, they are usually (though not always) repelled. Thus the wasps display both cooperation and conflict, but which of the two they show depends very much on the context and not so much on the identity of the wasps. Now their great propensity to make peace with insiders, even though they may be distantly related begins to make sense—it is to successfully make war with outsiders and protect their brood and their resources. Only by putting up a united front can they face outsiders. And the threat of outside invasion is ever present. A united front within the nest may not be very useful to deal with ants, ichneumonid wasps who inject their eggs into the wasp larvae, Tachinid flies who air-drop their larvae onto the nest or vespine wasps who eat up their larvae and pupae. But it must be useful when the enemy is an alien *R. marginata* wasp trying to sneak into the colony and usurp the queen's position. We have evidence that usurpers take their chances whenever there is some hope of success. Such conspecific usurpation is one of the most important causes of failure for queens of small colonies (Shakarad & Gadagkar, 1995). Indeed, that such usurpation is rarely seen in large colonies is testimony to the effectiveness of a united peaceful colony in thwarting the efforts of potential usurpers.

THE EVOLUTION OF ALTRUISM

As already mentioned the altruistic behaviour of members of a wasp family toward the queen and her offspring is an evolutionary paradox. What's in it for the workers? Why should they sacrifice their own chances of reproduction and help another individual to reproduce? In more technical language this conundrum may be re-stated as follows: how does evolution by natural selection promote genes that make their bearers behave in such an altruistic manner; why do such genes not disappear from the population, since they cannot multiply as fast their counterpart 'selfish' genes that make their bearers reproduce as fast as possible, without wasting time and energy helping someone else. A prominent theory that attempts to explain this paradox is called kin selection. It argues (and shows mathematically) that altruism may be favoured by natural selection if it is directed toward genetic relatives. This is because genetic relatives of the altruists are also likely to carry the same altruistic genes. Thus from a gene's point of view, altruistic genes are helping each other when altruists help their genetic relatives. Under certain conditions the loss of personal reproduction for the altruist may be more than compensated by the multiplication of altruistic genes through the reproduction

of the recipients of altruism (Hamilton, 1964a,b). We have found that this
theoretical framework provides a satisfactory explanation of the altruistic
behaviour in the *R. marginata* family. Using a model based on kin selection, we have correctly predicted that only a small proportion of the wasps
(~5%) should opt for the selfish solitary nest founding strategy while the vast
majority (~95%) should prefer to live in groups, even though it might mean
loss of personal reproduction for them. Even though distant relatives live in
extended families and altruism is sometimes directed toward not-so-close
relatives, because the cost of helping is very low, the benefits of helping are
very high and the prospects of selfish solitary nesting are very low, we find
that kin selection does a good job of predicting the behaviour of these wasps
(Gadagkar, 2001).

Kin selection, however, may not provide an adequate explanation for some
of the observed behaviours. For example, why should wasps mate with multiple males and thereby lower intra-colony relatedness; why should they found
new nests with non-nestmates; why should they admit young alien wasps into
their colonies; why should they not discriminate between close and distant
relatives in the family and dispense altruism preferentially to close relatives;
why should the workers continue to work in the absence of the queen and
in the absence of orders from the queen; why should they line up in orderly
queues and await their turn for direct reproduction as future queens; why
should they honour previous decisions and implement the reproductive queue
without conflict; why is there so much peace with insiders in the family in
spite of it being an extended family of close and distant relatives; why should
war be reserved for dealing only with outsiders, even though relatedness to
outsiders may sometimes not be very much less than relatedness to some
family members? Kin selection may work in spite of all these apparently
paradoxical behaviours, but what selects for these patterns of behaviour in
the first place? Perhaps there are other, better explanations, or other competing selection pressures involved in the evolution of the *R. marginata* family
system. This is the reason why I have argued that attempts to criticize kin
selection and propose alternate theories (Nowak, Tarnita, & Wilson, 2010)
should not be nipped in the bud (Gadagkar, 2010). In summary the evolution
by natural selection of the *R. marginata*-like family systems is far from being
understood. Much more new empirical and theoretical work is needed.

WHAT CAN WE LEARN BY STUDYING
THE WASP FAMILY SYSTEM?

Insect societies are being studied with many different motivations. They make
good model systems (proxies) for understanding biochemistry, development

and diseases of higher animals including humans. Their mechanisms of division of labour, task specialization, and self-organization provide inspiration and clues for organizing our own societies and institutions. Their systems of communication have inspired highly efficient algorithms in computer science, telecommunication and the internet, accounting for profits running into millions of dollars (for a review, see Gadagkar, 2009). Nevertheless my personal motivation is more modest. I study the *R. marginata* system for the same kinds of reasons that anthropologists study human societies. Anthropologists can inform us about the lives and mores of "primitive" and exotic human societies with thousands of years of experience independent of contemporary human societies. I will argue that biologists can teach us about social animals of all kinds with millions of years of independent evolutionary history. And those of us who study social insects can be privy to "wisdom" from an altogether different sub-kingdom of life on this planet. I would not for a moment suggest that we should blindly imitate a wasp family, but I am convinced that the wasps hold a mirror to us, and help us better understand ourselves (Gadagkar, 2011). And that is arguably worth more than millions of dollars.

I will end with two general remarks.

First, I am conscious of the fact that I have not used the word emotion, a word which appears in the subtitle of the book in which this essay is included, thanks to the intellectual generosity of the editors. Do the wasps feel any emotions when they choose to be solitary or social, when they accept the role of a sterile helper, when they mate, when they succeed in becoming queens, when they feed a hungry larva, when they cannibalize a larva, when they build a perfect hexagon, when they watch their brood being eaten by a predator, when they admit young aliens into their fold or when they aggressively dismember an invading alien queen? Of course we do not know and we will probably never know (Gadagkar, 1997). Needless to say the neural, hormonal and other biological machinery of the wasps is rather primitive in comparison to our own. If they nevertheless feel emotions similar to our own it would be remarkable indeed. On the other hand, if they can manage to do all that they do without emotions, it would be even more remarkable.

Second, as I have said in the beginning, here I have deliberately attempted to describe colonies of the social wasp *R. marginata*, using the language normally used to describe human families. This has been amusing no doubt, but also surprisingly instructive. It has allowed me to look at the wasps in a new light and revealed gap in our knowledge of the wasps. Although we often decry the use of anthropomorphism in describing animals, I certainly found the attempt to anthropomorphise the wasp colony very instructive. I would therefore argue that anthropomorphism might be a good tool to generate questions or hypotheses about animals, hypotheses that can then be tested using more rigorous scientific methods.

REFERENCES

Bang, A., & Gadagkar, R. (2012). Reproductive queue without overt conflict in the primitively eusocial wasp *Ropalidia marginata*. *Proceedings of the National Academy of Sciences*, 109 (36), 14494–99. doi:10.1073/pnas.1212698109.

Bhadra, A., & Gadagkar, R. (2008). We know that the wasps 'know': Cryptic successors to the queen in *Ropalidia marginata*. *Biology Letters*, 4, 634–37.

Bhadra, A., Mitra, A., Deshpande, S. A., Chandrasekhar, K., Naik, D. G, Hefetz, A., & Gadagkar, R. (2010). Regulation of reproduction in the primitively eusocial wasp *Ropalidia marginata*: On the trail of the queen pheromone. *Journal of Chemical Ecology*, 36, 424–31.

Bruyndonckx, N., Kardile, S. P., & Gadagkar, R. (2006). Dominance behaviour and regulation of foraging in the primitively eusocial wasp *Ropalidia marginata* (Lep.) (Hymenoptera: Vespidae). *Behavioural Processes*, 72(1), 100–103.

Deshpande, S. A., Sumana, A., Surbeck, M., & Gadagkar, R. (2006). Wasp who would be queen: A comparative study of two primitively eusocial species. *Current Science*, 91(3), 332–36.

Gadagkar, R. (1991). *Belonogaster, Mischocyttarus, Parapolybia*, and independent founding *Ropalidia*. In K. G. Ross and R. W. Matthews (Eds.), *The social biology of wasps.* (pp. 149–90). Ithaca: Cornell University Press.

Gadagkar. (1996). The evolution of eusociality, including a review of the social status of *Ropalidia marginata*. In *Natural History and Evolution of Paper-Wasps*, ed. Turillazzi, S., and West-Eberhard, M. J. Oxford: Oxford University Press, pp. 248–71.

Gadagkar, R. (1997). *Survival strategies: Cooperation and conflict in animal societies*. Cambridge, MA: Harvard University Press.

Gadagkar, R. (2001). *The social biology of Ropalidia marginata: Toward understanding the evolution of eusociality*. Cambridge, MA: Harvard University Press.

Gadagkar, R. (2009). What can we learn from insect societies? In R. Narasimha & S. Menon (Eds.) *Nature and culture*, (pp. 357–65). New Delhi: CSS & PHISPC.

Gadagkar, R. (2010). Sociobiology in turmoil again. *Current Science*, 99(8), 1036–41.

Gadagkar, R. (2011). War and peace: Conflict and cooperation in a tropical insect society. In M. Cockel, J. Billote, F. Darbellay, & F. Waldvogel (Eds.), *Common knowledge: The challenge of interdisciplinarity*, (75–96). Lausanne, Switzerland: EPFL Press.

Gadagkar, R., Chandrashekara, K., Chandran, S., & Bhagavan, S. (1993). Serial polygyny in the primitively eusocial wasp *Ropalidia marginata*: Implications for the evolution of sociality. In L. Keller (Ed.), *Queen number and sociality in insects*, (pp. 188–214). Oxford: Oxford University Press.

Gamboa, G. J, Wacker, T. L., Scope, J. A., Cornell, T. J. & Shellman-Reeve, J. (1990). The mechanism of queen regulation of foraging by workers in paper wasps (*Polistes fuscatus*, Hymenoptera, Vespidae). *Ethology*, 85, 335–43.

Hamilton, W. D. (1964a,b). The genetical evolution of social behaviour I & II. *Journal of Theoretical Biology*, 7, 1–52.

Kardile, S. P., & Gadagkar, R. (2002). Docile sitters and active fighters in paper wasps: A tale of two queens. *Naturwissenschaften*, 89, 176–79.

Lamba, S., Chandrasekhar, K., & Gadagkar, R. (2008). Signaling hunger through aggression-the regulation of foraging in a primitively eusocial wasp. *Naturwissenschaften*, 95, 677–80.

Muralidharan, K., Shaila, M. S. & Gadagkar, R. (1986). Evidence for multiple mating in the primitively eusocial wasp *Ropalidia marginata* (Lep.) (Hymenoptera: Vespidae). *Journal of Genetics*, 65, 153–58.

Naug, D., & Gadagkar, R. (1998). The role of age in temporal polyethism in a primitively eusocial wasp. *Behavioral Ecology and Sociobiology*, 42(1), 37–47.

Nowak, M. A., Tarnita, C. E. & Wilson, E. O. (2010). The evolution of eusociality. *Nature*, 466, 1057–62.

Premnath, S., Sinha, A. & Gadagkar, R. (1995). Regulation of worker activity in a primitively eusocial wasp, *Ropalidia marginata*. *Behavioral Ecology*, 6(2), 117–23.

Premnath, S., Sinha, A. & Gadagkar, R. (1996). Dominance relationships in the establishment of reproductive division of labour in a primitively eusocial wasp (*Ropalidia marginata*). *Behavioral Ecology and Sociobiology*, 39, 125–32.

Reeve, H. K. & Gamboa, G. J. (1987). Queen regulation of worker foraging in paper wasps: A social feedback control system (*Polistes fuscatus*, Hymenoptera: Vespidae). *Behaviour*, 102(3), 147–67.

Sarton, G. (1943). The feminine monarchie of Charles Butler. *Isis*, 34(6), 469–72.

Sen, R. & Gadagkar, R. 2006. Males of the social wasp *Ropalidia marginata* can feed larvae, given an opportunity. *Animal Behaviour*, 71, 345–50.

Shakarad, M., & Gadagkar, R. (1995). Colony founding in the primitively eusocial wasp, *Ropalidia marginata* (Lep.) (Hymenoptera: Vespidae). *Ecological Entomology*, 20, 273–82.

Sumana, A., Deshpande, S. A., Bhadra, A., & Gadagkar, R. (2008). Workers of the primitively eusocial wasp *Ropalidia marginata* do not perceive their queen across a wire mesh partition. *Journal of Ethology*. 26, 207–12.

Venkataraman, A. B., & Gadagkar, R. (1992). Kin recognition in a semi-natural context: Behaviour towards foreign conspecifics in the social wasp *Ropalidia marginata* (Lep.) (Hymenoptera: Vespidae), *Insectes Sociaux*, 39, 285–99.

Venkataraman, A. B., Swarnalatha, V. B., Nair, P., & Gadagkar, R. (1988). The mechanism of nestmate discrimination in the tropical social wasp *Ropalidia marginata* and its implications for the evolution of eusociality. *Behavioural Ecology and Sociobiology*, 23, 271–279.

Wilson, E. O. (1971). *The insect societies*. Cambridge, Mass.: Belknap Press of Harvard University Press.

Chapter 12

Ants and Families

LeAnn S. Howard and Deborah M. Gordon

Since 2004 we have been engaged in a fruitful and interesting conversation about the analogies between ant colonies and human families. LeAnn Howard has joined Deborah Gordon's field project in the Arizona desert each year, studying the behavior and ecology of desert seed-eating ants. Dr. Gordon has tracked a population of about 300 colonies per year since 1985. By following known colonies over their lifetimes, she has learned that colonies live for 25–30 years, each one founded by a single queen who mates early in life and then produces all of the ants of the colony each year. The colony consists of the queen and sterile female workers who do not mate or reproduce. Workers live about a year. The colony grows to a size of about 10,000 workers by the time it is 5 years old, and stays at this size until eventually the queen dies. Then once the workers die, the colony is dead; it does not adopt a new queen.

Colonies reproduce in an annual mating aggregation that occurs during the summer. In early summer, queens produce males and daughter queens. All of the colonies in the population send virgin queens and males to a mating aggregation. There they mate, the newly mated queens fly off to found new colonies, and the males die. Recently we have been able to identify which colonies were founded by daughter queens of known parent queens (Ingram et al., 2013). We learned that only about 25% of colonies succeed in reproducing, and we are working to understand why.

Dr. Gordon's investigation of ant colony organization centers on how colonies operate without central control (Gordon, 2010). No ant gives directions or instructions to another. No ant makes a global assessment of what needs to be done. Instead ants use their local, recent experience of interactions to make decisions about what to do next. In the aggregate this allows colonies to adjust their activity to changing conditions.

LeAnn Howard's work as a clinician centers on viewing the family as an interdependent unit rather than a collection of independent members. The family relationship system is central to the development of variation among individuals in overall adaptiveness. Individuals vary in the degree to which autonomy from the family is established. In addition, individuals vary in degree to which cognitive processes operate with relative autonomy from feeling states and more automatic responsiveness.

We decided to write this chapter as a conversation, summarizing our thoughts on comparing similarities and differences between ant colonies and human families in several ways: self-reflection or the lack of it, the role of contact in regulating behavior, interaction networks, generational influence of collective behavior, and variation in adaptation to changing conditions.

To compare ant and human behavior, we consider:

1. Self-reflection, and distinguishing facts from feelings.
2. The influence of contact and the outcomes of interaction networks.
3. Cross-generational influences.

COMPARING ANT AND HUMAN BEHAVIOR

LSH: There are many challenges when considering the relationship between human behavior and the behavior of other animals, particularly ants. A strong propensity for humans is to place ourselves at the center of nature and to assume all of life revolves around us. Another tendency is to place human attributes onto ants or to make the error of assuming that animals, including ants, are irrational and that humans are rational beings. The effort to observe and account for behavior between these two species requires the initial step of assuming that humans and ants are animals, a part of nature, and operating according to processes that are similar and uniquely different.

DMG: Ants are different from humans in crucial ways. They lack identity and any ongoing narrative about what is going on. All of these seem to me to be so important for humans that any story about what it is like to be an ant cannot be transferred to what we know from our own experience.
It is interesting to think about structural analogies. Some of the processes that regulate ant behavior might play out the same way, with similar dynamics, to analogous processes in humans. This is the idea that we explore below.

SELF-REFLECTION AND DISTINGUISHING
FACTS FROM FEELINGS

LSH: Ants are not observing humans or themselves. They don't think, feel, reflect, use language, or have personal identity. Ants respond to moment-to-moment shifts in the environment and to simple behavioral responses to other ants. This simple and somewhat chaotic process allows ants to achieve complex tasks that include reproducing, building a nest, repairing the nest, caring for young, gathering and storing food and competing with other colonies and other species.

Human beings, on the other hand, react, feel, and think. People appear to respond and react to processes that are evolutionarily older than feeling and thinking. Intense emotional experiences disrupt higher rational processes and more primitive brain control systems dictate behavior (Panksepp, 1998). This automatic process, while uniquely different from other species, may show evidence of fundamental processes held in common (Kerr, 2013).

An inactive ant responds automatically to another ant carrying a seed. A highly pressured offspring automatically moves away from a parent. The response is without thought. In addition, human beings are a feeling and thinking species. Humans feel sad, angry, frightened, etc. Thinking, the capacity to learn, reflect, and regulate behavior is more advanced in the human than in other primates. However, much of human thought, particularly as it pertains to self, is governed more by feeling states than objective thought. Feeling states can be completely internal and have little or no connection to external, factual reality (MacLean, 1978; Papero, 1990).

Human subjectivity is enormous. For example, people not only reflect on themselves inaccurately, but they also tell others about their behavior that many times does not match what, in fact, they actually do. Studies of the neural mechanisms in the human suggest that much of human behavior is out of awareness. In this sense humans and ants are not that different. One species doesn't reflect and the other reflects without accuracy much of the time.

DMG: How an ant responds to another is a mystery. We can see the outcome: when a forager waiting inside the nest for its next trip meets a returning forager coming back with food, it is likely to leave the nest. Even this simple interaction is not fully deterministic: an ant does not always do exactly the same thing in the same conditions. So our best generalizations about the outcome of interactions are probabilistic: we can say what an ant is likely to do in a particular situation. But we still don't know exactly what is happening for the ant, or even what it would mean to answer that question. How does an ant know to pick up a seed and bring it back to the nest? We have to recognize that we don't really know the answer to such questions about ourselves—why do I get angry and shout at my teenage daughter one morning, but laugh off the same behavior another morning? But at least we can talk about the answers to such questions about ourselves, while asking an ant would not get us very far.

LSH: A motivated person can begin to link automatic behavior with the facts of a system and to see their own family more realistically. This possibility concerns making a distinction between content and process. Ants, of course, don't focus on content. Human beings are extremely caught up in content and may miss how the process itself significantly influences the content and accompanying feeling states.

The capacity to function more autonomously depends on a person's ability to distinguish an intellectual process and feeling process (Bowen, 1978). More objective thinking and reflecting can overrule feelings as the basis for action. Self-regulation of the individual within the unit is at the heart of this process. Not all human beings are capable of this level of observation and choice in behavior. Clinical experience suggests that the most stuck together family units are not able to reflect and choose behavior. Families in which members are more independent of one another contain members who can reflect based on facts. These families tend to be more flexible and more stable. Those families are also freer of symptoms.

THE INFLUENCE OF CONTACT AND THE OUTCOMES OF INTERACTION NETWORKS

DMG: Ants respond to the rate at which they interact with other ants (Gordon, 2010). Most interactions are chemical. The best known example is when ants returning from a food source leave pheromone trails on the ground, and other ants respond to the chemical by staying near it, leading them back to the food. This is a chemical interaction between two ants with a lag between the time that one ant deposits the chemical on the ground and another ant finds it. There are more than 12,000 species of ants, and they differ in how they interact. Not all ant species use trail pheromone. Another form of interaction, seen in all ant species, is antennal contact. Ants smell with their antennae, and when one ant touches another with its antennae, it detects a layer of chemicals, cuticular hydrocarbons, on the other ants' body, that carries a colony-specific odor. Thus in a brief antennal contact one ant can assess if the other ant is a nestmate. In addition, because the cuticular hydrocarbons change according to conditions, ants performing different tasks in different conditions differ in odor. In harvester ants, antennal contact also allows one ant to assess the task group of the other.

This allows ants to behave according to a simple rule such as "I'm a forager. If I meet another forager with food often enough, I'm likely to leave the nest to forage". In the aggregate the response to interactions is enough to lead the colony to respond predictably to changes in the environment. For example, the regulation of foraging is based on simple positive feedback. If there is more food available, then foragers find it more quickly and return to the nest more quickly, leading more ants to go out.

Not all ants are the same. But we still know very little about how much differences among ants matter in interaction networks. From observing the contacts of individual ants, it looks as though whether an ant has many contacts depends only on whether it happens to go into an area, which we call an "interaction hotspot," where contact is frequent. We don't see any evidence so far that differences among ants lead to different kind of contacts. We don't see any evidence that it matters to ant #3 whether it meets ant #275 or ant #44. We humans also respond to contact with others, but for us each contact is laden with meaning in the narrative of the relations with particular others.

LSH: Human beings have physiological systems that are a part of each being and are also regulated by contact with other beings. Particularly impactful are patterns of contact and distance from family members. Humans have an affiliative response system. The neuropeptides of oxytocin and arginine vasopressin are key mediators of pair-bond formation and approach behavior (Carter, 2005; Heinrichs & Domes, 2008). Humans have a biological sensitivity to context. Parental care influences stress reactivity in an infant through its stress response system, which entails the HPA axis and the autonomic nervous system (McEwan, 2002). Also, the growing child's response impacts the parent. While this reciprocal process is far more complex than contact between ants, the core process of contact that modifies another underlies this phenomenon. The relationship between behavior and somatic process can be observed in the reported experience of falling in love. The process of "falling in love" appears to alter the perceptual framework of each individual such that potential future challenges are not observed (Carter, 2005).

Studies of the family suggest that relationship processes are the primary means of transmitting stress reactivity or calm (Noone, 2013). In addition, studies of physiological measures of family members interacting around intense topics point toward triangular patterns that repeat in periods of stress and calm (Harrison, 2013).

While interaction networks are extremely central to the functioning of both ants and humans, the process of each network has distinct differences. Interaction networks in ants depend on the pattern of encounter with other ants. An ant smells another and determines through smell if the ant contacted is a nestmate or not. An ant contacts another and this produces a change in state. The contact determines whether or not an ant continues doing the same task or switches to another. Rate of contact is also important. More ants coming in with a seed to the nest lead to more ants leaving the nest. Such patterns are connected to the availability of seeds on a given day. Simple patterns spread out to involve the entire unit of the colony.

In families the early mother-infant attachment is a normal state. Through developmental time a separation process of mother from offspring and offspring from mother leads to a continuum of very little separation to considerable separation. The separation process is both physical and emotional. Under optimal circumstances the child moves out to explore the world and the mother contains her own anxiety so that the offspring can achieve independent functioning that is age appropriate. The child becomes more self-regulating and the mother allows this while maintaining contact with the child (Kerr, 2013).

The mother-offspring pair is but a sliver of a process involving other family members and the degree to which each separates concerns the broader unit as well. Especially important to this process is the father. If the father steps away from active contact with his mate and offspring, it intensifies the involvement between mother and growing child. Each marriage produces offspring who are more or less involved in this process. Some children separate more than others. Extended family members and siblings are also a part of this process. The process goes beyond what any parent wishes to happen. It is automatic. The process in the human family unfolds through interlocking triangles in contrast to the contact of one ant with another. Fixed patterns of contact, distance, conflict, and overriding/accommodating behavior stabilize the family unit. Ants engage in contact, distance, and conflict.

Symptoms and Regression

The development of symptoms also distinguishes human families from ant colonies. Ants do not appear to experience stress and anxiety and do not demonstrate symptoms such as depression, anxiety, grief in the face of loss. Ant colonies do show variation in basic adaptiveness to changing conditions. Human families are uniquely different from ants in the tendency for family members to become symptomatic in the face of potentially stressful circumstances. Intensely interdependent family units or units exposed to ongoing periods of severe stress can show regression in members. As anxiety builds in the system members begin dealing with one another in increasingly reactive ways. Some systems regress for months or years at a time. Ant colonies, on the other hand, do not appear to get anxious. Less adaptive ant colonies will die.

One important question concerning similarities and differences between ants and humans is where to place the emphasis. Some psychological theories of human behavior place the emphasis on the unique differences. It is my opinion that noting the similarities leads to a more realistic view of what it takes for human beings to modify their behavior (Bowen, 1978).

GENERATIONAL INFLUENCE OF COLLECTIVE BEHAVIOR

DMG: Separated from its colony, an ant could not survive. No ant can take care of its own needs on its own. In this sense, an ant is never alone and never functions independently. In humans this is more ambiguous. We can live alone, and people can stay alive for years without much contact with others. But solitary confinement is acute torture, and even in that extreme situation, a person always lives with relations to others, even if they are only imaginary.

LSH: Families operate as single functioning interdependent units and some families are completely governed by the unit and exhibit no independence among members. In such families an individual is unable to observe, reflect accurately, and choose behavior. An example of this process would be a member unable to tell another no.

The relationship process leads to specific patterns in families that regulate the automatic functioning of individual members. Within-species variation in this process leads to variation in adaptiveness. It is speculated that family units significantly lacking in the emotional autonomy of its members provide the basis for intense symptoms such as schizophrenia or severe alcoholism. Human beings use language in complex and interesting ways, but often the language obscures the underlying display of behavior that is a more powerful driver of human behavior than most comprehend. Ant colonies and human families are both regulated by interaction networks. In the human it is the intensity of the process that governs the degree of interdependence. No human being in a family is fully independent of another.

In one sense it is obvious that ant colonies and human families are nothing alike. Humans beings walk on two legs, give birth to one or possibly two or three infants, write books, use the Internet, live in houses, cry, and study ants. Ants, on the other hand, live in the soil, feed and groom larvae, not children. Ants move pupae around. The queen reproduces all of the offspring, which number in the thousands. Each system, however, is an evolved natural system in which the functioning of the individual and unit are continually being balanced. It is therefore useful to contemplate what differences are of consequence.

The human being and possibly some primates appear to be the only species that can come to observe the processes in which they are a part. While it is very difficult for the human to do so, it is possible for one to begin to see a process, one's part in it, reflect on the part that self plays, and to begin to behave differently within the unit.

Human development occurs within the collective behavior of the family. Studies of early childhood experience suggest that the brain and behavior develop in tandem and continue to impact multiple generations of a family through the collective process or through change in the germline epigenome (Champagne, 2013). Trends in families toward greater or lesser stuck-togetherness can be observed through the facts and patterns of the system across generational time.

It is the multigenerational family process that transmits variation in levels of self to offspring. The transmission process is universal in all families as parents automatically pass their own immaturity on to their children. Siblings from the same family, however, tend to function with varying degrees of self. Many complex factors contribute to this difference: the facts in the system at the time of a child's birth, the state of the marital relationship, facts in the broader system, and current stressors at the time of the birth, for example (Bowen, 1978).

Through this process some children emerge from the family with a level of self that is higher than the parents, others may function at a similar level, and some may function below that of their parents. Through this automatic process generational lines of the family emerge with varying degrees of capacity to adapt to the stresses and challenges of living. It is this automatic process that produces a continuum of functioning in all families.

Unlike the ants, human beings can, with great effort, influence this automatic process. An example will illustrate this point. An adult daughter who has been working overtime to look after her depressed mother may find that her mother doesn't function better with all the extra "help." If that daughter is able to stay in contact with the mother, not help, and also not absorb the mother's anxiety, she is onto something significant. Family patterns operate in reciprocal relationship to one another. An over-functioning daughter, for example, unwittingly contributes to reciprocal under-functioning in her parent. The reciprocity, an outcome of anxiety, reduces the likelihood that each can function for self.

Once an individual begins to see the overall pattern and his or her own specific contribution to family difficulty, it becomes possible to see the automatic pattern in other important triangles: marriage and offspring, work systems, even societal patterns. The effort to modify self is lifelong, but the payoffs are significant. A small difference in functioning of an individual within a system can lead to a whole new order of lifestyle.

DMG: A harvester ant colony over time consists of many successive cohorts of worker ants, sisters that are produced by the same mother queen. The queen lives for 25–30 years. The workers live at most a year. So at any time, the ants in the colony are the younger sisters of the ants that were there the previous year.

Old, large colonies behave differently from younger, smaller ones (Gordon, 2000). A harvester ant colony begins with the founding queen, and grows to a size of about 10,000 ants by the time the queen is 5. It then maintains this size for the rest of the queen's life, as the queen continues to produce 10,000 ants year after year. The behavior of older, larger colonies, once they have reached the stable mature size, is more stable and more resilient than that of younger, smaller ones. In response to perturbations, older colonies are more likely to respond in a similar way, over and over. In addition, as the magnitude of perturbation increases, older colonies are likely to respond in a less extreme way. By contrast, younger, smaller colonies respond differently from one incident to another, and as the magnitude of disturbance increases, so does the magnitude of response.

Yet these differences between young, small colonies and old, large ones cannot be due to the experience of older, wiser ants, because the ants in an older colony are not any older than the ants in a younger one. It seems unlikely that the ants themselves transmit any of their experience to their younger sisters. There is one example of this: in red wood ants, an ant tends to use the same foraging trail over and over. Rosengren (1977) showed that old ants go out with young ants on a foraging trail. After the old ant dies in the winter, the younger ant tends to use the trail taken by the older ant. This should not be understood as the older ant telling the younger one anything, but at the colony level it has the consequence that the numbers of ants using foraging trails are preserved year after year.

In harvester ants, however, it seems that all that one group of workers transmits to its younger sisters is the nest. We are now working to learn more about how the shape of the tunnels, as the nest and colony grow older, may shape the flow of ants and thus influence the rate of interactions. The changes in colony behavior as the colony grows older and larger may be due to changes in colony size. In a larger colony, there are more ants for each ant to interact with. The apparent stability of the older colony may be due to the accumulation of more opportunities to interact.

Generations in ants are generations of colonies. Parent colonies produce offspring colonies. This is done in an annual mating aggregation, with virgin queens and males from many colonies represented. They mate and then the newly mated queens go off to found new colonies.

Recently we were able to use genetic variation to identify which colonies are the offspring of which parents. This is the first time this was done for any social insect population, and there were some interesting surprises. Only about 25% of the colonies on the site managed to produce offspring colonies. We are now working to understand why. It is clear that parents and offspring do not live near each other, because the newly mated queens fly a long distance to establish new colonies. Yet it appears that in some ways, offspring resemble their parents in the ways that they respond to environmental conditions. Perhaps what is inherited is a physiological response to heat and humidity.

Natural selection is currently acting on the regulation of foraging behavior in harvester ants. Over the past 15 years of intense drought conditions, it appears that colonies that regulate foraging activity so as to conserve water are having more offspring colonies. However, this is not due to transgenerational influence. Ant colonies are free of memory. A queen leaves her natal colony in the first few weeks of her life and after that, her offspring colony never meets her natal colony again.

LSH: It is useful to reflect on thoughts regarding the transgenerational impact of the family collective next to thoughts regarding ants. The exchange leads directly to a discussion of evolution.

DMG: Evolution is a complicated response to many combined influences, and it occurs in a changing environment that leads to frequent shifts in direction (Gordon, 2013). Although we know this about the evolutionary processes that we can follow, it is still often tempting to invoke evolution on a longer time scale as an explanation for traits that we see in nature. This often leads to misunderstanding. The most common form of misunderstanding is to assume that if we can see the function of something, we have identified the forces that led to its evolution. For example, harvester ant nests have tunnels at the entrance that lead to a chamber where the incoming and outgoing foragers meet. Many important interactions occur in these tunnels. But these gently sloping tunnels also keep water from flowing into the inner nest when heavy rains lead to flooding. We don't know which of these factors were most important in the evolution of nest construction in this species, or whether some other factors were more important than either of these. It's hard to imagine how we would ever find out, since we have no data on the harvester ant tunnels of earlier generations of colonies.

The same misunderstanding can be multiplied in comparisons between species, especially between humans and other animals. Analogies between the behavior of two species and an account of its function doesn't mean that the behavior evolved in the same way in the two species. Of course, we didn't evolve from ant ancestors, and our very ancient common ancestors don't resemble either ants or humans very much. The evolutionary tree is very bushy, with a lot of branches.

In asking evolutionary questions about the behavior of ants or other animals, it seems to me that at best we can look locally and recently, to ask how natural selection is acting now. By tracking colonies and their offspring over many years it's now been possible to do that for harvester ants. For humans, social influences, such as the transgenerational forces that LSH describes above are extremely powerful, interacting with genetic forces but often much more important.

Epigenetic processes are important in human health: one person might have genes that are regulated in such a way that environmental stress tips that person more toward cancer, while another person might have gene regulation that tips them more toward diabetes. Or some people express symptoms of stress in their shoulders and neck, and others in their digestive system, and so on, and it seems likely that this corresponds to some difference in their bodies. This is outside my expertise, just how things happen to look to me, but it seems to me that the environmental forces that do the tipping are probably much more powerful and important to understand than the biological processes, because bad environmental effects have such a strong effect that small differences in genes don't end up mattering as much. For example, we know that xenoestrogens, found in many products including some pesticides, lead to cancers of the reproductive system. It's possible that at small amounts, if two people are exposed to the same amount of pesticides, one will develop breast cancer and not the other because of epigenetic differences. But when the amount of toxin is high enough, the epigenetic variation is swamped and almost anyone would develop cancer. In the same sense, very strong social influences are likely to outweigh genetic differences. A person who genetically has no physical issues, living in very difficult social conditions, such as poverty or an extremely unhealthy family situation, is likely to face many more biological and life challenges than a person with some physical weakness that has very strong social support. Surely the social effects have become increasingly important for the people for whom medicine has provided more and more opportunities to live with mild physical issues. This makes it almost impossible to come to general conclusions about the action of evolution in recent generations of humans over the last 5–10K years in which we have records of human behavior.

LSH: The study of the family over the past sixty years has provided important knowledge regarding relationship systems as primary transmitters of vulnerability to stress reactivity or as transmitters of lower vulnerability. The study of epigenetic processes is adding to the understanding of the link between relationship processes and the vulnerability, under certain conditions, for cancer or depression, for example. While family process does not cause cancer or depression, family process is a powerful regulator of health, both emotional and physical. Under conditions of disruption within a family, individuals with lower levels of defined self are more vulnerable for the development of physical, emotional, or social symptoms. Under unusually calm family conditions, those same individuals may show no signs or symptoms at all (Kerr, 2013).

Highly adaptive individuals will generally be able to adapt to a range of more stressful life circumstances without the development of symptoms. Family interactions play an important regulatory role in the degree to which an individual is able to use higher cognitive processes to regulate the response to stress, thus allowing for more adaptive responses.

The clinical process from this perspective is radically different from a more traditional, individual-oriented perspective on human distress. Motivated individuals can and do increase the level of self through disciplined efforts to observe the automatic process, see their own part in it, and choose to function differently within the pressures of the unit. Therefore, family process is not destiny.

There are, however, limits to the adaptive capacity for all human beings. Current human-induced environmental changes are challenging the capacity of human beings to adapt. Individuals and family units that function at higher levels due to highly developed self will choose behavior that is less destructive of the environment and will adapt more readily to environmental change. There are limits on this capacity for all people as environmental shifts increase in intensity and frequency. It remains to be seen whether the human population will be able or willing to face and address the significant large-scale environmental challenges of the twenty first century.

SUMMARY EXCHANGE OF THOUGHTS

LSH: The exchange in this chapter is an outgrowth of 10 years of dialogue regarding human families and harvester ant colonies. Much of the exchange occurred initially in the field while making direct observations of harvester ants and continued through follow-up conversation in the lab, by phone, or email. Much more is left to learn about harvester ant colonies, human families, and fundamental processes of both. However, the effort to talk across disciplines and species has been worthwhile.

One of the greatest challenges for a family systems clinician is the fact that clinicians are people and therefore subject to the same tendencies as the families they see in their offices. In fact, many individuals who select psychotherapy as a profession have been long time "fixers" and "helpers" in their own families. Some are more objective than others but the pull of feeling states, what one has been trained to see, or the state of one's own family can impact how one interacts in one's office.

The pull of these forces is so great that an ethical requirement of any individual seeking to work with distraught and symptomatic families is to make a long-term research project out of the study of their own family and own tendencies within the system. Otherwise, one can become captive to a clinical family's inaccurate perceptions or a clinical family can become hostage to inaccurate perceptions by a clinician. In addition, the pull to "fix" another is powerful. Those clinicians who resist this pull are more useful to a family as the primary responsibility and capacity for change exists within the family itself.

I have found studying ants to be of notable value in my function as a clinician. Studying ants is a complex process but it is made easier by the fact that ants don't distract with feeling states and language. The process and the whole pattern come slowly into view through experiments designed to shift the environment and observe how the ants modify their behavior. Context is everything to ants and it is not possible to understand ant behavior without understanding this basic principle. Did it rain the night before? Is the nest entrance in disarray? How hot is it today? How many brood are there to feed? What are competing species up to? Where are the seeds today?

By observing ants I have become better able to tune out the distracting noise of feelings and language in order to observe the underlying pattern in a family. That doesn't mean that I am oblivious to feelings. Ignoring feelings is a means of distancing from another. Instead, what I mean is that I am able to remain available while stepping back enough to observe what relationship processes are driving the feelings. Most importantly I am able to carefully consider the context in which a particular behavior and feeling state is occurring. The most fundamental context for the human being is the family.

For example, if a spouse is yelling at their mate today and wasn't yelling a month ago, it is important to find out how, what, when and where conditions changed. No individual is highly reactive all the time and without understanding the conditions in which a behavior arises, a clinician is in the dark. The study of ant behavior has solidified the essential importance of context.

Learning about ants and learning about a family are similar processes. Each is an effort to make natural process objective through a long-term research study. A clinician who is able to maintain a research stance toward a clinical family is more effective than one who tries actively to change a family unit. It is a fact that efforts to change a family make the dilemmas of a family worse. A clinical principle is that a calm, neutral, and relatively objective clinician can assist a family to become more objective about itself leading to greater choice in behavior. A clinician learns about a family, the family learns about itself, and each is informed by the exchange. This is a basic difference in studying ants. Ants don't learn about themselves by humans studying them. They do, however, react to humans tampering with their environment.

DMG: I like how alien ants are, how they never get discouraged and trauma seems to leave no trace once it is over. I appreciate having no relation with them, giving me the opportunity to peer into their world unnoticed. Maybe the habits and skills of observing ants have influenced the way that I interpret interactions among people. As an ecologist I have learned that everything changes and most outcomes are the result of many overlapping processes. Watching ants I see that the colony is nothing more or less than a web of interactions, and it takes a constant effort to stick to what LSH calls "the facts" rather than the assumptions and beliefs that I bring with me. Learning from LSH about human families teaches me a unique perspective on what are the structures in the far simpler relations among ants, and I know that there is much more to learn from this conversation.

REFERENCES

Bowen, M. (1978). *Family theory in clinical practice.* New York: Jason Aronson.
Carter, C. S. (2005). Biological perspectives on social attachment and bonding. In Carter, C. S., L. Ahnert, K. E. Grossmann, S. B. Hrdy, M. E. Lamb, S. W. Porges, & N. Sacher, (Eds.), *Attachment and bonding: A new synthesis.* Cambridge, MA: The MIT Press.
Champagne, F. (2013). The transgenerational influence of social experiences: Implications for brain and behavior. *Family Systems,* 9(2), 154–155.
Gordon, D. M. (2000). *Ants at work.* New York: Norton Press.
Gordon, D. M. (2010). *Ant encounters: Interaction networks and colony behavior.* Princeton: Princeton University Press.
Gordon, D. M. (2013). The rewards of restraint in the collective regulation of foraging by harvester ant colonies. *Nature,* doi:10.1038/nature12137.
Harrison, V. (2013). Contribution of nuclear family triangles to variation in physiological reactivity. *Family Systems,* 9(2), 145–153.
Heinrichs, M., & Domes, G. (2008). Neuropeptides and social behavior: Effects of oxytocin and vasopressin in humans. *Progress in Brain Research,* 170, 337–50.
Ingram, K. K., Pilko, A., Heer, J., & Gordon, D. M. (2013). Colony life history and life time reproductive success of red harvester ant colonies. *Journal of Animal Ecology,* doi:10.1111/1365–265.12036.
Kerr, M. & Bowen, M. (1988). *Family evaluation.* New York: W.W. Norton & Company.
Kerr. M. (2013). The ultra-modern synthesis. *Family Systems,* 9(2). 133–142.
McEwen, B. (2002). *The end of stress as we know it.* Joseph Henry Press, Washington, D.C.
MacLean, P. D. (1978). A mind of three minds: Educating the triune brain. *Yearbook of the National Society for the Study of Education.* (pp. 308–349).
Noone, R. J. (2013). Commentary on use of the term solid self in Bowen theory. *Family Systems,* 10(1), 65–66.
Panksepp, J. (1998). *Affective neuroscience: The foundations of animal and human emotions.* New York: Oxford University Press.
Papero, D. V. (1990). *Bowen family systems theory.* Boston: Allyn and Bacon.
Rosengren, R. (1977). Foraging strategy of wood ants (*Formica rufa* group). Age polyethism and topographic traditions. *Acta Zoologi Fennica,* 149, 1–30.

Part III

EXAMPLES OF THE INFLUENCE OF A FAMILY EMOTIONAL SYSTEMS PERSPECTIVE ON RESEARCH AND PRACTICE

Chapter 13

Emotional Systems and the Regulation of Reproduction with Ovulation as an Illustration

Victoria Harrison

The regulation of human ovulation reflects the counterbalance of reactivity to relationships and the ability to function as a somewhat independent organism that is part of evolutionary heritage. Aspects of ovulation are regulated within the individual female, the function of an indwelling ovarian hormonal cycle. Aspects of ovulation are regulated in response to environmental cues but with far greater reactivity to relationships involved in reproduction and rearing young. Although contraception and reproductive medicine afford women what may appear to be greater thoughtful choice, this chapter describes how one might understand human reproduction in terms of an evolutionary lineage in which reactivity to relationships becomes a predominant influence over ovulation and mediates the impact of the natural environment over reproduction.

PHYLOGENETIC LINEAGE AND OVULATION: EARLY CELL LIFE

Earliest life reproduced without sex or ovulation. Each prokaryote cell replicates by itself. Environmental conditions and food supply in the great expanse of earth influenced rates of reproduction. Reproduction without sex occurs when (1) individuals are scarce, (2) there is little interaction between individuals or species, and (3) there is little species diversity (Trivers, 1985). Asexual reproduction produces greater numbers at a greater rate than sex, which involves relationships.

Over the first three billion years of life, increasing density of cell life and changing environmental conditions contributed toward evolution of complex nucleated cells, a cellular emotional system which integrates relationships.

201

Formerly independent cells join forces within a cell membrane, depend upon each other and are no longer able to survive alone. An animal's DNA is carried in the nucleus of each cell. Nucleated cells both replicate themselves and reserve DNA to fuse with the genetic material of another cell, then divide and produce an individual similar and somewhat different from the parent cells.

Male and female sex cells, and their relationship in reproduction, develop with eukaryotic cells. The germ cells provide future generations species-specific information for the developmental blueprint for life. Meiosis, assures that the number of chromosomes will be halved so that after fusion of egg and sperm the number of chromosomes will be restored to the original. Meiosis begins when the female is an embryo and is suspended until activated again at different times, in different ways in different species. With sexual reproduction, a single set of chromosomes from each gamete form a paired set so that the offspring have a combination of genes from both parents in every cell of the body (Margulis, 1987; Margulis & Sagan, 1986).

With sex, life acquires inheritance, the ability to reproduce individuals and relationships within the cell as well as those relationships that form between multicellular organisms. The transmission of genetic information through sex assures both continuity and diversity for future generations. Sex brings into play differential reproduction. Some cells reproduce. Others do not. Some individuals reproduce. Some do not. Reactivity to the environment and to relationships influence which reproduce, when, how many, and with what results. Cells maintain some independent capabilities and acquire a new degree of togetherness. Relationships become as important to adaptation and reproduction as does the individual.

PHYLOGENETIC LINEAGE AND OVULATION: MARINE INVERTEBRATE

This early form of animal life exhibits variations of asexual and sexual reproduction. The same species can exhibit asexual and sexual reproduction at different times in the lifecycle, depending primarily upon environmental conditions, with some influence from density. Asexual reproduction occurs without the involvement of ova or ovulation. Hermaphrodite reproduction involves the development of eggs without fertilization. Ovulation occurs with direct and indirect fertilization. There are increased number of ova and eggs, less maternal investment in egg development, less protection of eggs, and little coordination between males and females with indirect fertilization. Ovulation and spawning respond to temperature and photoperiod associated with food supply for the larvae.

Internal fertilization, either by direct or indirect means, is associated with fewer ova available for fertilization, greater maternal investment in nutrient rich eggs, fewer eggs, and greater coordination with males for fertilization. Females of some species retain embryos within or upon their body until young emerge more capable of independence. There is no evidence for the evolution of pair bonds or family relations over the lifetime (Pechenik, 1998).

PHYLOGENETIC LINEAGE AND OVULATION: FISH

Vertebrate species in which asexual reproduction is lost adapt to changing conditions through variation in emotional systems involved in reproducing and rearing young. Ovulation in fish illustrates the counterbalance between autonomous hormonal circuits within the female and reactivity to environmental conditions and to relationships. Endogenous rhythms within the female set in motion the development of ova, while the timing and frequency of the release of ova are under the influence of photoperiod, temperature, food supply, and relationships (predators, population density, and mates).

Fertilization for most fish is external and involves coordination of male and female for proximity and timing. Oocytes develop in ovaries regulated by hypothalamic responses to environmental cues that trigger sex hormones circulating through the brain and blood stream. Ovulation, prostaglandin activity, and spawning are activated by photoperiod and temperature and attract males to fertilize the eggs. Female pheromones, released at spawning, attract males, from a distance and stimulate nest building, competition with other males and courtship behavior. Male pheromones attract females from a distance and may induce ovulation in some species. The female produces a greater number of eggs than in species with internal fertilization and each egg is packed with nutrient necessary to support young with little parental care.

In fish that evolved internal fertilization, ovulation, estrogen levels and sexual receptivity are cyclical but there is greater synchrony between males and females. Pheromones and behavior synchronize males and females during courtship, copulation, and fertilization. Males and females may form long term pair-bonds, mate with each other exclusively, and provide care of young together (Connaughton & Katsumi, 1999; Stacey, 1987).

PHYLOGENETIC LINEAGE AND OVULATION: AMPHIBIAN AND REPTILE

Those species responsible for the transition of life from water to land increase maternal investment in development of more complex eggs and in care of eggs and young. Even under conditions of low density, amphibians produce fewer eggs than fish. Ovulation, though maintained by a hormonal circuit within each female, is governed far more by environmental conditions, day length, rainfall, and seasonal timing. There is little involvement between mates or between generations and ovulation is generally not under the influence of relationships. Ovulation may be stimulated, however, by territorial and court-ship behavior, particularly in the few species known for internal fertilization and male care of young (Brown, Morales & Summers 2010; Wake, 1999).

Reptiles assure life on land through amniotic development, eggs with shells, and internal fertilization in which sperms penetrate ova within the female. Ovulation most often occurs seasonally when temperature and day light also stir male sperm development and courtship behavior. Females can store sperm while ova develop and fertilization can occur months after copu-lation. A few species of lizards maintain cell division and egg development without fertilization by sperm and produce offspring with the same genetic makeup as the mother. Interaction between females and with males is associ-ated with stimulation of ovulatory hormones and egg development (Crews, 1983; 1987). Courtship behavior, with visual, tactile, and pheromonal cues, produces cooperation or tolerance for the proximity necessary for copula-tion. Copulation may stir ovulation for some species. A few recently discov-ered species of reptiles are known to maintain contact with mates and with the next generation of young (While, Uller & Wapstra, 2009; Davis et al., 2011).

PHYLOGENETIC LINEAGE AND OVULATION:
MAMMALS & PRIMATES

Variation in relationships between mates, between generations of kin and within the social group is a hallmark of mammalian evolution. Although mammalian brains and biology are adapted to climate, food supply and the natural environment, relationships with kin regulate individual physiology and behavior to an extent that is more pronounced and more prevalent that in more solitary species and phyla. Relationship patterns afford adaptation to food supply, density, and environmental conditions and regulate variation in number of young, in lifespan and development.

Neocortical development also distinguishes mammals from reptile and amphibian ancestors. Neuronal maps in the neocortex store information about the environment and about the organism so that warm-blooded high metabolism mammals can quickly locate food, resources, and relationships. Prolonged development and contact between kin shape patterns of neuronal connections for each species (Allman, 1999). Complex and counterbalancing hormonal and nervous system responses provide individuals within the same species a variety of alternative reactions in regulating ovulation.

Internal fertilization with various relationships between mates, internal retention of eggs and embryo, birth of more mature young with degrees of dependence upon parents, fewer young, lactation, and a wide variety of associations between generations and kin, distinguish mammalian emotional systems. Mammals lose asexual reproduction and external fertilization, which assured larger numbers of young. However mammals demonstrate the widest variety of relationships associated with adaptation and reproduction: solitude with multiple temporary mates and brief contact with young; one male with numerous females and offspring; one female with young and many mates; monogamy; family units within a larger group. Even a eusocial lifestyle, with a single reproducing female supported by males and offspring whose functions are determined largely by the group, has been discovered in the naked mole rat.

Martha McClintock (1987) illustrates the adaptive nature of varied responsiveness to the environment and to relationships through a comparison of the naked mole rat, the prairie and montane vole, the Norway rat, and the golden hamster, all species of rodents who live and breed in different ways. Naked mole rats, a colonial mammal, live in underground burrows where pheromonal, behavioral, and sensory signals regulate the social behavior and physiology of individuals. Workers or sentinels support the colony around one breeding female and the few males who mate with her. Ovarian development is suspended in females who are active in foraging, protecting the burrow, and caring for young. When the mother mole rat dies or is removed, competition rises among worker females. A breeding female, often larger than her sisters, will emerge and begin ovarian development.

Golden hamsters illustrate contrasting coordination between male and female with the natural environment. Individuals live alone in underground burrows. Female fertility is automatic and regular with minimal variation from spontaneous ovulation in four-day estrous cycles. The male hamster's testicular function is sensitive to day length. In the short days of winter, testes shrink. As daylight lengthens, testes grow and sperm production increases. When the solitary male and solitary female emerge from their respective burrows, males are drawn to female scent markings. After about an hour of mating, they part. Mother will bear and rear their pups alone.

For other rodent species, ovarian development occurs in each female, but fertility and reproduction are governed by relationships in other ways. Reproduction is suppressed by social signals from the mother in young prairie voles who remain in the nest of birth. Females become fertile when they migrate, when their mother dies, or when a strange male enters the territory. Within six days of contact with a male, a female will come into heat and mate. Ovulation occurs only in response to mating. When density is low, males and females remain together after mating and rear young together. Under conditions of increased density and competition for scarce resources, female voles live more often in female groups in which female suppression of fertility and mating is increased.

Female Norway rats come into heat whether they live alone or with other females or with groups of both males and females. The estrous cycle involves internally and individually controlled neuroendocrine feedback set in motion at puberty. Relationships, however, regulate the timing of puberty and fertility. When females live together, estrous is synchronized within the social group such that females tend to come into heat and ovulate on the same day. Pheromones from pregnant rats shorten the estrous cycle of other females, increasing the frequency of ovulation. Pheromones from lactating rats and their pups lengthen the cycle and reduce frequency of ovulation in others. When females separate, they begin to ovulate at different times. Fertility for the Norway rat is regulated by pheromonal cues about the social environment and not by length of light or food supply. If the source of light or food is dramatically disturbed, however, the estrous female stops spontaneous ovulation unless she is in direct contact with a fertile male (McClintock, 1987).

Patterns of neuroendocrine activity coordinate the patterns of relationships associated with adaptation to the environment and with reproduction. One study of two closely related species of vole illustrates the ways in which neuroendocrine responses support differences in degrees of connectedness between mates and with young. The monogamous prairie vole is characterized by long-term bonding, preference for close proximity between mates, and by increased care of young by both parents. Interaction between a monogamous pair maintains levels of oxytocin, vasopressin, and dopamine. Prairie voles exhibit elevated cortisol when separated from mate and kin.

The polyandrous montane vole lives in isolated burrows except when mating. The female provides what little parental care is provided. The montane vole does not exhibit elevated cortisol when separated from kin and mate. There are no differences in levels of oxytocin in the two species, but the monogamous prairie vole has more oxytocin receptors located in the forebrain than does the montane vole. The release of oxytocin occurs for prairie vole during courtship and copulation as well as during birth and lactation. Montane voles only release oxytocin during lactation following birth of pups (Young, 2014).

Most of the relationship patterns possible for mammals are evident in primates. The majority of primate species live in complex social groups that range in size from small families to hundreds of individuals. Even among more solitary species, often arboreal, individuals are in contact with a complex social network through olfactory and vocal communications (Smuts

1987). Dixon (1998) describes five major patterns of mating: *monogamy*, in which one male and one female establish a long-term, exclusive bond and in which each contributes toward rearing of young; *polygyny*, in which one male mates with several females and in which the relationships are persistent and consistent; *polyandry*, in which females mate with two or more males, forming long-term and consistent relationships; *polygynandry*, in which several males mate with several females in temporary, non-exclusive relationships within a consistent social group; and *dispersed*, in which several males mate with several females in short-term, non-exclusive relationships but in which individuals live at a distance from each other.

Allman's (1999) survey of the shape and function of primate brains indicate that both diet and relationships correlate with differences in size and complexity of the neocortex. Adaptation to the natural environment (food gathering and metabolism) and adaptation to the relationship system operate together. Those foods that require more work to locate and less work to digest fuel neuronal development in the cortex. Those species in which relationships between mates and young are more prolonged and complex develop a larger neocortex.

Neuronal links develop between the visual system and motor coordination, including muscles that govern facial expression unique to primate species. Prosimian species maintain an equally powerful olfactory communication that can operate over time and distance. Terrestrial apes and monkeys rely more on facial expression and socially mediated information available with greater proximity (Allman, 1999). Communication between individuals expands to include elaborate vocal messages, visual displays, facial expression, gestures, posture, touch, and the use of props (sticks and branches). Conflict and cooperation play a part in survival and reproduction. Alliances form and dissolve. There are friendships and pairs. A variety of dominance hierarchies are species-specific, either between males, females, or for the troop. Species-specific relationship patterns are active in the regulation of reproductive hormones and behavior related to ovulation and fertility.

Seasonal conditions set stereotypical hormonal and metabolic patterns in motion for estrous species of primates. Ovulation occurs most often around estrous. This is also the time when females solicit sex and are receptive to males. Neuroendocrine responses, physiology, and behavior are responsive to relationships with males, as well as to changes in temperature or climate (Hrdy, 1987).

Dixon (1998) describes evidence that New World monkeys are more regulated by relationship within the social group than directly by environmental factors. Relationship patterns such as dominance hierarchy, mating strategies, and cooperation in childcare, coordinate reproduction with resources necessary to support pregnancy and young. Ziegler and Snowdon (2009) describe, for example, how ovulation is suppressed in various ways for daughters in cooperative breeding species who remain with the family to assist in the care of younger siblings. Although daughters begin to mature while living with family, olfactory signals from their mother interrupt the feedback between LH and estrogen. Ovulation will not occur for a female who receives her mother's scent thus extending her availability for childcare and establishing experience in childcare when she does begin to reproduce (Ziegler, 2013).

Lasley and Shideler (1999) describe ways in which the shift from estrous to menstrual cycles in Old World monkeys anticipates human ovulation. "The menstrual cycle is associated with a trend toward decreasing hormonal and increasing neocortical control over behavior as well as prolonged infant dependency, maintenance of the mother-infant unit, continuous female receptivity, and the consolidation of the male-female pair bond" (p. 1060). Relationships between females, between males and females, and in the social group influence primate ovulation and fertility through stress reactions and synchrony in both estrous and menstrual species (Wasser & Barash 1983; Hrdy, 1987). The shift from estrous to menstrual cycles, however, can be viewed as one that operates more automatically and independently within the individual female, while still regulated by reactivity to the social and natural environment, that is, food, family, friends, and foes.

Increased complexity and variation in relationships involved in reproduction accompany increased responsiveness to those relationships and the ways they regulate hormones and physiology of ovulation. It appears that increased ability to function as a somewhat separate individual evolves to counterbalance the extent to which relationships regulate the physiology and behavior of individuals.

THE REGULATION OF HUMAN OVULATION

The human family is a product of uninterrupted reproduction along this phylogenetic lineage. Ovulation for the human female maintains many of the characteristics of her primate past along with differences conferred by expanding and varied relationship systems and greater capacity for self-regulation.

The human female has a pair of ovaries about the size of walnuts that sit on either side of the uterus near the entrance to fallopian tubes. While in utero, the female embryo sprouts her maximum number of oocytes which begin to decline in number until by birth, there are between 40 and 300 thousand ova suspended in the first stage of meiosis until puberty begins. The onset of menses, at between 9 and 18 years of age, follows a rise in adrenal activity which triggers nocturnal pulses of gonadotropin releasing hormone (GnRH) which in turn stimulate pituitary production of follicular stimulating hormone (FSH) and luteinizing hormone (LH). As FSH and LH levels build in the blood stream, they stimulate the ovary to produce estrogen and begin development of ova quiet since birth. As oocytes develop, the ovary increases estrogen production. If uninterrupted, a percentage of eggs will degenerate so that one will erupt from the ovary to be carried by fallopian cilia into and down the fallopian tube to the uterus for possible fertilization. Ovulation is announced by the spike in FSH that registers as an increase in basal body temperature. Ova are released about once a month from alternating ovaries.

Human ovulation is endogenous; it occurs within the individual in a monthly hormonal cycle marked by menstruation unless fertilization occurs. Knobil and Hotchkiss (1988) identified a "neuronal clock" that releases pulses of GnRH and FSH in precise 90-minute cycles. This is maintained within the individual, except when interrupted by pregnancy, lactation, or other experiences, on a monthly basis from menarche to pre-menopause. The monthly cycle itself is not activated by seasonal or environmental factors and it is not dependent upon relationships to stir the hormonal circuitry involved. The timing of ovulation, however, is now known to vary greatly (Martin, 2014).

The extent to which reproduction is sensitive to the natural environment is more of a controversy for the human species than for any other form of life on earth. Martin (2013) summarizes 75 years of research investigating evidence for seasonal patterns in conception and births. A variety of studies indicate historical evidence for birth seasonality but consider seasonal increases in conception to decline for people living in industrialized societies. Seasonal variation in ovulation, in today's world, is still observed in human populations where variation in rainfall, food supply, and energy expended to obtain food can delay menarche, delay ovulation, or prolong lactational amenorrhea (Bronson, 1995). Martin also cites research from reproductive medicine worldwide suggesting that "human breeding seasonality is linked to variation in day length, as in rhesus macaques" (p. 47).

The life history and biological energetics perspective on reproduction developed most extensively by Ellison and Lipson recognizes environmental influences over ovulation based on fluctuations in energy intake and energy expenditure that are mediated by relationships in the family and social group. Ellison's review of research (1990; 2003) on the energetics of ovulation establishes that lactation is not the only relationship factor with an impact on ovulatory hormones. Weight and weight loss, exercise, food supply and energy demands influence the age of puberty and ovulation throughout life. Ovulation may be delayed or inhibited as body weight drops and exertion rises. This is not a function of pathology but a counterbalancing system that enables female reproductive effort to respond to favorable or unfavorable conditions for survival and reproduction.

Caloric intake is not the only way nutrition can affect ovulation. Mathias, a neurogastroenterologist with a specialty in treatment of endometriosis, and his colleagues Franklin, Quast, Fraga, Loftin & Yates (1998) outlined the impact of high carb diet on prostaglandin pathways and blood sugar/insulin that interact with ovulatory hormones to produce symptoms that impact ovulation and fertility. Their observations are consistent with what Lipson (2001) describes as:

> The suite of responses to energetic stress that includes increased insulin sensitivity and increased concentrations of insulin-like growth factor-binding protein 1(IGFBP-1), with both insulin and IFG reduced, elevated cortisol, and reduced thyroid levels. . . . Thus, through their multiple effects, metabolic hormones coordinate the individual's response to stressful conditions by providing signals about how much energy is available to allocate to the demands of survival, growth, maintenance, and reproduction. (p. 241)

An extensive body of research on stress reactions provides clues to ways that ovulation is regulated in the human version of a family animal. Stress reactivity interacts with ovulatory hormones in various ways depending upon the timing and duration of change and challenge. An experience that is perceived as threatening will stimulate hypothalamic production of corticotrophin releasing factor (CRF). CRF activates four response pathways that can impact ovulation in various ways. CRF exerts a direct central nervous system effect upon FSH/LH production. Opiates, produced by the brain in response to rising CRF, can interrupt or inhibit FSH/LH secretion and delay or interrupt ovulation. Rising levels of CRF can also stimulate the pituitary to increase adrenocorticotropic hormone (ACTH) which stirs epinephrine and norepinephrine, the catecholamines that bring the sympathetic nervous system (SNS) into action. This rapid response system produces constriction and dilation of hollow vessel transportation of blood, oxygen, nutrition, waste and ova throughout the body. The smooth muscles of the reproductive organs are richly innervated with SNS fibers affording an immediate impact of stressful experiences. ACTH can also stir pituitary production of prolactin with the experience of sympathy for the plight of another. Elevated prolactin during nursing and as a stress response will interrupt and inhibit the hormones necessary for ovulation.

The impact of CRF on hypothalamic-pituitary-adrenal activity is the pathway most commonly considered to impact reproductive hormones, ovulation, and behavior. If rising levels of CRF are sustained over time, or repeatedly triggered, pituitary secretion of ACTH will stimulate a rise in adrenal production of cortisol which can inhibit pituitary sensitivity to FSH and interrupt hormonal interactions necessary for ovulation (Berga &Yen, 1999).

ACTH also stimulates adrenal production of androgens and testosterone in women associated with interruption or cessation of ovulation and with the shift of behavior toward survival and away from mating and reproduction (Steinberger et al., 1981).

Rising levels of cortisol will alert the pituitary to stop ACTH production and reduce the adrenal activity. When CRF stimulation of ACTH is chronic or ongoing, pituitary insensitivity to cortisol can develop. In the presence of high cortisol over time, the ability to produce ACTH can shut down. When the production of cortisol is suppressed or exhausted in the face of threat, the ability to postpone or delay ovulation may be lost. The inability to interrupt or delay ovulation contributes toward conceptions under duress and in circumstances that threaten successful pregnancy or the survival of mother or young, such as those documented by Shepler-Hughes (1992).

Patterns of relationships in the multigenerational family system transmit information about stress and resources and activate reactions that influence reproduction and ovulation. The family can serve as a support system to mediate natural conditions and minimize energy expended by women who are pregnant or nursing young. The presence of grandmothers to forage and feed a mother or her other children moderates the effort necessary to provide in some seasons. Hawkes' (2004) observations indicate that the presence of a grandmother is associated with more offspring and their improved survival. Paternal grandmothers are associated with greater number of young. Maternal grandmothers are associated with increased survival (Mace & Sear, 2004).

Puberty, with the onset of ovulation, is another example. The age at onset of puberty, the timing of the ovulatory hormonal relay, and thus fertility are under the influence of family relationships as resources or sources of stress. Geronimus (1996) documented earlier reproduction for girls whose mothers and grandmothers experienced difficult circumstances, poor health, and died at younger ages. Early fertility, and presumably ovulation, is one adaptation to a future of adversity and a short lifespan, predicted by past generations.

The absence of the father has also been associated with earlier age at menarche, earlier sexual activity, younger mothers, and shorter marriages (Quinlan, 2003). Ellis et al., (2011) propose that a daughter's reactions to the absence of father and disruption in the marriage reflects a fundamental variation in sensitivity to relationships that can impact ovulation and reproduction over the life course.

The absence of extended family under conditions of adversity may accelerate reproduction in ways described for primates by Wasser and Barash (1983) as loss of the ability to inhibit ovulation. In *Death Without Weeping*, Shepler-Hughes reports the reproductive impact of harsh lifestyle and migration from family under conditions of drought for young men and women living and working in sugar cane plantations. Women conceive and bear young, most of who die before age 2, without the inhibition of ovulation that is generally considered the consequence of such stress (1992).

Other studies indicate that contact and cutoff between generations of family members function to impact reproduction and ovulation. Harrison (2003) published a study of reproduction over seven generations in her own family. More children were born following migration in which one generation lost contact with past generations. The number of children declined as three or more generations of family remained alive and in contact with each other. These observations have not been investigated in enough families to distinguish how relationships between generations impact reproduction or ovulation as a stressor or as a resource.

One careful study (Harrison, 1997a,b) of ovulation patterns and family systems demonstrated that anovulatory cycles occurred for women who had little contact with family other than with their mother. These women reported more constant high levels of stress, in spite of few actual stressful life events. Women who had contact with many family members experienced delayed ovulation during months when stressful life events occurred. The one woman who ovulated on or near Day 14 for three months was actively working on self-regulation of stress reactions while increasing contact with her extended family. Flinn (1989) observed that tension and conflict between several generations of women living in the same household assured only one reproducing female among them.

Clinical work with about 500 women who experienced severe, recurring endometriosis inspired research by this author on stress reactivity and family relationships in the development of symptoms. It was possible to use biofeedback instruments to observe differences in physiological reactivity between families where ovulation and reproduction were disturbed by endometriosis and families without those symptoms. The presence and duration of high stress reactions for close family members appear to disrupt the hormones of ovulation, the immune system, and fallopian tube motility involved in development of endometriosis (Harrison 2005).

Stress reactions are not the only way relationships regulate reproduction. Synchrony in relationships between male and female and within social groups has been documented as another relationship influence. Other than the obvious necessity of sex between men and women for reproduction, the studies by Cutler et al., (1980) of sexual activity and ovulation patterns stand alone in suggesting that hormonal and pheromonal synchrony, in the absence of stress, between men and women influence ovulation patterns and fertility. Regular sexual intercourse between the same two people and contact with male pheromones are associated with higher frequency of fertile ovulatory cycles.

McClintock (1971) has documented menstrual synchrony among women living together in a dorm and identified pheromonal response as the mechanism by which several women cycle together, apparently "driven" by one of the group. Though there is little agreement upon the presence or function of synchrony in human reproduction, for other species this degree of responsiveness produces simultaneous breeding periods which make it easier to protect a group of young from common danger and at the same time intensify competition and pressure within the group. Synchrony also allows social suppression of reproduction at many levels, contributing toward both regulation of numbers and differential selection of those who will produce the next generation of young and those who will assist.

The investment in reproduction and rearing in the next generation varies more widely in the human than for any other family animal. A period of dependence on the family can range from infancy and childhood through adolescence to adulthood. Both future generations and past generations can function as a resource for reproducing and rearing children and as a stressor that inhibits or accelerates reproduction.

There is also evidence that human brain development, education, and intellectual development compete with reproduction in ways that impact physiology and ovulation. An increase in female literacy is associated with decreased birth rate through behavioral changes such as increased age at marriage, knowledge and practice of birth control, and greater control of personal economy (Akman, 2002; Martin & Juarez, 1995). Birth rate statistics suggest that women who pursue graduate school and professional careers delay childbirth until a later age and often rely upon fertility treatment at various points between conception and birth. No current research examines ovulatory functioning during sustained education or professional development however. Education and career pursuits also occur in the context of a family emotional system with complex influences over physiology and behavior.

SUMMARY AND DISCUSSION

Bowen theory views the family as more than a collection of individuals who impact each other like human billiard balls. He observed in his studies of family systems that family members vary in degrees of fusion between emotional reactivity and intellectual functioning that correspond to degrees of fusion in relationships between people. He called this differentiation of self.

There are varying degrees of fusion between the emotional and intellectual systems in the human. The greater the fusion the more life is governed by automatic emotional forces that operate. The greater the fusion between emotional and intellect, the more the individual is fused into the emotional fusions of people around him. . . . It is possible for man to discriminate between the emotions and

the intellect and to slowly gain more conscious control of emotional functioning.
(Bowen, 1978)

At lower levels of differentiation of self, fusion magnifies the reactivity to relationships, constrains self-regulation, and leaves functioning more at the mercy of what operates on automatic in biology and behavior. At higher levels of differentiation of self, individuals are better able to remain separate within their relationships, with a corresponding ability for thoughtful cortical activity, separate enough to influence automatic emotional reactions. This applies in reproduction and in ovulation. The ability of an individual to deal with stress, to accurately evaluate the nature of a threat and the reactions of others, and to respond effectively, will depend in large part upon his or her level of differentiation of self. The ability to maintain self-regulation affords greater resources in regulating ovulation.

Individuals are part of a family emotional system in which emotional fusion between family members and some ability to function as a separate individual mediate reactivity to relationships and to conditions of life. Responsiveness to the natural environment, food supply, climate, land, and water remains, but is mediated by the presence or absence of family and reactivity to patterns in those relationships. The physiology of ovulation is not fixed to depend upon environmental conditions nor upon any one relationship. The hormones and physiology of ovulation operate with degrees of separateness but are under the influence of reactivity to relationships, stress, and resources built into the brain and biology of each individual. Ovulation is responsive to the necessities of survival and adaptation for the individual and for the family of which she is part.

The human family is characterized by increasing involvement between generations of kin, between father, mother and young, between mates, and by increasing variability in those relationships. While mammals represent the widest range of relationships possible between generations and between mates, each species has a relatively fixed, species-specific pattern that does not vary much. Primates have increased variation between individuals within a species-typical pattern. Variability itself is the central feature for humans.

Bowen theory provides a conceptual framework for integrating knowledge about the family emotional systems and regulation of ovulation in clinical practice (Harrison, 2013). The scientific study of how family systems, with various levels of differentiation of self, govern details of ovulation and reproduction remains a lofty goal. What affords flexibility to populate the earth and flourish in the widest variety of conditions also is responsible for the suffering of infertility and over-population. Science, medicine, and advances of civilization that address human suffering would benefit from understanding the regulation of human reproduction in the context of Bowen theory. Ovulation can be an example.

REFERENCES

Akman, W. (2002). Women's education and fertility rates in developing countries, with special reference to Bangladesh. *Eubios Journal of Asian and International Bioethics,* 12, 138–143.

Allman, J. (1999). *Evolving brains.* New York: Scientific American Publications.

Berga, S. L. & Yen, S. S. C. (1999). Reproductive failure due to central nervous system-hypothalamic-pituitary dysfunction. In J. F. Strauss & R. L. Barbieri (Eds.) *Reproductive endocrinology* (pp. 537–595). Philadelphia: Elsevier Saunders.

Bowen, M. (1978). *Family therapy in clinical practice.* (p. 305). New York: Rowman & Littlefield.

Bronson, F. H. (1995). Seasonal variation in human reproduction: Environmental factors. *Quarterly Review of Biology,* June 70(2), 141–164.

Brown, J. L., Morales, V., & Summers, K. (2010). A key ecological factor drove the evolution of biparental care and monogamy in an amphibian. *American Naturalist,* 175, 436–446.

Connaughton, M. A. & Katsumi, A. (1998). Female reproductive system: Fish. In E. Knobil & J. D. Neil (Eds.), *Encyclopedia of reproduction, Vol. 2* (pp. 193–204). New York: Academic Press.

Crews, D. (1983). Regulation of reptilian reproductive behavior. In J. P. Ewert, R. R. Capranica, & D. J. Ingle (Eds.), *Advances in vertebrate neuroethology* (pp. 997–1032). New York: Plenum Press.

Crews, D. (1987). Diversity and evolution of behavioral controlling mechanisms. In D. Crews (Ed.), *Psychobiology of Reproductive Behavior* (pp. 88–119). Englewood Cliffs, N.J.: Prentice-Hall, Inc.

Cutler W. B., Garcia, C. R.; & Krieger, A. M. (1980). Sporadic sexual behavior and menstrual cycle length in women. *Hormones and Behavior,* 14, 163–172.

Davis. A. R., Corl, A., Surget-Groba, A. & Sinervo, B. (2011). Convergent evolution of kin-based sociality in a lizard. *Proceedings of the Royal Society of London*-B 278: 1507–1514.

Dixon, A. (1998). *Primate sexuality.* Oxford: Oxford University Press.

Ellis, B. J., Shirtcliff, E. A., Boyce, W. T., Deardorff, J., & Essex, M. J. (2011). Quality of early family relationships and the timing and tempo of puberty: Effects depend on biological sensitivity to context. *Development and Psychopathology,* 23, 85–99.

Ellison, P. T. (1990). Human ovarian function and reproductive ecology: New hypotheses. *American Anthropologist, New Series,* 92(4), 933–952.

Ellison, P. T. (2003). Energetics and reproductive effort. *American Journal of Human Biology,* 15, 342–351.

Flinn, M. V. (1989) Household composition and female reproductive strategies. In A. Rasa, C. Vogel & E. Voland (Eds.), *Sexual and reproductive strategies.* (pp. 206–233). London: Chapman and Hall.

Geronimus, A. T. (1996). What teen mothers know. *Human Nature,* 7(4), 323–352.

Harrison, V. (2003). Reproduction and emotional cutoff. In P. Titleman (Ed.), *Emotional cutoff* (pp. 245–272). New York: Haworth Press.

Harrison, V. (2005). Stress reactivity and family relationships in the development and treatment of endometriosis. *Fertility Sterility*, 83, 857–864.

Harrison, V. (1997a). Family emotional process, reactivity and the regulation of ovulation. *Family Systems*, 4(1), 49–62.

Harrison, V. (1997b). Patterns of ovulation, reactivity and family emotional process. In C. S. Carter & I. I. Lederhendler (Eds.), *The integrative neurobiology of affiliation* (pp. 522–524). New York Academy of the Sciences Annals Vol. 807.

Harrison, V. (2013). A wider lens: Bowen theory and a natural systems view of symptoms. *CAPA Quarterly*, 1, 10–13; 34.

Hawkes, K. (2004). The grandmother effect. *Nature,* 11(428), pp. 128–129.

Hrdy, S. B. & Whitten, P. L. (1987). Patterning of sexual activity. In B. Smuts, D. L. Cheney, R. M. Seyfarth, R. W. Wrangham, & T. T. Struhsaker (Eds.), *Primate societies* (pp. 370–384). Chicago: University of Chicago Press.

Knobil, E. & Hotchkiss, J. (1988). The neuroendocrine control of ovulation. *Human Reproduction*, 3(4). 469–472.

Lasley, B. & Shideler, S. (1999). Nonhuman primates. In E. Knobil & J. D. Neill. (Eds.), *Encyclopedia of reproduction, Vol. 3* (pp. 1058–1063). New York: Academic Press.

Lipson, S. F. (2001). Metabolism, maturation, and ovarian function. In P.T. Ellison (Ed.), *Reproductive ecology and human evolution* (p. 241). New York: Aldine de Gruyter.

Mace, R. & Sear, R. (2004). Are humans communal breeders? In E. Voland, A. Chasiotis, & W. Schiefenhoevel (Eds.), *Grandmotherhood–the evolutionary significance of the second half of female life.* (pp. 143–159). New Brunswick, NJ: Rutgers University Press.

Margulis, L. & Sagan, D. (1986). *The origins of sex.* New Haven: Yale University Press.

Margulis, L. (1987). *Symbiosis in cell evolution.* New York: Freeman Press.

McClintock, M. (1987). A functional approach to the behavioral endocrinology of rodents: Diversity in the social regulation of fertility. In D. Crews (Ed.), *Psychobiology of reproductive behavior* (pp. 176–203). Englewood Cliffs, NJ: Prentice-Hall.

McClintock, M. (1971). Regulation of ovulation by human pheromones. *Nature,* 12 (392), 177–9.

Martin, T. C. & Juarez, F. (1995). The impact of women's education on fertility in Latin America: Searching for explanations. *International Family Planning Perspectives,* 21(2).

Martin, R. (2013). *How we do it: The evolution and future of human reproduction.* New York: Basic Books.

Mathias, J. R., Franklin, R., Quast, D. C., Fraga, N., Loftin, C., & Yates, L. (1998). Relationship of endometriosis and neuromuscular disease of the gastrointestinal tract. *Fertility Sterility*, 70, 81–88.

Pechenik, J. A. (1998). Marine invertebrates, modes of reproduction. In E. Knobil & J. D. Neill (Eds.), *Encyclopedia of reproduction Vol. 3* (pp. 98–103). New York: Academic Press.

Quinlan, R. (2003). Father absence, parental care, and female reproductive development. *Evolution and Human Behavior,* 24, 376–390.

Shepler-Hughes, N. (1992). *Death without weeping: The violence of everyday life in Brazil.* Berkeley, CA: University of California Press.

Smuts, B. (1987). *Primate societies.* Chicago: University of Chicago Press.

Stacey, N. E. (1987). Roles of hormones and pheromones in fish reproductive behavior. In D. Crews (Ed.), *Psychobiology of reproductive behavior* (pp. 28–60). Englewood Cliffs, NJ: Prentice-Hall.

Stebbins, R. C. & Cohen, N. W. (1995). *A natural history of amphibians.* Princeton, NJ: Princeton University Press.

Steinberger, E., Smith, K. D., & Rodriguez-Rigau, L. J. (1981). Hyper-androgenism and female infertility. In P. G. Crogsignani & B. Rubin (Eds.), *Endocrinology of human infertility: New aspects* (pp. 327–342). London, England: Academic Press.

Trivers, R. (1985). *Social evolution.* Menlo Park, CA: The Benjamin/Cummings Publishing Co.

Wake, M. (1999). Amphibian reproduction: Overview. In E. Knobil & J. D. Neill (Eds.), *Encyclopedia of reproduction* (pp. 161–166). New York, NY: Academic Press.

Wasser, S. K. & Barash, D. P. (1983). Reproductive suppression among female mammals: Implications for biomedicine and sexual selection theory. *Quarterly Review of Biology,* 58(4), 513–38.

While, G. M., Uller, T., & Wapstra, E. (2009). Family conflict and the evolution of sociality in a non-avian vertebrate. *Behavioral Ecology,* 20, 245–250.

Young, L. J. (2014). The chemistry between us: Brain mechanisms of social bonding. Paper presented at Bowen Center for the Study of the Family 51st Annual Symposium. Washington, D.C.

Ziegler, T. E. & Snowdon, C. T. (2009). The endocrinology of family relationships in biparental monkeys. In P. T. Ellison & P. B. Gray (Eds). *Endocrinology of social relationships* (p. 142). Cambridge: Harvard University Press.

Ziegler. T. E. (2013). Social effects via olfactory sensory stimuli on reproductive function and dysfunction in cooperative breeding marmosets and tamarins. *American Journal of Primatology,* 75(3), 206.

Chapter 14

Mating and Parental Care

The Influence of Gender on the Primary Triangle

Margaret G. Donley

The formation of enduring relationships between parents and children and between mates is an integral part of the human family. Indeed, pair-bonds are particularly important in mammalian monogamy where they provide the core of the family unit (DeVries et al., 1996). Many assume that human relationships are unique in nature and involve processes too complex to exist in other mammals. However, clinicians know that people struggling in their marriage and/or family, have difficulty accessing the most complex and human aspects of the brain—the prefrontal lobes of the cerebral cortex—when dealing with relationship problems. Ask any person who knows s/he should stop an affair, but continues it; or any mother who cannot stop focusing on a child, even though she knows it makes the situation worse. This is not surprising given that our cortex was added later in evolution and does not always exert control over our primitive emotional states (Carter, 2011).

Couples and families enter therapy primarily because their emotional reactivity contributes to relationship patterns that are increasingly unproductive and inflexible. Although emotional processes drive this relationship intensity, it is by no means uniquely human. What people say and talk about may be distinctly human, but how they act and react is based, in part, in the neuroendocrine system that the human shares with other pair-bonded mammals. Since families are held together by social bonds, it makes sense that the research on the neurochemical systems involved in attachment, can contribute important information to understanding how marriages and families function.

The purpose of this chapter is to examine how the neurobiology of social affiliation and pair-bonding can better inform clinicians in their work with couples and families. How the anxiety and stress that impact relationship dynamics between men and women share common features with the behavior patterns evident in other pair-bonded mammals. With this in mind, I will highlight a particular relationship pattern that has emerged repeatedly from my clinical work with families: *Under conditions of stress, men tend to automatically move towards a woman for well-being, while women tend to automatically move towards their children.* This chapter will explore the neurobiological underpinnings of this relationship pattern.

To better understand the connection between stress and attachment, the first section of the chapter will adopt an evolutionary perspective in considering the ways in which positive social bonds reduce stress. The second reviews the literature on pair-bonding in mammals with regards to the differing influence neuropeptides have on males and females. The third section will explore how gender differences in stress reactivity and affiliation provide a way of thinking about how the primary triangle in the human family operates to manage anxiety.

I conclude this chapter by considering how research from the field of neurobiology can be applied to clinical work with couples and families. Understanding how family processes are rooted in the neurobiology of social affiliation and pair-bonding offers insights into how anxiety operates through triangles to regulate the family emotional unit.

STRESS AND ATTACHMENT

From an evolutionary perspective, social attachments function to facilitate reproduction, provide a sense of security, and reduce feelings of stress (Carter, 1998). Attachments are essential for survival—without social relationships we suffer, get depressed, and fail to thrive. Very few things are as painful as losing someone we love. Feeling both the comfort of being attached and the distress over losing an attachment are built into the emotional core of our nervous system and evolved long before what we think of as modern cognition (Carter & Porges, 2013).

One reason relationships exert such a powerful influence over us is because they function to attenuate our very sensitive stress response system. A principal factor in motivating us to engage in social bonds is that they make us feel secure and less stressed in the face of threat. Humans, and other pair-bonded mammals, are unique in the degree to which their stress response system is influenced by social factors. This heightened sensitivity is mediated in part by the fact that pair-bonded mammals have higher basal levels of stress hormones (adrenal corticoids) than do non-monogamous animals (Carter, 1998). This is one reason why the social buffering of the stress response is limited to species that have selective social attachments (DeVries, 2002). The long and short of it is that evolution designed pair-bonded animals (like humans) to be exquisitely sensitive to social threats and/or loss of social contact. Stress, therefore, encourages bonding because those attachments are calming.

Neuropeptides and Attachment

How do social relationships decrease stress and anxiety? Two neuropeptides central to understanding how social bonds develop, and how these bonds impact the stress response, are oxytocin (OT) and arginine vasopressin (AVP). There is strong evidence that in mammals, maternal-infant bonding and adult pair-bond formation rely, in part, on these two neuropeptide hormones (Panksepp, 1998; Young & Wang, 2004; Carter, 1998). Both are important in promoting social engagement and are essential in the expression of what we think of as love. What appears evident is that OT and AVP are key players, along with the brain's reward system, in the development and maintenance of love relationships.

Oxytocin and AVP promote social engagement in a number of ways. Not only are they implicated in social memory, but they also down-regulate reactivity of the hypothalamic-pituitary-adrenal (HPA) axis (Carter, 1998). One defining characteristic of pair-bonded mammals is that they a have a stress response when faced with social separation. When reunited, the stress response is turned off due to the release of OT and activation of the reward system. In essence, the activation of the HPA axis by separation is a protective in maintaining social bonds and is one reason why there is a strong association between the stress response and the expression of social behaviors and attachment. Oxytocin, and in some cases AVP, also help promote social interactions by decreasing anxiety and fear, which results in an increased ability to tolerate stress (DeVries, 2002; Carter & Porges, 2010). The ability to turn off fear and anxiety is a necessary prerequisite for pair-bonding, parental behavior, and sexual expression.

Although OT and AVP play a key role in social bonding, these peptides do not act alone. The motivational aspects of social bonding, including both pair-bonding and parental attachment, inevitably involve the activation of the reward system (Panksepp, 1998). The endogenous opioid system (the "reward system") plays a substantial role not only in pair-bonding, but also in human parental care where the emotional component of engagement is highly rewarding (Fernandez-Duque et al., 2009).

There is a tight coupling between attachment and the neuronal system for reward. Unlike promiscuous animals, those that form pair-bonds have higher densities of OT and AVP receptors in the brain regions associated with the reward system (DeVries, 2002). These peptides are positioned to increase the brain's sensitivity to opioids, which intensify the sense of pleasure one receives from social bonds. Therefore, it is not just OT and AVP that are important to bonding, but rather where their receptors are located in the brain that makes a difference between attachment and non-attachment.

The sensitivity people have to their attachments, along with their reactivity to relationship shifts, is generally what motivates people to seek out therapy. The more these bonds are threatened (by either real or imagined threats) the more distressed people become and the more pressure they exert on the relationship in an effort to restore comfort and security. How this occurs in people has important implications for understanding the development of symptoms within families.

GENDER DIFFERENCES AND ATTACHMENT: THE IMPACT OF NEUROPEPTIDES

The way stress impacts relationships is not gender neutral. There are some interesting details of OT and AVP that warrant further examination in so far as they suggest potential differences in the way males and females manage stress. Although both neuropeptides are associated with social behavior, parental care, and pair-bonding, their actions are often in opposite directions (Carter, 1998). For example, OT tends to promote positive social bonds by decreasing reactivity to stress and exerting a calming effect. Oxytocin is implicated in nurturing and supportive behaviors, which are particularly evident in parental care. In contrast, AVP is associated with arousal, vigilance, and defense behaviors (such as territoriality and mate guarding), equally important components of attachment behavior (Carter & Porges, 2010).

Oxytocin and AVP are differentially weighted in males and females. Females have more extensive OT circuits (under the control of estrogen) and men have a higher prevalence of AVP circuits (under the control of testosterone) (Panskepp, 1998). These peptides contribute to gender differences that are observable in the psychological traits and behavior of males and females (Panksepp & Biven, 2012). Examples of these differences in males and females can be seen in their sexual, pair-bonding, and social behavior.

Sexual Behavior

Higher levels of AVP in males account for many of the gender differences seen in the social behavior of monogamous prairie voles (Carter, 1998). For example, AVP is important in facilitating many aspects of male sexual persistence, such as territoriality, vigilance, and aggression (Panskepp, 1998; Carter, 1998). In pair-bonded species, mating actually changes the male brain by increasing AVP receptors in the brain (Young & Alexander, 2012). Vasopressin regulates pair-bonding in male prairie voles and if it is blocked males will not form a pair-bond (Wang & Aragona, 2004). Unlike females, who will form a pair-bond after extended cohabitation without mating, males require mating for pair-bond formation (Wang & Aragona, 2004). Not surprisingly, stress increases sexual motivation in male rats (Lepton & Stewart, 1996) and pair-bond formation in male prairie voles (DeVries et al., 1996) largely due to AVP, which biases the male brain towards sex (Young & Alexander, 2012). In addition to promoting sexual arousal, AVP is also implicated in the defense behavior of males (e.g., mate guarding), a significant indicator of attachment. Given the effect of AVP, it is not surprising that when male sexual desire has no outlet, it can promote feelings of tension and frustration (Panksepp & Biven, 2012).

The release of OT following ejaculation enables males to demonstrate nurturing behaviors (Panskepp, 1998). This may account for why men are more inclined towards nurturing behavior following sex. The relation between sexual behavior and OT has also been observed in nonhuman primates. In cotton-top tamarins (a nonhuman primate), OT levels in males are related to the frequency of sexual behavior, whereas with females, OT levels are more related to the amount of contact and grooming they received from the male (Snowdon et al., 2010).

Indeed, male and female sexualities are organized differently within the brain (Panksepp, 1998). For example, AVP, so strongly implicated in male sexual arousal, actually inhibits sexual arousal in females, perhaps due to the fact that it increases aggression. In contrast, OT is key to a female's sexual receptivity–both in the courting and copulatory phases (Panksepp, 1998).

Furthermore, there is evidence to suggest an overlap between brain circuits involved in the stress response and ones involved sexual behavior (Young & Alexander, 2012). For women sexually receptive behavior is tied to the brain's stress response. Research suggests that married women who are stressed are less interested in sex compared to married men who are stressed (Bodenmann et al., 2007). Moreover, only 25% of women report a desire for sex to relieve tension as compared to 80% of men (Baumeister et al., 2001). For women high levels of estrogen (e.g., during ovulation) tend to dampen down the stress response (Lindheim et al., 1992) enabling them to become more interested in sex. In other words, turning down anxiety can help females become more sexually receptive. In contrast, stress affects males' sexual interest differently, as indicated by studies that suggest mild-to-moderate anxiety promotes sexual arousal in men (Barlow et al., 1983).

One characteristic of pair-bonded primates is that they have sex throughout a female's cycle. Frequent sex likely enables pair-bonded adults to maintain their relationship and provide reassurance when the relationship is challenged. Regular sexual activity may enhance the circuits underlying bonding, thus strengthening the pair-bond (Young & Wang, 2004).

Examining whether men are more interested in sex than women is germane to the observation raised initially of whether men focus on women for well-being. For men, sex, love, and aggression are inextricably mixed in the brain (Young & Alexander, 2012) and there is evidence that strong emotions and heightened anxiety increase sexual responses in males (Dutton & Aron, 1974). Since sex may be one way that males experience stress relief (due to an increase in OT), focusing their attention on females as a way of managing anxiety makes sense. A literature review by Baumeister et al., (2001), supports the idea that men think about sex more often, report more frequent arousal, and have more fantasies about sex than women. Studies that included a large sample of men, with all levels of relationship longevity, also confirm that men desire more sex than they were currently having in their relationships as compared to women (Baumeister et al., 2001).

Pair-Bonding

In pair-bonded species, mating is generally necessary for the formation of a pair-bond. Following mating, males become territorial and selectively aggressive towards intruders (Carter & Porges, 2010; Carter 1998). As noted above, mating influences AVP levels in males and AVP plays a key role in a male's ability to form a pair-bond. As with sexual behavior, AVP has little effect on a female's interest in forming a pair-bond, at least in prairie voles. Rather, the development of partner preference in a female relies almost exclusively on OT. Endogenous OT, released during mating, facilitates pair-bonding in females. In fact, OT is so important that without it females will not form a pair-bond (Insel & Hulihan, 1995). Whereas OT is the "pair-bond hormone" for females, AVP is the "pair-bond hormone" for males.

Stress also impacts pair-bond formation differently in males and females. For instance, stress facilitates partner preferences in male prairie voles, whereas it has the opposite effect on females (DeVries et al., 1996; Carter, 1998). When male prairie voles are placed in stressful conditions they tend to form stronger bonds with a female. In contrast, a stressed female is disinterested in forming a pair-bond with a male and instead tends to develop an increased preference for other females and her natal nest (Carter, 1998).

In tamarins, males work harder to maintain the pair-bond than do females (Snowdon & Ziegler, 2007). A female's presence can function as a calming agent when a male is faced with a threat (Bosch et al., 2008; Kaiser et al., 2003). These differences were also seen in the way pair-bonded mammals responded to loss. For example, males had a significant grief response when separated from their bonded female; whereas females had an equally intense response to being separated from any partner, including other females (Bosch et al., 2008; Young & Alexander, 2012). Research on monogamous guinea pigs yielded similar results. A male's hormonal stress response can only be ameliorated by the presence of his partner, whereas the female's can be reduced by familiar females in addition to her mate (Kaiser et al., 2003).

The literature that examines differences relating to social support in marriages is clear: men rely on their wives as confidants more than women rely on their husbands. According to Antonucci & Akiyama (1987) women have a large variety of people in their social networks whereas "the network structure of men appears considerably more limited, consisting predominantly of a single person, the wife" (p. 738). Men tend to invest their emotional capital in their partner, whereas women equally rely on the emotional support of other women (Young & Alexander, 2012). Similarly, men receive more support from women than women receive from men (Schwarzer & Gutierrez-Dona, 2005). And, lastly, when the wife is stressed, both husbands and wives are less happy in the marriage. However, when husbands are stressed, only the husbands are less happy (not the wives), suggesting that wives' stress may play a greater role in shaping the family atmosphere (Neff & Karney, 2007).

There is ample evidence that marriage is more protective for men than for women (Kalmijn, 2007). The loss of a spouse is known to be more damaging to the physical and mental health of men than it is to women (Stroebe & Stroebe, 1983). Furthermore, men have more difficulty with the loss of their spouses than women do (Helsing & Szklo, 1981). Women, however, seem to benefit more from the support of other women, including family and friends (Taylor et al., 2000; Taylor, 2006). Collectively these studies suggest that social contacts have a stronger protective benefit for women then for men.

Social Relationships

A female's inclination to move towards relationships under stress is supported by a number of studies that have looked at the way isolation affects males and females differently (Palanza, 2001; McCormick et al., 2005; Grippo et al., 2007). For example, male and female rodents are affected differently by housing conditions. If you crowd males, their stress response increases, whereas crowded females are less stressed than those housed separately (Brown & Grunberg, 1995). Similar differences were also seen in prairie voles and guinea pigs, leading some to speculate that the female's stress response is more sensitive to social isolation than is the male's. Such studies suggest that females may be more susceptible to social stressors than males and more vulnerable to the consequences of social isolation (Palanza, 2001; McCormick et al., 2005; Grippo et al., 2007).

The fact that OT is manufactured in greater quantities in the female brain has led to speculations that men and women have different ways of responding to stress. For instance, men, who produce more AVP, tend to demonstrate a "fight/flight" response to stress, in contrast to women, who are more likely to "tend and befriend," that is, to affiliate under stress (Taylor et al., 2000). Taylor's argument is based on neuroendocrine evidence from animal and human studies that suggest that OT plays a more important role in influencing women's social behavior than men's, especially under stress (Taylor, 2006). According to one analysis, 25 out of 26 studies revealed consistent findings that women, in contrast to men, move towards affiliation as a coping mechanism (Taylor, 2006). In general, women seek safety with other women.

Although the study of pair-bonds in other animals cannot allow us to fully understand the complexity of human attachments, they do offer insights into the neural systems that form the foundation of human social behavior. The fact that pair-bonding co-occurs with biparental care (both parents engaged in rearing the young) is an example of how these neuropeptides, in conjunction with activation of the reward system, have evolved to influence social behavior.

THE FAMILY AS A SYSTEM

Mating and Parental Care

Paternal care is relatively rare in mammals. Evidence from both human and nonhuman research suggests that when paternal care exists, it hinges on the pair-bond relationship, which notably influences paternal responsiveness and care of offspring (Snowdon & Ziegler, 2007; Jean-Baptiste et al., 2008; Fernandez-Duque et al., 2009). Unlike the female brain, that has deeply embedded maternal circuits that prepare females to care for infants (Panksepp, 1998), paternal behavior evolved through different mechanisms. Although the evolutionary process leading to paternal care is beyond the scope of this paper, it is clear that biparental care co-occurs in mammals that form pair-bonds. In many cases male care of young is often induced through mating and cohabitation (Terleph et al., 2004). The male's affiliation with the female during her pregnancy and postpartum influences not only his physiology (through hormonal shifts) but also his behavior in ways that facilitate paternal involvement. For example, in monogamous rodents paternal care and responsiveness increase in response to cohabitation with a female (Brown et al., 1995; Jean-Baptiste et al., 2008), suggesting that the sensory stimulus from the female modifies the male's behavior toward the offspring.

Evidence that paternal behavior is related to the pair-bond relationship has also been found in nonhuman primates. For example, hormones implicated in paternal behavior in marmosets and tamarins increased as a result of the cues the male received from the pregnant female and, in some cases, from the increase in affiliation prior to birth. This research by Snowdon & Ziegler (2007) raised the question of a communication system "whereby the fetus communicates through the mother to induce changes in their father's hormones to prepare for birth" (p. 52). As with monogamous rodents, paternal effort in nonhuman primates was influenced by the quality of the pair-bond. There is reason to believe, as Snowdon & Ziegler (2007) suggest, that the same principles of "family dynamics" apply to the human species.

The expression of paternal care in humans can range from nonexistent on one end, to close intimacy and direct care on the other (Fernandez-Duque et al., 2009). Nonetheless, when human paternal care is evident, it is remarkably similar to how paternal care is demonstrated in other monogamous mammals. For instance, research suggests that men are willing to invest in the offspring of their current mate, even in the absence of genetic relatedness (Anderson et al., 1999). Evidence that males' provide care to their partner's offspring (in the absence of genetic relatedness) is considered by some to be an indication of a primary interest in mating (Anderson et al., 1999; Fernandez-Duque et al., 2009) and further emphasizes the idea that male-infant care may have evolved as a form of mating effort rather than paternal investment (Smuts & Gubernick, 1992). Human studies echo findings in non-human primates confirming the association between a strong pair-bond and paternal behavior (Snowdon & Ziegler, 2007). Hewlett (1992) found that the time the father spent with the mother predicted paternal behavior as measured by his involvement with his children. This is consistent with findings from Belsky (1979) that the marital relationship influenced the father's involvement with his children. There exists, then, a large body of research that illuminates how the mother influences the father-child relationship (DeLuccie, 1995; Fagan & Barnett, 2003).

Nowhere is there more evidence of how the mother influences the father's relationship with children than in the literature relating to divorce. Fathers have less contact with their adult children than fathers who did not divorce; whereas for mothers the effects of divorce are small (Stewart, 1999). In addition, a father's re-marriage predicts even less contact with his biological children as compared to men who remain in the original marriage (Kalmijn, 2007). Not surprisingly, wives are more influential in regulating the father's involvement with children than are husbands in influencing their wives in parenting (Belsky, 1979; DeLuccie, 1995). Whether or not a couple is married, mothers have an influence on men's involvement in their children's lives, further buttressing the idea that the mother's support is a key factor in the father's involvement with their children (Fagan & Barnett, 2003). Although these studies provide empirical support for the idea that the pair-bond relationship significantly influences the father's behavior, it would be inaccurate to think of this as a one-way process. Parent-child relationships are continuously influenced by the relationship between the parents—whether they are married or divorced.

The relationship between parents impacts their children. The theoretical framework used to explain this has historically been attachment theory (Hazan & Shaver, 1994). Although this perspective made advances in understanding relationship interdependence, it lacks the theoretical groundwork for how the primary triangle operates in the family emotional unit to regulate anxiety and stress.

The Primary Triangle

A primary assumption of Bowen theory is that the family relationships are not only interdependent, but they functions as an emotional unit (Bowen, 1978). One concept of the theory, the triangle, provides a theoretical way of understanding how the relationships within the mother-father-child system function to manage anxiety and tension.

The concept of the triangle rests on the observation that any relationship between two individuals is inherently unstable and easily disturbed by the forces within and outside of it (Bowen, 1978). Disturbances in the balance of a relationship can trigger anxiety, causing one person to initially seek more togetherness to restore comfort. The pull for togetherness in one is often met with reactive distancing in the other. The process revolves around emotional attachment and the way anxiety impacts attachment (Kerr & Bowen, 1988). A three-person system has a higher level of flexibility and adaptability to deal with anxiety.

The differences in how males and females automatically move to relieve stress and anxiety have implications for how this triangling process unfolds. Whereas women generally rely on their children, family and friends for support, men more likely tend to put their principal emotional capital into their female partner. The fundamental differences in how males and females function contribute to some predictable ways that triangles take shape as tension arises within families. Triangling often becomes more intense and fixed in marriages where spouses have a strong reliance on a relationship to calm anxiety, and where an individual's well-being is exclusively tied to the connection with his/her mate and/or child. How much a person is governed by a relationship is influenced by the family of origin and is referred to in Bowen theory as differentiation of self (Bowen, 1978), and has an impact on how intense and fixed certain patterns, such as triangles, become within families.

Triangling essentially helps to regulate the development of stress and chronic anxiety within the family unit. If the mother is especially anxious, she can focus on the child to stabilize her functioning, often leaving her husband in an outside position in the triangle. A male's sensitivity to the relationship with his wife can take the shape of avoiding conflict and/or working to please her by focusing on the children. His sensitivity to her needs, and his interest in pleasing her, can stabilize the marriage. However, if she begins to feel smothered by his anxious need to help, she will likely react by pulling away and withdrawing from him even more.

On the other hand, if the wife's affection and sexual interest in her spouse have diminished, the triangle can unfold differently. The husband's sensitivity and vigilance may result in emotional distance and anger towards her. This withdrawal will often extend to the children. The growing emotional distance in the marriage will propel the mother to move towards her children and become even less interested in affection and/or sex. The triangle involving a child and his/her parents is considered the "primary triangle" in Bowen theory. A person's development occurs within this primary triangle and it establishes the relationship patterns for that person that remains relatively fixed in all relationships (Bowen, 1978).

Men are particularly sensitive to their wives and often respond to the children based on emotional state of the marriage. Because mothers are most often the gatekeepers to the children, men often relate to their children based on the cues they receive from their wives. A common scenario, illustrating triangles, is one where the father, based on his sensitivity to his wife's upsetness with the children, punishes them. This is distinctly different from how a mother often reacts when she finds her husband upset with the children. Frequently her immediate reaction is to think that her husband must have done something wrong to make the children so difficult.

In situations where women are overfocused on their children, they think less about sex and more about how they need help with raising the children. Men, on the other hand, who are often heavily invested in their wives, think more about sex/affection and less about the details of their children's lives. This can often lead to growing resentment and blaming the other for the problem without seeing one's part in creating it. The focus on the other can lead to escalating reactivity that can contribute to intense conflict or emotional cut-off/withdrawal. This reactivity is fueled by the sensitivity each has to the other, growing out of the intensity in the attachment.

CLINICAL IMPLICATIONS

Couples seeking therapy often blame each other for the stated problems and describe themselves as having "communication problems." It is a challenge to sort through the content of what is said to get to an understanding of the relationship dynamics driving the process. The ability to see how relationships function to regulate people, by providing security and stability, is an essential step in clarifying the nature of the disruption that creates reactivity. In marriages with children, this often involves understanding how males and females automatically move to manage the tension within their relationship by recruiting others into the process, via triangles.

There appears to be certain themes that arise in marriages (with children) that seek therapy. Women, for example, frequently complain that their husbands do not help enough, are disengaged and too focused on sex. Men, on the other hand, often complain that their wives are too focused on their children's needs, critical of their attempts to help, and no longer interested in sex. These themes, though not exhaustive, speak to the common genders differences that manifest themselves in the clinical setting.

Clinical Case

The following case illustrates the points presented in this chapter. Mr. and Mrs. Blunt presented in the initial session with "communication problems" and "tension" that had been growing for over four years. Married for 12 years, they have three children (ages 9, 6, 4) and both work full time in professional jobs. Based on comments of their previous therapist, Mrs. Blunt reported that her husband had a "narcissistic" personality, focused on his needs, rather than the needs of the family. Mr. Blunt confirmed that he was probably "self-centered" but that his family was the most important thing in his life. He expressed frustration that his wife was overly judgmental of him and that she cared more about the children, parents, and her job than him.

Mr. Blunt was an only child and his parents were deceased. His father died over 10 years ago and his mother died six months after the birth of their last child. He has little contact with a maternal aunt and his two cousins. Mrs. Blunt is the oldest of three children, with two younger sisters. Her parents reside in the area and often help with child care. She has frequent contact with her siblings. Mr. Blunt has a conflictual relationship with his wife's mother (with whom Mrs. Blunt is very close), which causes additional tension in the marriage.

Mr. Blunt is anxious that his wife is not attracted to him and at times worries that she will leave him. Since the birth of the third child, the couple has rarely had sex (2–3 times a year). Mrs. Blunt states she is not interested in having sex as she has "too much on her plate" with the kids and her job, and all she wants to do at night is sleep. She believes her husband is too self-centered, focused on needing affection/sex more than on the needs of the family and children.

Formulation of Presenting Problem

Although the knowledge presented in the preceding sections does not address the many details of how to manage oneself as a therapist, it does inform a way of thinking about human behavior that is based more on what people do, rather than what people say. It offers a way for a clinician to begin to clarify the emotional process and reactivity between spouses. For example, teaching couples about the differences between the way males and females automatically move as tension increases enables people to see the process between them in a less personal and more objective manner. This is particularly true with sex, which can become emotionally charged in a relationship. At its best, this dovetails into a clinician's ability to teach about emotional systems and assist people in thinking about their situation and controlling their emotional reactivity (Papero, 1990). Lastly, and perhaps most importantly, it can help the clinician to develop neutrality when faced with highly emotionally charged issues in a clinical session. The following ideas from the research above are relevant regarding this clinical case.

Relationships in marriages are co-created. How Mr. and Mrs. Blunt operate in the marriage is based on a fairly high degree of emotional attachment, manifested in an intense mutual sensitivity and years of reactivity to each other. Focusing on one person as having a "diagnosis" implies that one is causing the problem for the other. The initial complaints from Mrs. Blunt were around Mr. Blunt being needy and self-centered, "he is like my fourth child" (under-functioning) and she saw herself as "having to do it all" (over-functioning). Mr. Blunt complained that his wife was overly involved with her children and parents and had no time for him. The process in the relationship is reciprocal—the more she acts one way, the more he acts the other way (and vice versa). Mr. Blunt's self-centeredness goes hand in glove with Mrs. Blunt's over-giving to others (children, parents, and friends). If one person could change his/her part in the problem, the other person would have more flexibility to be different.

Gender differences in managing stress. Mr. Blunt is an only child and the death of his mother left him with no viable connection with his extended family. This intensified his emotional involvement in his nuclear family. The birth of the third child followed six months later, after which the couple rarely had sex. Over the past several years, Mr. Blunt had difficulty managing his stress (no sexual outlet) which contributed to his being more vigilant, defensive (jealous), demanding, and preoccupied about his wife leaving him (mate-guarding). The lack of sex and affection signaled to Mr. Blunt that the relationship was under threat, leading to more anxiety and a prescription for anti-anxiety medication.

Mrs. Blunt felt constrained and impinged upon by her husband's focus on her and his need for more togetherness (affection and sex). The tension in the marriage led to increased conflict (less OT in Mrs. Blunt's brain). She became less interested in sex and resentful of his making it an issue (one more pressure). As her stress increased, she distanced and focused more on her children. In addition, Mrs. Blunt put more into the emotional support she gave to and received from her mother and sisters. She admits that she considered divorce, but that she does not want to put her children through the process. This confirms Mr. Blunt's fear that she is ready to leave and propels him to focus more of his attention (vigilance) on his wife.

Triangles. The birth of their third child, coupled with Mr. Blunt's lack of an available extended family, was the tipping point that escalated anxiety in the marriage. As the relationship became more uncomfortable, due in part to Mr. Blunt's pull for togetherness and affection, Mrs. Blunt moved emotionally towards her mother who helps with the children. She confided in her mother about her husband's "narcissistic" needs and her mother supported her view that her husband has the problem. Mr. Blunt's reactivity to his wife manifested itself in becoming more critical and resentful of her. His anger at his mother-in-law's special status with his wife, led to negative encounters with Mrs. Blunt's mother, further intensifying the alliance between mother and daughter, with Mr. Blunt on the outside of the triangle. Mrs. Blunt spends her free time involved with her children and is critical of her husband's lack of involvement with them. She enjoys a closer relationship with the kids than does Mr. Blunt who feels that his wife "controls everything", including how he should interact with the children (e.g., he cannot give the kids soft drinks, "even on vacation"). Over time, she has become the gatekeeper to the kids, while he has pulled away and silently sulked. The marriage stabilized into an emotional divorce.

CONCLUSION

The human family is not unique in nature, as evidenced by other pair-bonded mammals that form long-lasting social relationships, have biparental care of young, and live in extended family units. The preceding sections have investigated the neurobiological basis for the gender-based relationship patterns that are observable in species that form pair-bonds, including humans. Consistent with the research is the observation that in marriages with children, males tend to automatically move towards a female for well-being and females tend to automatically move towards their children for well-being. Understanding this process provides a way of thinking about how triangles operate in the human family to manage chronic anxiety.

REFERENCES

Anderson, K. G., Kaplan, H., & Lancaster, J. (1999). Paternal care by genetic fathers and stepfathers I: Reports from Albuquerque men. *Evolution and Human Behavior*, 20(6), 405–431.

Antonucci, T. C., & Akiyama, H. (1987). An examination of sex differences in social support among older men and women. *Sex Roles*, 17(11–12), 737–749.

Barlow, D. H., Sakheim, D. K., & Beck, J. G. (1983). Anxiety increases sexual arousal. *Journal of Abnormal Psychology*, 92(1), 49.

Baumeister, R. F., Catanese, K. R., & Vohs, K. D. (2001). Is there a gender difference in strength of sex drive? Theoretical views, conceptual distinctions, and a review of relevant evidence. *Personality and Social Psychology Review*, 5(3), 242–273.

Belsky, J. (1979). The interrelation of parental and spousal behavior during infancy in traditional nuclear families: An exploratory analysis. *Journal of Marriage and the Family*, 41, 749–755.

Bodenmann, G., Ledermann, T., & Bradbury, T. N. (2007). Stress, sex, and satisfaction in marriage. *Personal Relationships*, 14(4), 551–569.

Bosch, O. J., Nair, H. P., Ahern, T. H., Neumann, I. D., & Young, L. J. (2008). The CRF system mediates increased passive stress-coping behavior following the loss of a bonded partner in a monogamous rodent. *Neuropsychopharmacology*, 34(6), 1406–1415.

Bowen, M. (1978). *Family therapy in clinical practice*. New York: Jason Aronson.

Brown, R. E., Murdoch, T., Murphy, P. R., & Moger, W. H. (1995). Hormonal responses of male gerbils to stimuli from their mate and pups. *Hormones and Behavior*, 29(4), 474–491.

Brown, K. J., & Grunberg, N. E. (1995). Effects of housing on male and female rats: Crowding stresses males but calms females. *Physiology and Behavior*, 58(6), 1085–1089.

Carter, C. S. (1998). Neuroendocrine perspectives on social attachment and love. *Psychoneuroendocrinology*. 23(8). 779–818.

Carter, C. S. (2011). The "love" hormones and the ways they impact our nurturing and attachment . *Family Therapy Magazine*, 10(3), 12–16.

Carter, C. S., & Porges, S. W. (2013). The biochemistry of love: an oxytocin hypothesis. *European Molecular Biology Organization,* 14(1), 12–16.

Carter, C. S., & Porges, S. W., (2010). Social bonding and attachment. *Encyclopedia of Behavioral Neuroscience,* 257–262.

DeLuccie, M. F. (1995). Mothers as gatekeepers: A model of maternal mediators of father involvement. *Journal of Genetic Psychology*, 156(1).

DeVries, A. C. (2002). Interaction among social environment, the hypothalamic–pituitary–adrenal axis, and behavior. *Hormones and Behavior*, 41(4), 405–413.

DeVries, A. C., DeVries, M. B., Taymans, S. E., & Carter, C. S. (1996). The effects of stress on social preferences are sexually dimorphic in prairie voles. *Proceedings National Academy of Science,* 93, 11980–11984.

Dutton, D. G., & Aron, A. P. (1974). Some evidence for heightened sexual attraction under conditions of high anxiety. *Journal of Personality and Social Psychology,* 30(4), 510–517.

Fagan, J., & Barnett, M. (2003). The relationship between maternal gatekeeping, paternal competence, mothers' attitudes about the father role and father involvment. *Journal of Family Issues,* 24(8), 1020–1043.

Fernandez-Duque, E., Valeggia, C. R., & Mendoza, S. P. (2009). The biology of paternal care in human and nonhuman primates. *Annual Review of Anthropology,* 38, 11.

Grippo, A. J., Gerena, D., Huang, J., Kumar, N., Shah, M., Ughreja, R., & Carter, C. S. (2007). Social isolation induces behavioral and neuroendocrine disturbances relevant to depression in female and male prairie voles. *Psychoneuroendocrinology,* 32(8), 966–980.

Hazan, C., & Shaver, P. R. (1994). Attachment as an organizational framework for research on close relationships. *Psychological Inquiry,* 5, 1–22.

Helsing, K. J., & Szklo, M. (1981). Mortality after bereavement. *American Journal of Epidemiology,* 114(1), 41–52.

Hewlett, B. S. (1992). Husband-wife reciprocity and the father-infant relationship among Aka pygmies. In B. S. Hewlett (Ed.), *Father-child relations: Cultural and biosocial contexts* (pp. 153–176). New York: Aldine de Gruyter.

Insel, T. R., & Hulihan, T. J. (1995). A gender-specific mechanism for pair bonding: oxytocin and partner preference formation in monogamous voles. *Behavioral neuroscience,* 109(4), 782.

Jean-Baptiste, N., Terleph, T. A., & Bamshad, M. (2008). Changes in paternal responsiveness of prairie voles (Microtus ochrogaster) in response to olfactory cues and continuous physical contact with a female. *Ethology,* 114(12), 1239–1246.

Kaiser, S., Kirtzeck, M., Hornschuh, G., & Sachser, N. (2003). Sex-specific difference in social support—a study in female guinea pigs. *Physiology and Behavior,* 79(2), 297–303.

Kalmijn, M. (2007). Gender differences in the effects of divorce, widowhood and remarriage on intergenerational support: Does marriage protect fathers? *Social Forces,* 85(3), 1079–1104.

Kerr, M., & Bowen, M. (1988). *Family evaluation.* New York: W. W. Norton and Company.

Lepton, M., & Stewart, J. (1996). Acute and repeated activation of male sexual behavior by tail pinch: opioid and dopaminergic mechanisms. *Physiology & Behavior,* 60(1), 77–85.

Lindheim, S. R., Legro, R. S., Bernstein, L., Stanczyk, F. Z. Vijod, M. A., Presser, S. C., & Lobo, R. A., (1992). Behavioral stress responses in premenopausal and postmenopausal women and the effects of estrogen. *Annual Journal of Obstetrics and Gynecologymerica,* 167(6), 1831–1836.

McCormick, C. M., Robarts, D., Kopeikina, K., & Kelsey, J. E. (2005). Long-lasting, sex-and age-specific effects of social stressors on corticosterone responses to restraint and on locomotor responses to psychostimulants in rats. *Hormones and Behavior,* 48(1), 64–74.

Neff, L. A., & Karney, B. R. (2007). Stress crossover in newlywed marriage: A longitudinal and dyadic perspective. *Journal of Marriage and Family*, 69, 594–607.

Palanza, P. (2001). Animal models of anxiety and depression: how are females different? *Neuroscience and Biobehavioral Reviews*, 25(3), 219–233.

Panksepp, J. (1998). *Affective neuroscience: The foundations of human and animal emotions.* New York: Oxford University Press.

Panksepp, J., & Biven, L. (2012). *The archaeology of mind: Neuroevolutionary origins of human emotions.* New York: WW Norton & Company.

Papero, D. (1990). *Bowen family systems theory.* Boston: Allyn and Bacon.

Schwarzer, R., & Gutiérrez-Doña, B. (2005). More spousal support for men than for women: A comparison of sources and types of support. *Sex Roles*, 52(7–8), 523–532.

Smuts, B. B., & Gubernick, D. J. (1992). Male-infant relationships in nonhuman primates: Paternal investment or mating effort? In B. S. Hewlett (Ed.), *Father-child relations: Cultural and biosocial contexts* (pp. 1–30). New York: Aldine de Gruyter.

Snowdon, C. T., Pieper B. A., Boe, C. Y., Cronin, K. A., Kurian, A. V., & Ziegler, T. E. (2010). Variation in oxytocin is rated to variation in affiliative behavior in monogamous, pairbonded tamarins. *Hormones and Behavior*, 58(4), 614–618.

Snowdon, C. T., & Ziegler, T. E. (2007). Growing up cooperatively: Family processes and infant care in marmosets and tamarins. *Journal of Developmental Processes*, 2(1), 40–66.

Stewart, S. D. (1999). Nonresident mothers' and fathers' social contact with children. *Journal of Marriage and the Family*, 61, 894–907.

Stroebe, M. S., & Stroebe, W. (1983). Who suffers more? Sex differences in health risks of the widowed. *Psychological Bulletin*, 93(2), 279.

Taylor, S. E., Klein, L. C., Lewis, B. P., Gruenewald, T. L., Gurung, R. A., & Updegraff, J. A. (2000). Biobehavioral responses to stress in females: Tend-and-befriend, not fight-or-flight. *Psychological Review*, 107(3), 411.

Taylor, S. E. (2006). Tend and befriend biobehavioral bases of affiliation under stress. *Current Directions in Psychological Science*, 15(6), 273–277.

Terleph, T. A., Jean-Baptiste, N., Bamshad, M. (2004). Mechanism and time course for induction of paternal behavior in prairie voles. *Journal of Mammalogy*, 85(6). 1124–1129.

Wang, Z., & Aragona, B. J. (2004). Neurochemical regulation of pair bonding in male prairie voles. *Physiology and Behavior*, 83(2), 319–328.

Young, L. J., & Wang, Z. (2004). The neurobiology of pair bonding. *Nature Neuroscience.* 7(10), 1048–1054.

Young, L. J., & Alexander, B. (2012). *The chemistry between us: Love, sex and the science of attraction.* London: The Penguin Group.

Chapter 15

Understanding Autonomic Physiology and Relationship Processes in High-risk Families

Elizabeth A. Skowron

The capacity for self-regulation is essential for mature parenting, given the nature of strong emotion that is often elicited in the parenting context (Dix, 1991). Problems with self-regulation—defined as the ability to modulate emotion, shift and focus one's attention, inhibit undesirable behavioral responses, and perform actions in spite of strong desires to avoid so (Cole et al., 2004; Rothbart et al., 2000)—form the core of many physical and psychological disorders in parents and children.

Impairments in self-regulation contribute to significant risk for child maltreatment (CM) perpetration, and exacerbate the negative parenting interactions observed in CM families (Dodge, Bates, & Pettit, 1990; McCanne & Hagstrom, 1996; Rogosch, Cicchetti, & Aber, 1995). Likewise for children, exposure to CM exerts detrimental effects on their developing capacities to regulate attention, emotion, physiology, and behavior. These deficits lead to a host of problem behaviors that confer heightened risk for subsequent regulatory impairments (e.g., Pollak, 2008; Trickett 1993). According to data available through NCANDS, over 80% of CM incidents are perpetrated by a child's parent. These numbers suggest that CM is largely rooted in the day-to-day interactions between parents and their children (Reid, Taplin, & Lorber, 1981). Thus, research that focuses on understanding parents' capacities for self-regulation in the immediate context of parenting is needed to shed light on the intrapersonal and interpersonal mechanisms that underlie at-risk parenting, such as risk for CM perpetration, and to provide clues about why CM and other relational disorders of regulation are so resistant to most therapeutic interventions (Skowron & Reinneman, 2005).

Child maltreatment (CM), defined as harsh physical punishment and abuse, or neglect of a child's basic physical needs, constitutes a violation of the sense of safety and stability in children's early typical experiences with caregivers. CM exposure undermines healthy regulatory development (Shonkoff et al., 2012), and leaves children at great risk for experiencing traumatic stress reactions, internalizing problems such as anxiety, depression, and social withdrawal, and externalizing disorders such as aggression and conduct problems (Cicchetti & Lynch, 1995; Cicchetti & Toth, 2005; Rogosch et al., 1995; Trickett, 1993) . Research on the long-term consequences of CM into adulthood has documented that CM-exposure heightens later risk for family violence, alcohol and drug abuse, self-injury, and suicidal behaviors (Malinosky-Rimmel & Hansen, 1993).

Exposure to CM is particularly detrimental for children's developing stress response systems, and leads to fundamental changes in their physiology (DeBellis, 2005; Shonkoff & Phillips, 2000). For example, CM children's low morning cortisol levels appear to reflect ongoing exposure to CM, while more severe forms of CM function to increase children's cortisol set points (Gunnar & Fisher, 2006). Children who are victims of CM also show dysregulated emotion and heightened autonomic responding to interpersonal hostility (Pollak, 2008). Although heightened physiological reactivity may serve an adaptive function for CM-exposed children living in high-threat contexts, over time it may interfere with the development of higher order cognitive functions including executive attention, inhibitory control, and problem solving (e.g., DePrince, Weinzierl, & Combs, 2009; Pears, Fisher, Bruce, Kim, & Yoerger, 2010; Pollak, Vardi, Putzer Bechner, & Curtin, 2005). Several excellent reviews on this topic exist (e.g., DeBellis, 2005; Pollak, 2008; Watts-English, Fortson, Gibler, Hooper, & DeBellis, 2006), all of which note that many questions remain regarding the pathways through which violence exposure affects children's neurodevelopment and their subsequent outcomes.

In this chapter, we explore the evidence from studies conducted with high risk families that employ behavioral observations and measures of autonomic physiological regulation informed by our understanding of Bowen theory's constructs of differentiation of self, family emotional process, and multigenerational transmission process. Differentiation of self reflects the capacity for deep and meaningful connection with important others, skill in maintaining a clear sense of one's self within relationships, and a willingness to assert a self in one's close relationships. In short, differentiation of self is characterized by a capacity to regulate one's affective and behavioral responses, and an ability to achieve *both* an independent sense of self and deep intimacy with significant others. We review findings that inform our understanding of (a) differentiation of self and child maltreatment, the (b) development of differentiation of self in early childhood and in the (c) role of self-regulation in parenting, which until very recently has received little attention in the research literature.

DIFFERENTIATION OF SELF, AUTONOMIC
PHYSIOLOGY, AND CHILD MALTREATMENT

Recent decades have witnessed the development of increasingly sophisticated models for understanding risk factors for perpetrating child maltreatment (CM), but despite significant progress, the etiology of CM is still not well understood. Leading models of the etiology of CM include *developmental, ecological* and *transactional* approaches that frame the causes and consequences of CM along multiple levels of analysis (i.e., characteristics of individual children, their parents, parent-child processes, and the broader social and cultural context). The developmental-ecological perspective considers many pathways through which CM can occur, with risk for CM ultimately resting on the balance of stressors and supports present in the family (Belsky, 1993). CM reflects a pathogenic relational environment that undermines biological and psychosocial development, with the balance of potentiating factors (i.e., those that increase risk for CM) and compensatory factors (i.e., processes that lower CM risk) determining whether CM occurs and the seriousness of its outcomes (Cicchetti & Rizley, 1981). In other words, when stressors outweigh supports in a family, the probability of CM increases, whereas when enough protective factors are present, risk for CM decreases.

Bowen family systems theory (i.e., Bowen, 1978; Kerr & Bowen, 1988) builds on these leading frameworks through its emphasis on the role of relational and neurobiological systems necessary for understanding family transactional processes underlying CM and its developmental outcomes. From a systems perspective, the phenomenon of CM is characterized by pervasive deficits in the capacity to self-regulate in the act of parenting one's child. CM parents are more emotionally reactive and less able to think clearly under stress (Skowron & Platt, 2005, Skowron et al., 2010). Although CM parents' deficits in positive parenting practices and greater reliance on aversive control occur as a result of high emotional reactivity, and result in harm to their children, including physical and psychological injury, use of these maladaptive practices may actually calm parents and serves a maladaptive stabilizing function in the family system (e.g., Skowron & Woehrle, 2011; Smith, 2001).

Murray Bowen's family systems theory provides a rich framework for conceptualizing the phenomenon of self-regulation particularly as it is expressed in relationships with important others. Bowen's concept of differentiation of self is defined as the capacity to manage emotional reactivity, think clearly in the midst of strong emotion, which taken together enable and support the achievement of "autonomy-in-connection" (i.e., to assert autonomy and achieve deep intimacy in one's most significant relationships, such as the family system (Bowen, 1978; Kerr & Bowen, 1988)). Parents who are better differentiated are better able to regulate emotion, think clearly under stress, more capable of remaining connected with their children while also providing support for their children's age-appropriate autonomy. More highly differentiated parents score higher on indices of effortful control (Skowron & Dendy, 2004), and their children demonstrate greater academic and socioemotional competence, compared to children of less differentiated parents (Skowron, 2005). Family systems characterized by greater differentiation of self are more flexible and adaptive systems under stress, because they are more capable of modulating emotional arousal and thinking clearly in the midst of stress/strain, allow for more intimate contact, tolerate differences of opinions, and have members who are not typically overwhelmed by their emotional experiences.

Parents who perpetrate CM and those at risk of perpetrating CM score lower on measures of differentiation of self (Skowron, 2010; Skowron & Platt, 2005), and they are much less likely to support their children's autonomy, than either non-CM or neglectful parents (Skowron et al., 2011). Meta-analysis documents that CM parents are stricter and more harshly controlling than non-CM parents (Wilson et al., 1998). Such parents are challenged by robust and difficult-to-modulate emotional arousal and as such, may be less capable of supporting "autonomy-in-connection" in their children. Instead, they are more likely to resort to harsh, controlling parenting practices in order to calm themselves, thus leaving them at greater risk of perpetrating acts of CM when faced frustrated or overwhelmed. Unrealistic expectations for mature behavior in their children also may activate high levels of negative emotion in CM parents (Bugental, 2009), which in turn, likely contributes to disturbed parenting through overreliance on use of harsh control. Parents at greater risk for CM initiate more relationship ruptures while interacting with their children, and are less likely to initiate repair of those ruptures than their children, and achieve fewer successful repairs than non-CM families (Skowron et al., 2010). The experience of strong negative reactivity together with limited regulatory capacities may function to disrupt positive parenting because they lead parents to attend more to their own self-focused motives (i.e., manage and calm self) and decrease their attention to child-focused goals (i.e., support and care for child's needs; e.g., Dix, 1991).

Of particular relevance to informing our knowledge of self-regulation in the context of parenting are Bowen's core ideas about differentiation of self on both the behavior and autonomic levels of functioning. Bowen (1978) asserted that differentiation of self operates on both physiological and behavioral levels. He explained that:

> Emotional functioning includes the automatic forces that. . .biology defines as instinct, reproduction, the automatic activity controlled by the autonomic nervous system, subjective emotional and feeling states, and the forces that govern

relationship systems. . . . It is deep in the phylogenetic past and is much older than the intellectual system. . . . There are varying degrees of 'fusion' between the emotional and intellectual systems in the human. The greater the fusion, the more the life is governed by automatic emotional forces that operate. . .the greater the fusion, the more man is vulnerable to physical illness, emotional illness, and social illness, and the less he is able to consciously control his own life. (1978, pp. 304–305)

Indeed, countless studies have shown that self-regulation of emotion and behavior show predictable neurophysiological substrates (e.g., Beauchaine, 2001; Graziano & Derefinko, 2013). Meta-analysis indicates that parents at high risk for CM have difficulty regulating their emotional and behavioral responses (Cicchetti & Toth, 2005), and display deficits in executive function, and greater autonomic reactivity to child-specific and neutral stimuli in the form of higher resting heart rate, greater sympathetic activation, and lower galvanic skin response at rest and in response to child-related stimuli (McCanne & Hagstrom, 1996).

CARDIAC VAGAL TONE AND CHILD MALTREATMENT

The parasympathetic nervous system (PNS) has been proposed as a biological system underlying many crucial facets of social self-regulation (e.g., Beauchaine, 2001; Porges, 1995; 2001; Thayer & Lane, 2000). The function of the parasympathetic branch is to maintain homeostasis by regulating sympathetic excitation and rapidly down-regulating autonomic arousal as needed to engage with environmental demands (Porges, 2001). According to Porges' (2011) polyvagal theory, mammals have evolved physiological systems for responding to threat and facilitating positive social engagement. Porges argues that the parasympathetic nervous system (PNS), mediated by the vagus nerve, exerts neural control over the autonomic nervous system in order to regulate arousal in response to environmental cues (Porges, 1995, 2001). Vagal control of heart rate thus enables rapid regulation of emotional states in social contexts, and as such is of particular interest for understanding how individual differences in biologically based regulation may correspond with measures of differentiation of self, and shape variations in parent-child processes, children's developing capacities for regulating arousal, and broader family systems functioning.

Parasympathetic or vagal tone can be assessed by isolating the variability in heart rate due to respiration, or RSA (Berntson, Cacioppo, & Quigley, 1993), with greater variation in heart rate across the cycle of inhalation and exhalation indicative of parasympathetic activation, or greater vagal tone.

Our research on CM parenting has focused on vagal tone as a neurophysiological indicator of regulatory processes, because of its importance to social
functioning, and the co-localization of behavioral regulation and autonomic
function systems in the brain (Oschner & Gross, 2007; Posner & Rothbart,
2007).

Of particular interest to the phenomenon of CM and its adverse effects on
children, are Porges' propositions in his polyvagal theory regarding the role
of threat and safety in the development of strong parasympathetic (i.e., vagal)
tone. Porges' posits a neurophysiological-based social engagement system
whose development is predicated on experience of safe social relationship
systems through vagally mediated control of heart rate arousal. Not only
does the vagus nerve dynamically mediate arousal via lowering heart rate, it
also enervates the musculature in the face and upper neck central to social
behavior, including facial muscles that control displays of eye gaze and facial
affect muscles of the inner ear that distinguish high frequency tones within
the human vocal range from lower frequency tones. Thus strong parasympathetic tone is enabled by and in turn supports the capacity for positive social
engagement with caregivers and others.

Much of the existing research on RSA has characterized the role of resting
or "baseline" values, and changes in response to challenge (e.g., Beauchaine,
2001; Berntson, Cacioppo, & Quigley, 1993; Porges, 1995; Thayer & Lane,
2001). Resting vagal tone is considered an index of one's capacity for physiological regulation (Beauchaine, 2001). In children and adults, higher resting vagal tone is associated with greater regulatory capacity and attentional
control (Beauchaine, 2001), whereas lower resting vagal tone is thought to
be a nonspecific marker of dysregulated emotion (Beauchaine, 2001) and
linked to increased risk for a range of socio-emotional problems (Graziano
& Derefinko, 2013).

Changes in vagal tone in response to challenge are referred to in terms
of vagal augmentation (i.e., RSA increases) or vagal withdrawal (i.e., RSA
decreases) from baseline levels, due to their association with increases and
decreases in activation of the parasympathetic nervous system, respectively
(e.g., Beauchaine, 2001). Decreases in RSA index the withdrawal of vagal
(PNS) influence on the heart, leading to cardiac acceleration to support
mobilization and attentional engagement, while increases in RSA index an
augmentation of vagal influence on the heart, resulting in a slowed heart
rate that promotes calm behavioral states, self-soothing, and social engagement (e.g., Porges, 2001; Berntson et al., 1993). Increases in vagal tone (i.e.,
RSA augmentation) typically relate to increased efforts to regulate one's
emotions (Butler, Wilhelm, & Gross, 2006), and a number of findings have
documented associations between RSA augmentation and elevated levels of
social engagement and positive emotionality (Geisler, Kubiak, Siewert, &

Weber, 2013; Kok & Frederickson, 2010; Skowron et al., 2011). Conversely, decreases in vagal tone (i.e., RSA withdrawal) have been associated with exposure to stress (Berntston, Cacioppo, Quigley, & Fabro, 1994) and expressions of negative emotionality (Beauchaine, 2001).

A growing number of studies focused on understanding the autonomic physiology of children exposed to CM and other forms of early adversity support Porges' assertion that the experience of safe environment is essential for developing optimal vagal functioning (Graziano & Derefinko, 2013; Porges, 2001). Among preschool children exposed to significant early adversity, high vagal tone and vagal augmentation are associated with greater self-regulation and fewer behavioral problems (e.g., Calkins, Graziano, & Keane, 2008; Obradovic, Bush, Stamperdahl, Adler, & Boyce, 2010; Skowron, Loken, Gatzke-Kopp, Cipriano, Woehrle et al., 2011; Skowron et al., 2013). For example, several studies from our lab found that greater vagal withdrawal during challenge tasks was associated with better outcome among children from lower risk contexts, including better inhibitory control (Skowron et al., 2013) and fewer behavioral problems (Cipriano-Essel et al., 2011).

Also consistent with Bowen's propositions regarding the autonomic substrates of differentiation of self, more sensitive, skillful parenting is uniformly associated with higher resting vagal tone (e.g., Musser, Ablow, & Measelle, 2012; Perlman, Camras, & Pelphrey, 2008), and marital quality (Smith et al., 2012). Likewise, our research shows that higher resting vagal tone is observed among neglectful and non-maltreating mothers who engage in positive parenting, but predicts more hostile controlling parenting in abusive mothers (Skowron et al., 2013). Yet few studies of parenting to date have focused on understanding the role of vagal function observed during parenting and whether it varies for healthy versus. at-risk parenting. Further, findings are mixed in regards to whether optimal parenting is associated with vagal increases or decreases. Our research on CM parenting uses time-synchronized assessment of physiology and micro-social coding to examine moment-by-moment transactions between parent and child. In this work, we found that both CM and non-CM mothers display a pattern of increasing vagal tone from rest to engagement in a challenging task with their preschool child, suggesting that vagal augmentation occurs in the context of social engagement when parents are required to suppress arousal in the service of relational engagement (Skowron et al., 2011). Several other studies of vagal tone in the context of parenting support the notion that increased vagal tone signals positive social engagement and social self-regulation. For example, Hill-Soderland et al., (2008) monitored episode-by-episode RSA responding of mothers and their avoidant or securely attached infants during the Strange Situation procedure, and observed increases in mothers' vagal tone during the final reunion with their child, and when engaging with the stranger,

Elizabeth A. Skowron

and signaling positive social engagement and greater regulation. Likewise, experimentally induced increases in parent-child engagement via oxytocin administration were associated with increased RSA in parents and children during free play (Weisman, Zagoory-Sharon, & Feldman, 2012).

Other studies have reported vagal decreases associated with positive parenting of distressed infants and children. For example, decreases in maternal RSA are linked with more sensitive (Moore et al., 2009) and less intrusive parenting (Mills-Koonce et al., 2009) of infants while they are exhibiting distress or other negative affect. Another study (Mills-Koonce, Gariepy, Propper, Sutton, Calkins et al., 2007) documented that larger decreases in maternal vagal tone in response to high levels of infant negativity were associated with higher maternal sensitivity in mothers of avoidantly attached children. Hill-Soderlund et al., (2008) found that mothers of both secure and insecure infants showed significant decreases in their vagal tone during separations from their child. However, Lorber and O'Leary (2005) found greater vagal withdrawal among mothers who display harsh over-reactive discipline with their preschool children, and greater vagal withdrawal has also been observed in partners during marital conflict discussions (Nealey-Moore et al., 2007).

Looking beyond static measures of vagal tone, we have also employed multi-level modeling (MLM) methods to track dynamic changes in RSA associated with positive interactive synchrony in mother-child interactions (Giuliano, Skowron, & Berkman, 2015). As shown in Figure 15.1, greater positive synchrony in mother-child dyadic exchanges during a joint laboratory challenge was associated with a trajectory of vagal withdrawal in

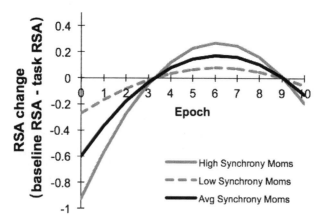

Figure 15.1 Growth Models of Mother's Changes in Vagal Tone (RSA) Reactivity as a Function of Task-Average Dyadic Synchrony. *Source*: Giuliano, Skowron, & Berkman, 2015

mothers at the onset of interaction, followed by vagal augmentation through the remainder of interaction. In other words, mothers who achieved high levels of positive synchrony with their child showed vagal withdrawal at the task onset—likely to orient and focus, and then proceeded to increase their vagal tone over the remainder of the interaction—likely to support positive engagement and joint problem-solving with their child (e.g., Porges, 2001). In contrast, mothers who achieved little positive synchrony with their child displayed a flat or blunted pattern of vagal reactivity over the course of the task. Interestingly, CM status did not moderate the relationship between dyadic synchrony and growth trajectories in parent vagal tone. The dynamic vagal response patterns observed in these mothers are consistent with tenets of neuroviseral integration theory (Thayer & Lane, 2000; Friedman, 2007) which state that healthy physiological processes are characterized by greater variability or flexibility in biological response, whereas pathological states are characterized by low variability or flat response profiles. Within this perspective for example, anxiety is characterized by the restricted physiological response range observed among its sufferers. In further support of this notion, results from dispersion tests on maternal vagal tone over the course of ten 30" joint task epochs revealed significantly greater epoch-to-epoch variability in non-CM mothers' vagal tone over time and less variability, or greater consistency, in vagal tone observed in physically abusive and neglectful mothers (Skowron et al., 2013). In other words, physically abusive and neglectful parents showed flatter RSA over time when interacting with their children, whereas non-maltreating mothers showed greater physiological variability during interactions. These findings suggest that healthy adaptive physiology is characterized by high levels of variability, while maladaptive profiles are better characterized by low variability or greater consistency over time (Appel et al., 1989; Goldberger, 1992, 1996). Given research documenting inconsistency/unpredictability in CM parenting behaviors, we wonder whether this results from CM parents' efforts to dampen their physiological arousal during parenting, thus revealing greater concern with their own internal states and an anxious disregard of their child's needs.

Relatedly, we used MLM to document patterns of significant coupling in parents' physiology and behavior during the act of parenting, that vary across physically abusive, neglectful, and non-CM families (Skowron et al., 2013). In physically abusive mothers, joint patterns of time-ordered physiology and parenting behavior suggested that positive parenting was more physiologically taxing for abusive mothers and harsh parenting was more reinforcing. Specifically, person-level increases in positive parenting were associated with vagal withdrawal (i.e., greater arousal) in abusive mothers. Vagal withdrawal then led to subsequent increases in abusive mothers' strict/harsh control of their child. This pattern of significant coupling in physiology and behavior observed among the abusive mothers while parenting provides support for both Porges' (2011) polyvagal theory and suggests that abusive mothers' impaired social engagement skills may derive from experiencing the parenting context as more threatening on an autonomic level than their lower-risk peers. These findings highlight the heightened arousal that abusive mothers face in providing adequate caregiving, and suggest that the parenting capacities of abusive mothers are uniquely challenged by deficits in physiological regulation. Given that abusive parents are also predisposed to making threat-biased attributions of their child and greater vigilance (e.g., Bugental, 2009), we wonder if abusive mothers tend to exert harsh control of their child because they are driven by autonomic arousal and perceptions of the parenting context as threatening.

In contrast, we found that the kind of parenting behavior displayed by neglectful mothers predicted subsequent changes in their physiology response. When neglectful mothers increased their positive parenting, it led to subsequent increases in their vagal tone. Conversely, increases in harsh control led to subsequent decreases in neglectful mothers' vagal tone. These findings are promising and suggest that neglectful parents—who comprise the largest proportion of families involved with Child Welfare—may experience some physiological reinforcement for engaging in more adaptive parenting.

DIFFERENTIATION OF SELF DEVELOPMENT
IN EARLY CHILDHOOD

According to Bowen theory (1978; Kerr & Bowen, 1988) levels of differentiation of self are transmitted across generations of a family, with the previous generation's level of differentiation roughly constraining the level of differentiation achieved in the next generation. Bowen wrote about the development of differentiation in childhood, noting that:

> All things being equal, you emerge with about the same basic level of differentiation your parents had. This is determined by the process before your birth and the situation during infancy and early childhood. (Bowen, 1978, p. 409)

Security and Bio-behavioral Synchrony. We theorize that children's developing self-regulation of emotion and behavior unfolds as part of their experiences with safety, support, and efforts to define a self in the context of connections with caregivers. Together, these experiences form the core of children's developing capacities for differentiating a self in their family system. The development of differentiation of self in early childhood begins with the fundamental provision of safety via parent-led bio-behavioral synchrony that promotes bonding and basic security. Well-differentiated parents serve as external regulators of children's bio-behavioral states in early infancy by creating and sustaining the infant's experience of positive interactive synchrony with caregiver. In other words, the experience of positive bio-behavioral synchrony between caregiver and child is thought to serve homeo-static regulation and social bonding functions in infancy (Tronick, 1989). Although Bowen labeled this "undifferentiation" between caregiver and child, he acknowledged it as developmentally typical and appropriate given the important function that such early coordination serves. Research has documented patterns of concordance in vagal tone over time between mother and child from infancy to early childhood in a sample of typically developing children (Bornstein & Suess, 2000). Likewise, we have reported significant concordance in mother and preschooler contemporaneously measured heart rate (HR) and vagal tone at rest: Greater maternal HR was associated with greater child heart rate and lower child vagal tone (Creaven et al., 2013). Further, there is evidence that early synchrony in parent-infant interactions supports developing self-regulation and capacity for empathy as children age (e.g., Feldman, 2007; Tronick, 1989).

Autonomy-in-Connection. The transition from infancy into the preschool years reflects a particularly important time for the emergence of children's capacities to manage and regulate themselves (e.g., Grolnick & Ryan, 1989). The developmental needs of a child evolve over time from infancy, and as such, the quality of caregiver-child interactions shifts over time toward promoting preschoolers' developing autonomy-in-connection, self-regulation, and social competence (Harrist & Waugh, 2002). Bowen emphasized the importance of experiencing autonomy-in-connection as foundational for the development of differentiation of self. From a family systems perspective, parents' own abilities to regulate their own emotions, think clearly under stress, and promote both intimacy and autonomy among family members, taken together provide optimal support for their children's developing differentiation.

As they age, children increasingly internalize the regulatory functions once performed by caregivers. This transition from other-regulated to increasingly self-regulated functioning is supported by the fact that positive, interactive synchrony occurs only about half of the time during parent-child interactions (Harrist & Waugh, 2002), and it is interspersed with manageable "failures," or brief relationship ruptures that are quickly repaired by parent. This experience of relationship ruptures and repairs enable children over time to gradually internalize the regulatory functions once served primarily by caregivers (Tronick, 1989). Research conducted with humans and primates has documented powerful negative effects of relational control and subordinance/submission on one's stress response and autonomic function (Sapolsky,

2004). For example, relational experiences characterized by subordinate status and low control (i.e., low support for autonomy-in-connection) have been linked to elevated sympathetic tone, heightened anxiety, and vigilance (Repetti et al., 2002; Sapolsky, 2004). In contrast, early experiences with parent support for age-appropriate and prosocial autonomy promote developing self-confidence, and capacities for self-regulation of affect, physiology, and behavior (Bernier, Carlson, & Whipple, 2010; Bowen, 1978; Grolnick, Deci, & Ryan, 1997; Grolnick & Farkas, 2002). Children who experience more parental support for their developing autonomy display better effortful control (Lengua, Honorado, & Bush, 2007) and executive functioning abilities (Landry, Miller-Loncar, Smith, & Swank, 2002). We found that even after considering effects of CM-exposure, that parent's autonomy promotion predicted greater inhibitory control among temperamentally exuberant children (Cipriano-Essel et al., 2011). Warm autonomy support may provide children with opportunities to practice implementing self-generated solutions for task completion, facilitating development of successful goal directed behavior (Blair, 2002).

More differentiated parents are thought to be better able to support and encourage their preschool child's budding autonomy strivings, and engage in supportive, comforting behaviors that are adaptive when their child experiences stress. For example, our findings indicate that children whose efforts to assert autonomy were more often met with maternal affirmation (i.e., warm support for their independent ideas and actions), showed higher vagal tone in the context of a joint challenge (Skowron et al., 2011). In contrast, when children's autonomous behavior is more often responded to with maternal criticism and harsh control, children show lower vagal tone during those interactions. The negative effects of maternal harsh control were particularly strong when it was experienced by child immediately following an effort to assert autonomy-in-connection. In sum, our data suggest that children showed physiological sensitivity to the quality of parenting they experience, particularly in response to their efforts to assert age-appropriate autonomy.

We think that preschoolers in more differentiated families may experience a smoother transition from early parent-regulation of their internal states and needs, toward their increasing self-regulation of internal states and behavior. It also stands to reason that a child's capacity for differentiation of self or "autonomy-in-connection" emerges and consolidates earlier in children who are growing up in more differentiated families. Evidence in support of this notion would take the form of decreasing bio-behavioral concordance over time between parent and child and growing independence in the physiology and behavior observed in parents and their children.

Related to this, we examined latent profiles of dyadic interaction in another study incorporating multilevel observations of neurophysiology and parenting processes and three latent interactive profiles emerged: positive coordination (PC); child-led coordination (CLC), and dyadic miscoordination (DMC) (Skowron, Khurana, & Gatzke-Kopp, under review). As shown in Figures 15.2a and b, preschool children who experienced greater positive interactive coordination with their caregiver (i.e., high rates of positive synchrony, low rates of mother-initiated ruptures, and short latencies to repair) displayed significantly higher resting vagal tone and inhibitory control scores. In contrast, children in dyads characterized by chronic miscoordination with mother (i.e., lower positive behavioral synchrony and long latencies to repair following rupture) showed the lowest resting vagal tone and inhibitory control. Perhaps of greatest interest was the latent profile "Child-Led Coordination," that was characterized by moderately high levels of positive synchrony, high rates of mother-initiated ruptures and high rates of child-initiated repairs of those ruptures. Children in the Child-Led Coordination dyads displayed low vagal tone and inhibitory control scores on par with children in chronic, dyadic miscoordination dyads. Rather, it appears that for these children, positive synchrony with mother was being maintained through an inordinate level of responsibility on the child's part to repair relationship ruptures initiated by the parent. Our findings indicate that the responsibility taken by these children to maintain synchrony in the relationship appears costly to their developing self-regulation, suggesting that the experience of positive interactive synchrony is not experienced as uniformly positive or adaptive in all cases. Consistent with Bowen theory, some forms of interactive synchrony may not be helpful for children's development.

Likewise among the subset of CLC dyads, we observed evidence of bio-behavioral sensitivity between parent and child that appear consistent with Bowen's notions about anxious attunement found in less-differentiated families. Specifically, increases in compliant child behavior during moderately challenging puzzle task led to subsequent increases in maternal vagal tone, only among CLC dyads. These associations suggest that CLC parents are physiologically calmed when their children act in more compliant ways. Likewise, other studies have shown that CM-exposed children appear to be more sensitive to their caregiving context (Pollak & Kistler, 2002; Skowron et al., 2013).

In sum, parents and children in less differentiated families may experience relational conditions that promote ongoing fusion between biological and behavioral response systems within and between parent and child through experiences that heighten children's sensitivities/reactivity to caregivers or parent reliance on children's behavior to manage their own internal states. Are children raised in high-risk, poorly differentiated contexts essentially learning to remain more biologically/behaviorally sensitive to relationships than their peers being raised in more differentiated families? Much remains

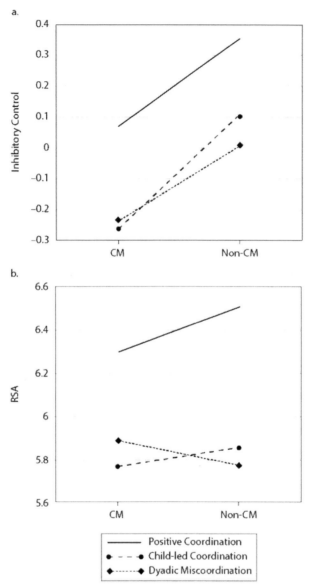

Figure 15.2   a. Children's Inhibitory Control varies as a function of dyadic coordination profile and CM exposure. b. Children's Resting Vagal Tone (RSA) varies as a function of dyadic coordination profile. *Source*: Skowron, Khurana, & Gatzke-Kopp, under review

to be clarified about the timing and developmental of bio-behavioral syn-chrony between caregiver and child and its role in healthy child development. Whether or not forms of synchrony continue to be adaptive over time as chil-dren mature is an important question in need of further inquiry.

SUMMARY AND NEXT STEPS

According to Bowen theory, an individual comes to acquire the level of differentiation of self in one's family system, and that level, give or take a few points, is transmitted across generations of the family. Yet, there are no longitudinal studies that have empirically tested this assumption. Research is needed to understand how differentiation of self begins to develop in infancy and early childhood and sound measures are needed to assess this construct at these ages.

Evidence from studies employing micro-social coding and autonomic function in parents and children supports Bowen's theoretical propositions regarding the behavioral and autonomic substrates of differentiation of self. For example, parenting behavior that is characterized by greater dif-ferentiation of self—namely the capacity for positive interactive synchrony and the ability to provide support for children's expressions of "autonomy-in-connection" predicts early developing capacities for physiological regulation (i.e., greater vagal tone) and behavioral control in preschool children. Likewise, harsh controlling parenting has adverse implications for children's early regulatory development. Because CM children showed higher vagal tone when their mothers parented in ways which affirmed their autonomous bids, a plausible interpretation for physically abused, neglected, and non-CM children alike, is that positive parenting which also supports children's autonomy may facilitate the development of physi-ological and behavioral regulation, thus serving a protective function for maltreated children.

Well-differentiated parents show patterns of parenting behavior that are by and large independent of their physiological response. In contrast, less differentiated parents—physically abusive and neglectful mothers—show time-ordered patterns of association between their parenting behaviors and their physiological responding. These findings suggest that insight-oriented interventions alone (i.e., approaches to increasing awareness and understand-ing of forces in family system that influence behavior) may be insufficient for strengthening differentiation of self in the lowest functioning parents. Instead, efforts to strengthen these parents' capacities to physiologically calm them-selves in the context of positive parenting may be essential for successful intervention. This remains an empirical question for future inquiry. Ongoing, cross-disciplinary research is needed to inform our understanding of key family processes that unfold on biological and behavior levels of experience, that shape the course and timing of differentiation development in the family system.

REFERENCES

Beauchaine, T. (2001). Vagal tone, development, and Gray's motivational theory: Toward an integrated model of autonomic nervous system functioning in psychopathology. *Development and Psychopathology*, 13, 183–214.

Belsky, J. (1993). Etiology of child maltreatment: A developmental–ecological analysis. *Psychological Bulletin*, 114, 413–434.

Bernier, A., Carlson, S. M., & Whipple, N. (2010). From external regulation to self-regulation: Early parenting precursors of young children's executive functioning. *Child Development*, 81, 326–339. doi:10.1111/j.1467–8624.2009.01397.x

Berntson, G. G., Cacioppo, J. T., & Quigley, K. S. (1993). Respiratory sinus arrhythmia: autonomic origins, physiological mechanisms, and psychophysiological implications. *Psychophysiology*, 30(2), 183–196.

Berntson, G. G., Cacioppo, J. T., & Quigley, K.S., & Fabro, V. T. (1994). Autonomic space and psychophysiological response. *Psychophysiology*, 31, 44–61.

Blair, C. (2002). School readiness: Integrating cognition and emotion into a neurobiological conceptualization of children's functioning at school entry. *American Psychology*, 57, 111–127. doi:10.1037//0003–066X.57.2.111.

Bornstein, M. H., & Suess, P. E. (2000). Child and mother cardiac vagal tone: continuity, stability, and concordance across the first 5 years. *Developmental Psychology*, 36(1), 54.

Bowen, M. (1978). *Family therapy in clinical practice*. New York: Jason Aronson.

Bugental, D. B. (2009). Predicting & preventing child maltreatment: A biocognitive transactional approach. In A. Sameroff (Ed.), *The transactional model of development: How children and contexts shape each other* (pp. 97–115). Washington, DC: American Psychological Association.

Butler, E. A., Wilhelm, F. H., & Gross, J. J. (2006). Respiratory sinus arrhythmia, emotion, and emotion regulation during social interaction. *Psychophysiology*, 43, 612–622.

Calkins, S. D., Graziano, P. A., Berdan, L. E., Keane, S. P., & Degnan, K. A. (2008). Predicting cardiac vagal regulation in early childhood from maternal-child relationship quality during toddlerhood. *Developmental Psychobiology*, 50(8), 751–766.

Cicchetti, D., & Carlson, V. (Eds.), *Child maltreatment: Theory and research on the causes and consequences of child abuse and neglect*. New York, NY: Cambridge University Press.

Cicchetti, D., & Rizley, R. (1981). Developmental perspectives on the etiology, intergenerational transmission, and sequelae of child maltreatment. *New Directions for Child Development*, 11, 31–55.

Cicchetti, D., & Toth, S. L. (2005). Child maltreatment. *Annual Review of Clinical Psychology,* 1, 409–438.

Cipriano-Essel, E. A., Skowron, E. A., & Gatzke-Kopp, L. M. (2011). Preschool children's cardiac reactivity moderates relations between exposure to family violence and emotional adjustment. *Child Maltreatment,* 16, 205–215. PMC3582334.

Cole, P. M., Martin, S. E., & Dennis, T. A. (2004). Emotion regulation as a scientific construct: Methodological challenges and directions for child development research. *Child development,* 75(2), 317–333.

Creaven, A. M., Skowron, E. A., Hughes, B., Howard, S., & Loken, E. (2013). Dyadic concordance in mother–preschooler resting cardiovascular function varies by risk status. *Developmental Psychobiology,* 56, 142–152.

DeBellis, M. D. (2005). The psychobiology of neglect. (2005). *Child Maltreatment,* 10, 150–172.

DePrince, A. P., Weinzierl, K. M., & Combs, M. D. (2009). Executive function performance and trauma exposure in a community sample of children. *Child Abuse & Neglect,* 33, 353–361.

Dix, T. (1991). The affective organization of parenting: Adaptive and maladaptive processes. *Psychological Bulletin,* 110, 3–25.

Dodge, K. A., Bates, J. E., & Pettit, G. S. (1990). Mechanisms in the cycle of violence. *Science,* 250, 1678–1683.

Feldman, R. (2007). Parent-infant synchrony: Biological foundations and developmental outcomes. *Current Directions in Psychological Science,* 16, 340–345.

Geisler, F., Kubiak, T., Siewert, K., & Weber, H. (2013). Cardiac vagal tone is associated with social engagement and self-regulation. *Biological Psychology,* 93, 279–286.

Giuliano, R. J., Skowron, E. A., & Berkman, E.T. (2015). Growth models of dyadic synchrony and mother–child vagal tone in the context of parenting at-risk. *Biological Psychology.* 105, 29–36.

Graziano, P., & Derefinko, K. (2013). Cardiac vagal control and children's adaptive functioning: A meta-analysis. *Biological Psychology,* 94(1), 22–37.

Grolnick, W.S., Deci, E. L., & Ryan, R. M. (1997). Internalization within the family: The self-determination theory perspective. In J. E. Grusec and L. Kuczynski (Eds.), *Parenting and the internalization of values* (pp. 135–161). NewYork: Wiley.

Grolnick, W. S., & Farkas, M. (2002). Parenting and the development of children's self-regulation. In M. H. Bornstein (Ed.), *Handbook of parenting: Vol. 5: Practical issues in parenting (2nd ed.),* pp. 89–110. Lawrence Erlbaum Associates: Worcester, MA.

Gunnar, M. R., Fisher, P. A., & The Early Experience, Stress, and Prevention Network (2006). Bringing basic research on early experience and stress neurobiology to bear on preventive interventions for neglected and maltreated children. *Development and Psychopathology,* 18, 651–677.

Harrist, A. W., & Waugh, R. M. (2002). Dyadic synchrony: Its structure and function in children's development. *Developmental Review,* 22(4), 555–592.

Kerr, M. E., & Bowen, M. (1988). *Family evaluation.* New York, NY: Norton.

Kok, B. E., & Fredrickson, B. L. (2010). Upward spirals of the heart: Autonomic flexibility, as indexed by vagal tone, reciprocally and prospectively predicts positive emotions and social connectedness. *Biological Psychology,* 85, 432–436.

254   *Elizabeth A. Skowron*

Landry, S. H., Miller-Loncar, C. L., Smith, K. E. & Swank, P. R. (2002). The role of early parenting in children's development of executive processes, *Developmental Neuropsychology,* 21, 15–41. doi:10.1207/S15326942DN2101_2.

Lengua, L. J., Honorado, E., & Bush, N. R. (2007). Contextual risk and parenting as predictors of effortful control and social competence in preschool children. *Journal of Applied Developmental Psychology,* 28, 40–55. doi:10.1016/j.appdev.2006.10.001.

McCanne, T. R., & Hagstrom, A. H. (1996). Physiological hyperreactivity to stressors in physical child abusers and individuals at risk for being physically abusive. *Aggression and Violent Behavior,* 1, 345–358.

Malinosky-Rummell, R., & Hansen, D. J. (1993). Long-term consequences of childhood physical abuse. *Psychological bulletin,* 114(1), 68.

Musser, E. D., Ablow, J. C., & Measelle, J. R. (2012). Predicting maternal sensitivity: The roles of postnatal depressive symptoms and parasympathetic dysregulation. *Infant Mental Health Journal,* 33(4), 350–359.

Obradović, J., Bush, N. R., Stamperdahl, J., Adler, N. E., & Boyce, W. T. (2010). Biological sensitivity to context: The interactive effects of stress reactivity and family adversity on socioemotional behavior and school readiness. *Child Development,* 81, 270–289

Ochsner, K. N., & Gross, J. J. (2007). The neural architecture of emotion regulation. *Handbook of emotion regulation,* 1, 87–109.

Pears, K. C., Fisher, P. A., Bruce, J., Kim, H. K., & Yoerger, K. (2010). Early elementary school adjustment of maltreated children in foster care: The roles of inhibitory control and caregiver involvement. *Child Development,* 81, 1550–1564.

Perlman, S. B., Camras, L. A., & Pelphrey, K. A. (2008). Physiology and functioning: Parents' vagal tone, emotion socialization, and children's emotion knowledge. *Journal of Experimental Child Psychology,* 100(4), 308–315.

Pollak, S. D. (2008). Mechanisms linking early experience and the emergence of emotions: Illustrations from the study of child maltreatment. *Current Directions in Psychological Science,* 17, 370–375.

Pollak, S. D., & Kistler, (2002). Early experience is associated with the development of categorical representations for facial expressions of emotion. *Proceedings of the National Academy of Sciences,* 99, 9072–9076.

Pollak, S. D., Vardi, S., Putzer Bechner, A. M., & Curtin, J. J. (2005). Physically abused children's regulation of attention in response to hostility. *Child Development,* 76, 968–977.

Porges, S. W. (1995). Orienting in a defensive world: Mammalian modifications of our evolutionary heritage: A polyvagal theory. *Psychophysiology,* 32, 301–318.

Porges, S. W. (2001). The polyvagal theory: Phyologenetic substrates of a social nervous system. *International Journal of Psychophysiology,* 42, 123–146.

Porges, S. W. (2011). The polyvagal theory: Neurophysiological foundations of emotions, attachment, communication, and self-regulation. New York: Norton.

Posner, M. I., & Rothbart, M. K. (2000). Developing mechanisms of self-regulation. *Development and Psychopathology,* 12, 427–441.

Reid, J. B., Patterson, G. R., & Loeber, R. (1981). The abused child: Victim, instigator, or innocent bystander? In *Nebraska symposium on motivation*. University of Nebraska Press.

Repetti, R. L., Taylor, S. E., & Seeman, T. E., (2002). Risky families: Family social environments and the mental and physical health of offspring. *Psychological Bulletin*, 128, 330–366.

Rogosch, F. A., Cicchetti, D., & Aber, J. L. (1995). The role of child maltreatment in early deviations in cognitive and affective processing abilities and later peer relationship problems. *Development and Psychopathology*, 7, 591–609.

Rothbart, M. K., Ahadi, S. A., & Evans, D. E. (2000). Temperament and personality: Origins and outcomes. *Journal of Personality and Social Psychology*, 78, 122–135.

Sapolsky, R. M. (2004). Social status and health in humans and other animals. *Annual Review of Anthropology*, 393–418.

Shonkoff, J. P., & Fisher, P. A. (2013). Rethinking evidence-based practice and two-generation programs to create the future of early childhood policy. *Development and Psychopathology*, 25, 1635–1653.

Shonkoff, J. P., Garner, A. S., & The Committee on Psychosocial Aspects of Child and Family Health, Committee on Early Childhood, Adoption, and Dependent Care, and Section on Developmental and Behavioral Pediatrics (2012). The lifelong effects of early childhood adversity and toxic stress. *Pediatrics*, 129, 2011–2663.

Skowron, E. A., Khurana, A., & Gatzke-Kopp, L. (under review). *Latent classes of dyadic rupture-repair processes predict children's RSA and inhibitory control.*

Skowron, E. A. (2005). Parent differentiation of self and child competence in low-income, urban families. *Journal of Counseling Psychology*, 52, 337–342.

Skowron, E. A., & Reinemann, D. H. S. (2005). Psychological interventions for child maltreatment: A meta-analysis. *Psychotherapy: Theory, Research, Practice, and Training*, 42, 52–71.

Skowron, E. A., Cipriano-Essel, E. A., Benjamin, L. S., & Pincus, A. L., & Van Ryzin, M. (2013). Maternal cardiac vagal tone and parenting behaviors display concurrent and time-ordered associations that diverge in abusive, neglectful, and non-maltreating mothers. *Couple and Family Psychology: Research and Practice*, 2, 95–115.

Skowron, E. A., Cipriano-Essel, E. A., Gatzke-Kopp, L. M., Teti, D. M., & Ammerman, R. T. (2014). Early adversity, RSA, and inhibitory control: Evidence of children's neurobiological sensitivity to social context. *Developmental Psychobiology*, 56, 964–978. doi: 10.1002/dev.21175.

Skowron, E. A., Loken, E., Gatzke-Kopp, L. M., Cipriano, E. A., Woehrle, P. L., Van Epps, J. J., Ammerman, R. T. (2011). Mapping cardiac physiology and parenting processes in maltreating mother–child dyads. *Journal of Family Psychology*, 25, 663–674. PMCID 3582338.

Skowron, E. A., & Dendy, A. K. (2004). Differentiation of self and attachment in adulthood: Relational correlates of effortful control. *Contemporary Family Therapy: An International Journal*, 26, 337–357.

Skowron, E. A., & Platt, L. F. (2005). Differentiation of self and child abuse potential in young adult college students. *The Family Journal,* 13, 281–290.

Skowron, E. A., & Woehrle, P. L., (2012). Child maltreatment. In N. Fouad, J. Carter, & L. Subich (Eds.), *APA Handbook of Counseling Psychology, vol. 2: Practice, Interventions and Applications* (pp. 153–180). Washington, DC: American Psychological Association, doi: 10.1037/13755–007.

Smith, T. W., Cribbet, M. R., Nealey-Moore, J. B., Uchino, B. N., Williams, P. G., MacKenzie, J., & Thayer, J. F., (2012). Matters of the variable heart: Respiratory sinus arrhythmia response to marital interaction and associations with marital quality. *Journal of Personality and Social Psychology,* 100, 103–119.

Thayer, J. F., & Lane, R. D. (2000). A model of neurovisceral integration in emotion regulation and dysregulation. *Journal of Affective Disorders,* 61, 201–216.

Thayer, J. F., Friedman, B. H., & Borkovec, T. D. (1996). Autonomic characteristics of generalized anxiety disorder and worry. *Biological psychiatry,* 39(4), 255–266.

Trickett, P. K. (1993). Maladaptive development of school-aged, physically abused children: Relationships with the child-rearing context. *Journal of Family Psychology,* 7, 134–147.

Tronick, E. Z. (1989). Emotions and emotional communication in infants. *American psychologist,* 44(2), 112.

Watts-English, T., Fortson, B. L., Gibler, N., Hooper, S. R., & DeBellis, M. D. (2006). The psychobiology of maltreatment in childhood. *Journal of Social Issues,* 62, 717–736.

Wilson, S. R., Rack, J. J., Shi, X., & Norris, A. M. (2008). Comparing physically abusive, neglectful, and non-maltreating parents during interactions with their children: A meta-analysis of observational studies. *Child Abuse and Neglect,* 32, 897–911.

Index

Skowron, Elizabeth A., 237–56
SLC6A4 gene, 78
smoking, 93
Snowdon, Charles T., 103–22
social brain hypothesis, 5, 10
social competence, 146, 154, 247–48
social networks:
    coalitions and alliances, 146,
        150, 154;
    gender differences, 225–26, 228;
    primates, 206–7.
    See also kinship networks
social neuroscience development, 5
social wasps. *See* wasps, social
societal emotional process, 9
Sociobiology (Wilson), 5
solid self, 46, 49, 52
solitary living, 164, 190–91, 191
spawning, 203
sports, 146
stability and plasticity of epigenetics,
    74, 91, 92
staff and anxiety transfer, 6, 44, 48, 60.
    See also clinicians
Strange Situation, 243–44
stress:
    anxiety and depressive disorders, 94;
    attachment and, 152, 220–22, 228;
    autonomic function, 247–48;
    child abuse and neglect, 74, 78, 239;
    child development, 74–75, 247–48;
    context-dependent epigenetic
        modifications, 94–95;
    family emotional system, 19–21,
        23–25, 96, 189, 195–96, 225;
    gender difference in reactivity and
        sex, 220, 223–26, 231–32;
    marmosets and tamarins, 106;
    ovulation in humans, 210–12;
    puberty regulation, 211;
    reactivity in infants, 189;
    reactivity in non-human primates, 75,
        247–48;
    reactivity in rodents, 56, 75–76, 79,
        88, 97, 114;

SEEKING system, 130;
    vagal tone, 242–43
stroke, 132
suicide, 130, 131
symbiosis, mother-infant, 43
symbiotic regulation, 32
sympathetic nervous system and
    ovulation, 210
sympathy, 210
synchrony:
    differentiation of self, 246–47, 251;
    estrus in rats, 206;
    menstrual, 212–13;
    parent-child coordination, 249;
    vagal tone, *244,* 244–45, 247, 249,
        250, 251

tamarins:
    compared to human family systems,
        116–17;
    cooperative breeding, 104, 108–11;
    family system, 103–17;
    mate selection and pair bonding,
        105–8, 223, 224;
    paternal care, 32, 111–14, 226–27
tend and befriend response, 226
tension. *See* anxiety; stress
termites, 161
territoriality, 222, 224
tertiary-process higher-order mental
    activities, 132
testosterone:
    California mouse, 112;
    human fathers, 117, 153, 154;
    human male coalitions, 154;
    LUST system, 130;
    marmosets and tamarins, 106,
        109–10, 112, 113, 114;
    production from estrogen, 112, 114;
    in women, 211
three-way relationships. *See* triangles
tickling rats, 130–31, 134, 137
titi monkey, 115
top-down epigenetics, 89
trail pheromone, 188

traits. *See* epigenetics
transcription factor A (NGFI-A), 93
transfer anxiety, 6–7, 24, 44, 47, 55–56
transgender, 130, 133–34
triangles:
    differentiation of self, 48–49, 228;
    family emotional process, 25, 190,
        192, 228–29;
    family of origin, 53–54, 55;
    family projection process, 35–36;
    fixed, 21, 34, 228;
    influence of gender on primary
        triangle, 219–32;
    overview, 9, 19–21, 228–29;
    predictability, 47–49;
    staff, 48
trust and bi-parenting, 105, 116

undifferentiated family ego mass, 17

vagal tone and child abuse and neglect,
    241–51, *250*
vagus nerve, 241–46
vasopressin. *See* arginine vasopressin
    (AVP)
ventral palladium and pair bonding in
    voles, 153
ventral striatum dopaminergic response
    to stress, 74
vervet monkeys, 114
Vespa, 169
visual system development, 128

voles, 107, 153, 205–6, 222–23,
    224, 225

Waddington, Conrad, 90
wasps, parasitic, 168
wasps, social:
    conflict and cooperation, 178–79;
    family components, 162–67;
    family systems, 161–81;
    nest, *162,* 167–68;
    reproduction, 160–74, *168, 173,*
        174, 178;
    workers, 164–66, 167, *167,*
        174–78, *177*
wasps, *Vespa,* 169
water conservation by ants, 193–94
weight loss/gain:
    human ovulation, 209;
    marmoset and tamarin
        fathers, 112
Weiss, August, 90
wild lion tamarins, 115–16.
    See also tamarins
Wilson, Edward O., 5
Woltereck, Richard, 90
workers:
    ants, 188;
    naked mole rates, 205;
    social wasps, 164–66, 167, *167,*
        174–78, *177*

xenoestrogens, 195

About the Contributors

Robert J. Noone, Ph.D. maintains a practice in psychotherapy in Evanston, IL. He is co-founder of and faculty at the Center for Family Consultation in Evanston, IL and served as Executive Director of the Family Service Center of Wilmette, Glenview, Northbrook, and Kenilworth, IL, for 28 years. He is currently editor of the journal *Family Systems* and a faculty member at the Bowen Center for the Study of the Family in Washington, D.C. He is author of published articles and book chapters on Bowen family systems theory and psychotherapy.

Daniel V. Papero, Ph.D. is a Senior Faculty Member at the Bowen Center for the Study of the Family in Washington, D.C. He is the author of the book *Bowen Family Systems Theory* as well as numerous book chapters and journal articles. He lectures both nationally and internationally on the Bowen theory and maintains a clinical practice in Washington, D.C.

John Butler, Ph.D. maintains a private practice at Rose Street Mental Health Care in Wichita Falls, TX. He is editor of *The Origins of Family Psychotherapy: The NIMH Family Studies Project* (2013) and the author of several professional articles on family theory and psychotherapy.

Frances A. Champagne, Ph.D. is Associate Professor, Department of Psychology and Director of the Champagne Lab, Columbia University, New York. Dr. Champagne's main research interest concerns how genetic and environmental factors interact to regulate maternal behavior, and how natural variations in this behavior can shape the behavioral development of offspring through epigenetic changes in gene expression in a brain region specific manner. She is also interested in the impact of fathers on mothers and offspring and the epigenetic mechanisms through which this interplay occurs.

James Curley, Ph.D. is Assistant Professor, Department of Psychology, Columbia University. His general area of research is behavioral neuroscience and development. Dr. Curley has conducted and published research at molecular, systems, organismal and evolutionary levels of analysis in both animals and humans. The focus of his lab at Columbia is on the development of social behavior, especially in how both inherited genetic variability and social experiences during development can shift individual differences in various aspects of social behavior and the neuroendocrinological basis of these differences.

David Crews, Ph.D. is Ashbel Smith Professor of Zoology and Psychology, University of Texas at Austin. He is the Director of The Reproductive Biology Laboratory of David Crews at the University of Texas, Austin. Dr. Crews is Director, National Institute of Mental Health Training Program in Neurobiology and Behavior, John Wiley Distinguished Speaker, International Society of Developmental Psychobiology (2001); Fellow, American Psychological Association; and Fellow, The American Academy of Arts and Sciences (1996).

Margaret G. Donley, MSW maintains a private practice in Prairie Village, KS. She is the author of several professional articles on family theory and psychotherapy and is co-director of Bowen Family Systems Clinical Seminars in Kansas City, where she is involved in supervising and teaching area clinicians in family systems theory and therapy.

Marina Farinelli, M.D. is a member of the Department of Psychology at the University of Bologna, Italy. Dr. Farinelli has been working with neurological patients since 1996 at "Villa Bellombra" Rehabilitation Hospital in Bologna, Italy. She has established and coordinates a Clinical Psychology Service which supports patients and their caregivers and contributes to clinical practice and research from a psychosomatic and neuropsychoanalytical perspective in collaboration with the Department of Psychology of the University of Bologna, Italy and other Italian and International Research Centers.

Mark V. Flinn, Ph.D. is Professor and Chair of the Department of Anthropology, University of Missouri, Columbia, MO. He is the principal investigator of a 27-year longitudinal study on the impact of stress on the health of families and children. Dr. Flinn is currently President, Human Behavior & Evolution Society; Fellow, Association for Psychological Science; and Fellow, American Association for the Advancement of Science.

Randall T. Frost, M. Div., RCC is Director of Training and Research at Living Systems in Vancouver, BC, a pastoral counselling center that uses Bowen theory as its primary approach to counselling, training, education and research. He is a member of the faculty of the Bowen Center for the Study of the Family in Washington, D.C., and author of professional articles and book chapters on family theory and psychotherapy.

Raghavendra Gadagkar, Ph.D. is Bose Research Professor and JC Bose National Fellow at the Centre for Ecological Science, Indian Institute of Science, Bangalore, India. Dr. Gadagkar is currently President of the Indian National Science Academy, Chairman, Centre for Contemporary Studies, Bangalore; Foreign Associate; National Academy of Sciences, USA; Member, German National Academy of Sciences Leopoldina. Dr. Gadagkar has published over 250 scientific papers and articles in international journals and is the author of the books *Survival Strategies: Cooperation and Conflict in Animal Societies* (2001), and *The Social Biology of Ropalidia marginata: Towards Understanding the Evolution of Eusociality* (2001).

Deborah M. Gordon, Ph.D. is Professor, Department of Biology, Stanford University and Senior Fellow, Woods Institute for the Environment. Dr. Gordon is the Director of The Gordon Lab at Stanford. She has studied ant colony behavior and ecology for more than two decades, focusing on the developing behavior of colonies, even as individual ants change functions within their own lifetimes. Dr. Gordan is the author of numerous scientific publications and of the books *Ant Encounters: Interaction Networks and Colony Behavior* (2010) and *Ants at Work: How an Insect Society is Organized* (2009).

Victoria Harrison, MA, LMFT is founding Director of the Center for the Study of Natural Systems and the Family in Houston, TX. She maintains a practice of psychotherapy based in Bowen theory and uses biofeedback and neurofeedback for the study of reactivity. She is also Senior Faculty at the Bowen Center for the Study of the Family in Washington, D.C. She conducts research on physiological reactivity in the family and its impact on health and reproduction.

LeAnn Howard, LSCSW maintains a private practice of family therapy in Kansas City. She was founding director of Menninger, Kansas City. She has taught Bowen family systems theory for more than 35 years and speaks locally, regionally, and nationally.

Jaak Panksepp, Ph.D. is Baily Endowed Chair of Animal Well-Being Science and Professor, Integrative Physiology and Neuroscience, Washington State University, Pullman, WA. Dr. Panksepp is author of the books *The Archaeology of Mind: Neuroevolutionary Origins of Human Emotion* (2012), *Affective Neuroscience: The Foundations of Human and Animal Emotions* (1998), and editor of many books including: *A Textbook of Biological Psychiatry*, (1998), and *Advances in Biological Psychiatry*, Vol. 2, (1996).

Elizabeth A. Skowron, Ph.D. is Associate Professor, Department of Counseling Psychology and Human Services, University of Oregon, Eugene, OR. Dr. Skowron is the Lead Investigator on a NIMH-funded study of parenting processes and children's regulatory and behavioral outcomes in at-risk families. Dr. Skowron's expertise is in family systems, interpersonal, and dynamic approaches to intervention. She is particularly interested in the neurobiology of at-risk parenting, differentiation of self (i.e., autonomy & attachment), self-regulation, and the ways in which family systems promote children's competence.

Charles T. Snowdon, Ph.D. is Hilldale Professor of Psychology and Zoology University of Wisconsin, Madison. Currently editor of the *Journal of Comparative Psychology*, he was previously North American Editor of *Animal Behaviour* and has served as President of the Animal Behavior Society. He has held a Research Scientist Award from the National Institute of Mental Health since 1977. His research interests are in vocal and chemical communication, reproductive behavioral biology, parental care and infant development in cooperatively breeding primates.